PUBLIC ADMINISTRATION
(PROBLEMS AND PROSPECTS)

PUBLIC ADMINISTRATION
(PROBLEMS AND PROSPECTS)

Compiled & Edited
by
Dr. R.K. Pruthi

DISCOVERY PUBLISHING HOUSE
NEW DELHI-110002

First Published – 2005

Reprinted – 2026

ISBN: 978-81-8356-008-5

Publlic Administration
Problems and Perspectives

Published by:
DISCOVERY PUBLISHING HOUSE
4383/4B, Ansari Road, Darya Ganj
New Delhi-110 002 (India)
Phone: +91-11-23279245; 23253475; 43596065
Mobile: +91 9811179893 / +91 9871656464
E-mail: discoverybooksindia@gmail.com
orderdphbooks@gmail.com
namitwasan9@gmail.com
web: www.discoverypublishinggroup.com

Printed at:
Infinity Imaging Systems
Delhi

Preface

What are the problems of public administration? How can it be improved? What are its future perspectives? How to promote efficiency in administration?

Different view points have emerged regarding introducing change in the practice of administration in response to the rapidly changing environment. Several measures of administrative reorganisation and reforms have been suggested to strengthen administrative capacity and responsibility. Object of this book is to compile material on the subject for the use of students and teachers?

We record our respectful acknowledgements to the authorities on the subject.

Librarians and their staff members have been kind and co-operative. We thank them.

Hard work by my publisher and his staff members has been a matter of great relief for me. If our humble labour satisfies our readers, we shall feel adequately rewarded.

R.K. Pruthi

Contents

1

Introduction

In regard to the theory and practice of Public Administration rethinking and suggestions for reform took place among individual intellectuals as well as at common forums of the scholars and administrators. For instance, F.C. Mosfier edited a publication, entitled "Governmental Reorganisation: Cases and Commentaries (1967)"

The book dealt with the common theme of administrative reorganisation and reform to strengthen administrative capability and responsibility. The discussions at the various forums did not always result in any consensus among the participants about any set formulae for administrative change. However, several valuable view points did emerge, regarding introduction of changes in the theory and practice of Public Administration in response to the rapidly changing environment. This urge for change has resulted in the organisation of several conferences in America. Of these conferences one organised at Philadelphia in 1967 and the second organised at Minnowbrook in 1968 are the most important.

Changing Environment of Social Unrest

In the second half of the present century rapid environmental changes taking place in U.S.A. enabled her to achieve greatest prosperity and power. But at the same time more and more social tensions and unrest among several sections of people began to take place. The social dissatisfaction and protests were mostly confined to the minority groups, the unemployed and certain highly sensitive youth groups. These became a matter of growing concern to the elected officials, the administrators, the intellectuals and the public leaders. A good deal of public debate and discussion began to take place as how to solve the challenging societal and technological problems. Several changes in policies and institutions began to be undertaken and some others were debated to strengthen political and administrative capabilities for coping with the rapidly changing environments: economic, social, political, technological and human.

Philadelphia Conference

Major viewpoints expressed at his conference about the subject and practice of Public Administration are summarised below:

(a) With the progressive transformation of, the limited function state into a welfare state, the responsibilities and functions of its government have increased very considerably. This implies growth in the dimensions and functions of the administration. Since this growth is to be a continuous process, it would be erroneous to demarcate rigidly the boundaries of the study of Public Administration. The scope of the subject should remain flexible to facilitate its growth. Again, it being obvious that administrators are involved in policy making process as advisers and facilitators besides being primarily concerned with policy implementation, the dichotomy between policy and administration and therefore between the study of government and study of Public Administration is meaningless.

(b) Too much emphasis on perfection of hierarchy and internal processes in administrative organisations results in rigidities in administrative performance which detract from its relevance and efficacy in rapidly changing environments; organisational innovations and management flexibility are therefore appropriate.

(c) The subject and practice of Public Administration should pay increased attention to the social problems of urban squalor, unemployment, poverty, environmental pollution and degradation.'

(d) There are great socio-economic disparities between classes of people. Hence, social equity should be given due attention.

For promoting equity as an administrative value alongwith the existing values of efficiency and accountability, as well as for improving administrative responsiveness, people's participation in administrative decision-making and activities should be institutionally provided in a recognised administration. This would also mean that the study of Public Administration should also include social equity as one of the themes.

(e) Education and training programmes in Public Administration should not only provide management abilities and technique skills but should also deepen the social sensitivity or consciousness of students/trainees as well of the public personnel at work in various governmental agencies. Moreover, administrative ethics needs due emphasis in education programmes so as to prevent or minimise the chances of malpractices and corruption.

Minnowbrook Conference

A year later in 1968 comparatively young scholars and practitioners of Public Administration met at Minnowbrook to critically review the relevance of the study and practice of Public Administration in terms of rapidly changing environment posing challenging problems before the government and social system in the country. Several viewpoints were expressed vigorously. Though these were not much dissimilar to the ones expressed at the Philadelphia Conference or by some individual academics at times, it was the passionate character of discussions which was the distinctive feature of the meet at Minnowbrook. Moreover, this was followed later on by small group meets of the participants to keep up the tempo of their view points as well as to elucidate these for general publicity or dissemination. The essence of the various viewpoints articulated by the young participants was the advocacy for a normative approach in place of the value-free efficiency approach of the classical theory. This normative approach stresses that the purpose of governmental administration should be reduction of economic, social and psychic suffering and the enlargement of life opportunities both for the employees of the government as well as for citizens. In other words, concerned sections of people should be freed from deprivations, wants and social disabilities. For this purpose, it was suggested that administrative organisations and administrative systems should be continuously adapted to the environmental changes and should also facilitate clientele or citizen involvement in administrative processes to improve administrative effectiveness.

FEATURES OF NEW PUBLIC ADMINISTRATION

George Frederickson has summarised, in several of his writings, the main features of the new approach to Public Administration passionately advocated at Minnowbrook Conference and afterwards According to him, social equity is the key concept stressed as an additional administrative value by the advocates of the new approach. He even titled one of his books as New Public Administration. According to him the various features of the New Public Administration are as stated below.

Change and Administrative Responsiveness

The social, political, economic and technological environments are changing rapidly. Administrative organisations should, therefore, develop clear criteria by which the effectiveness and relevance of their decisions and actions can be judged in the changing context. They should also set up an appropriate device and procedure to effect appropriate change regularly within themselves so as to be responsive to the environment. In other words, organisational and operational flexibility or adaptability to meet environmental changes should be in-built in the administrative system and in each of its departments and agencies.

Rationality

In Public Administration there is a good deal of emphasis on rationality as the main criterion for administrative decisions and actions. But this rationality really refers to the rationality of the administrator and not as people would interpret it. The administrator needs to consult the citizens as well not only about what is proposed to be done but also about what ought to be done and by whom.

Management-Worker Relations

It is true that human relations approach within an administrative organisation enhances both morale and productivity (efficiency) among employees but these are not to be end in themselves. The main objective should be the satisfaction of the citizens with the performance and attitudes of the administrative employees whose morale and productivity would have risen due to any human relations approach within an organisation.

Structures

There is a need for adopting a dynamic approach to organisational structure. Appropriate decentralisation of authority and modification of hierarchies of control and subordination, for instance, need continuous review so that the structure becomes relevant to the changing needs of environment. In other words, there should be alternative structures to be chosen from the above inventory of organisations rather than one standardised organisational structure based upon POSDCORB or other principles stressed by the advocates of the traditional approach to Public Administration. Small decentralised and flexible hierarchies, for instance, can be suitable for administrative organisations concerned with programmes of intimate concern to the people or some of their actions.

Education in Public Administration

The subject of Public Administration has been enriched by several streams of knowledge (concepts, ideas and insights). Heterogeneity is characteristic of this subject. The management approach, the human relations approach, political approach and public participative or choice approach continue to contribute to its growth. This is how it should be. Since public affairs, in which the government is engaged, are highly varied and complex no single approach or theory or concept would be adequate to guide action or understand its rationale.

Goals of New Public Administration

New Public Administration literature has stressed four important goals—namely, relevance, values, equity and change.

Relevance

Public Administration has always emphasised efficiency and economy. Public Administration is criticised as having little to say about contemporary problems and issues. At the Minnowbrook Conference, the participants focused attention on the need for policy-oriented Public Administration and emphasised that Public Administration must explicitly deal with political and normative implications of all administrative actions. Another aspect of relevance that was voiced was Public Administration knowledge. At the Minnowbrook Conference, some of the following questions were raised:

(a) What standards of decision do we use to select?

(b) Which questions ought to be studied and how to study them?

(c) Who defines our questions and priorities for us?

(d) To what extent are we aware of the social and moral implications of knowledge in Public Administration?

(e) What are the uses of Public Administration as a social and political science?

(f) Does Public Administration presently yield knowledge used to certain institutions in society (usually the dominant ones) and not to others?

These are very disturbing questions challenging the status quo in Public Administration.

Values

New Public Administration is explicitly normative. It rejects value concealing behaviouralism as well as procedural neutrality of traditional Public Administration. The participants at the Minnowbrook Conference, clearly espoused that value neutral Public Administration is impossible. The emphasised that public officials have to advocate the interests of disadvantaged people.

Social Equity

Public Administration is indicated as an instrument of status quo, denying social justice to the less privileged groups. The leaders of New Public Administration emphasise the principle of social equity. Realisation of this principle should be the purpose of Public Administration. Frederickson himself explains the concept of social equity much more boldly when says: "A Public Administration which fails to work for changes, which tries to redress the deprivation of minorities, will likely to be eventually used to repress those minorities". Client-focus administration is a major goal of New Public Administration. Other goals are debureaucratisation, democratic decision-making and decentralisation of administrative process in the interest of more effective and humane delivery of public services.

Change

Achievement of social equity requires promotion of change by the public administrators. Change is necessary to prevent Public Administration from coming under the dominance of powerful interest groups. New public administrators should regard change as a constant fact of administrative life.

In conclusion, what the New Public Administration movement focused was that the administrator should be given less "generic" and more "public" than his predecessor, less "descriptive" and more "prescriptive", less "institution oriented" and more "client-impact oriented", less "neutral" and more "normative", and it is hoped, no less scientific.

COMMENTS ON NEW PUBLIC ADMINISTRATION

According to Alan Campbell many of the issues brought to the surface vigorously by advocates of New Public Administration were not new. These have been raised by other scholars from time to time. But these have been raised by proponents of New Public Administration very forcefully and with a strong commitment to social change. Their strong emphasis on citizen's participation in decision-making, on normative value of social equity, and human relations approach oriented largely to service to people is once again a reminder about the need for reorientation of theory and practice of Public Administration.

Dwight Waldo, in his book titled "Enterprise of Public Administration (1980)" has pointed out that New Public Administration projects three perspectives clearly—client (citizen) oriented bureaucracy, representative bureaucracy and people's participation. These public perspectives if woven into Public Administration appropriately would tend to democratise it even more than before.

Carter and Duffey, writing on New Public Administration in the International Journal of Public Administration, (1984), have expressed doubt whether the objective of social equity is actually getting recognised as a well-established administrative objective or value in addition to the existing ones of efficiency, effectiveness and public accountability. The great disparities of wealth and income continue in USA to a large extent. Due to recent curtailment of government spending on social welfare programme in USA the deprived sections of the people still do not have adequate access to all the requisite economic and social facilities for their substantial betterment.

We are of the view that since in USA the main emphasis has been on free competition and individual initiative, adoption of social equity as a policy and administrative objective is not an easy proposition. In course of time, perhaps the progress towards its adoption may become more encouraging due to social pressures.

Recent trends in the study and practice of Public Administration in several countries, both developed (e.g. France, Sweden and Britain) and developing (e.g., India, Pakistan) also indicate similar revision and additions. The intensity and extent of the impact of the trends however, vary from one country to the other, depending upon their respective historical heritages, national resources, character of political system, cultural and demographic patterns and role of the state in national development. The impact is very weak in some countries at one extreme and very strong at the other due to their differing national profiles. On the whole, these trends indicate:

(a) growing emphasis on social equity in public policies and administrative actions;

(b) devising of institutional arrangements to facilitate increased public participation in administrative processes (i.e. decision-making, operations, etc.) at local and grassroot levels;

(c) strengthening of political direction of administration as well as administrative accountability to the political authorities within the government;

(d) adoption of innovative (new) types of organisations as well as of modern management practices, and techniques and technologies to raise the administrative capability (i.e. efficiency and effectiveness) to deal with highly diverse, complex and numerous governmental tasks.

e) growth of unionism among the public personnel (government employees) of various grades and making of organised arrangements for government-employees consultation and negotiations as well as for arbitration of disputes.

Because of these trends in administrative systems, the scope of the study of the subject of Public Administration has increased considerably. Moreover, the study is no longer content with the description and analysis of administrative phenomena, policies, organisations and processes. It is also becoming increasingly normative as it now deals with questions of social equity orientation, democratic orientation, ethical behaviour and citizen's participation within continuously expanding administrative systems. Besides, it is also beginning to be increasingly comparative as it now examines and conceptualises the administrative policies and organisations and operations in various national environments comprising several aspects—political, social, economic, demographic physical and technological.

In short, the New Public Administration, both in practice and theory tends to be comprehensive in scope, descriptive-cum normative in character and comparative besides multi-disciplinary in substance.

2

Importance of Public Administration

Today most of the countries in the world are adopting the concept of a Welfare State. Formerly, the State was a 'Police State', it had to perform functions relating to maintenance of peace and security. Although a few welfare activities were also performed at that time; they were not principal functions of the State. The Encyclopaedia of Social Sciences has described a Welfare State as a State which takes the responsibility to provide minimum standard of subsistence to its citizens. According to Pt. Jawaharlal Nehru, "The fundamental features of a Welfare State are to provide equality of opportunity to all, to abolish disparity between rich and poor and to raise standard of life. While we talk of individual liberty in democracy, the opportunities for enjoying freedom for all the people are however, provided only in Welfare State." Prof, Kent has remarked that by a Welfare State we mean that State, which provides extensive services to the people. Thus, in a Welfare State, the administration enters into economic, political, social and educational life of individuals.

Wide Activities of State

By adoption of the concept of welfare the field of activities of administration in a State are expanding every day. The narrow scope of public administration is now discarded. Public administration touches upon all aspects of life of an individual. It provides services for an individual, right from his birth to death. In normal period it plays the role of guide; in the period of emergency, it turns a true friend, philosopher and guide. The State is to serve the old, sick, orphans, widows, helpless, oppressed and disabled people, and each of them is benefited by State services. By serving a pregnant woman, the State gets ready to serve an individual before his birth. After his death, it arranges for his cremation through electric crematorium. It makes arrangement for registration of death and issues a death certificate, so as to enable his children to inherit his estate, and have his bank accounts transferred. There is a provision of family pension. In some of - the government departments, one relative of the deceased is provided employment in government service. Under employees assurance a huge amount is paid to the family on the sudden death of an employee. Thus, in a Welfare State, public administration serves an individual from cradle to the grave. The State is everywhere; it leaves hardly anything untouched.

Characteristics of a Welfare State

1. Expanding Functions of a State. The State has completely entered into men's life. Today the administration faces new challenges at every step. In the age industrialisation, the administration, has of the prepare itself to face new challenges.

2. Increase in Number of Personnel. The State has to recruit an army of personnel to meet the new challenges and to perform expending activities. Many functions performed by voluntary organisations have been taken over by the Welfare State. It has naturally increased the State expenditure.

3. Dependence upon Administration. For every activity or work, one has to depend upon the Sate. Even for the supply of food, milk, water, housing, medical facilities and means of transportation one has to depend upon State.

4. Positive Concept. The negative concept of the Sate has been converted into a positive one. The administration cares for the health and security of citizens through anti-malaria drive, cleanliness and many such activities.

5. Bureaucracy. The civil service is getting converted into bureaucracy. 'Work to rule' and strikes have become the order of the day. The significance of the public administration

is greater in those countries which are economically, politically and educationally backward. If the administration fails to create a favourable atmosphere, the life of people shall not be secure. The fundamental aim of Five-Year Plans, in India is to provide medical and health facilities, sanitation, electricity, transport and communication to every man. According to Prof. A.D. Gorwala, "In democracy, for the success of plans a healthy, neutral administration is essential. Prof. Karve has observed that in a Welfare State where there is a planned economy, and a democratic constitution, the latter cannot function unless there is a public administration based upon integrated structure. Prof. Ordway Tead has observed, "Public administration is a moral activity and administration is a moral agent."

Role of Public Administration

In a modern State the public administration has to play a significant role. The complex nature of society and expansion of activities of the modern State have increased its importance. The administration of modern State has to care for integral development of the personality of an individual. Planned economic and social development is taking place in every country. Efficient administration is required to advance this progress and development and to withstand the problems. Being the watch dog of civilised life the public administration has become a tool of change and reforms. Prof. A. D. Gorwala has rightly remarked, "In Democracy, for the success of plans, clean, neutral and efficient administration is essential." To quote Prof. Demock, "Public administration is an integral part of civilised society and a part of our life in modern society; it has led to a new form of state-called the 'administrative state'.

Characteristics of Democratic Administration

1. Respect of Public Will. In democracy the administration is for the people, and not the people for the administration. The success of administration depends upon analysis of public wishes, and in adapting itself accordingly. The more deeply the administration grasps the public opinion, more successful

it shall be. The administration has to spread a complete network of public relations. Thus ultimately administration is a human problem.

2. Propaganda and Broadcasting. In democracy the administration is not a secret. The more information is extended to the people, greater is the success of administration in achieving public cooperation. Opportunity is provided for free expression taking help of propaganda and means of communication to learn public opinion about government decisions and, to learn how much public support is expected.

3. Equality and Cooperation. In democracy the feelings of friendship and fraternity should be developed. The days of Bossism and Feudalism are over. The administrators are public servants and not their masters. As democracy is based upon the concept of cooperation and equality, the administration should be familiar with the economic and social problems of people.

4. Control on Arbitrariness. In democracy the administration cannot be insolent and arbitrary but under the limits of social control. It is controlled by the Legislature. It is under the judicial review.

Public Administration in Modern World

Today the world has been grouped into two categories:

(i) *Development Countries.* These include Anglo-American countries, which are influenced by the western civilisation and those countries like U.S.S.R., China, Korea, Yugoslavia etc. Which are under the impact of Marxism-Leninism.

(ii) *Developing Countries.* These are countries of Asia, Latin America, Africa etc. Which are under the process of development. They are also called the 'third world'. India, Bangladesh, Sri Lanka, Indonesia, Algeria, Pakistan, Ghana, Egypt etc. Are the developing countries. They have been liberated after a long struggle against the colonial rule. Suffering from all sorts of weaknesses they have not yet been able to finally choose and determine the form of their

governments. Traditions play a significant role in the formation of their political system. The political power in these countries is centralised into the hands of a few classes.

Salient Features of Developing Countries

1. Instability. Instability is the destiny of developing countries. The political systems suffer from the public unrest, economic exploitation, multi-party system etc. Diverse religions, cultures and nationalities exercise contradictory impact upon these systems.

2. External Aggression. The problem of external aggression is always there before the developing countries. The politicians are always engaged in securing power. Government are always in danger. Elections are never free and fair. The governments freely make use of armies to solve internal security problems. The democracy is passing through the phase of instability. Corruption is increasing under the cloak of democracy.

3. Paper Plans. In developing countries plans are formulated on paper, whose execution is doubtful. The perpetual intervention of external powers makes the success of plans all the more doubtful.

Problems of Developing Countries

1. Lack of Management Ability. Being newborn States, the developing countries lack ability of management. They have yet to develop their own efficient administration structure.

2. Lack of Administrative Structure. The aspiration of people are fast increasing, but they could not yet achieve proper ability to organise appropriate administration structure.

3. Lack of Professional Standard. The administration has not been able to adapt itself to time and public demands. Economic backwardness, lack of specialists and education are the hurdles in their advancement.

4. Lack of Administrative Leadership. The Administration in these countries do not consider themselves to be public

servants. Due to the want of efficient political leadership, the administration has not been able to achieve its objectives. Corruption, dishonesty and red-tapism are posing a problem to leadership.

5. Lack of Moral Values. There is lack of moral values. The administrative class makes use of policies for its selfish ends, public interest is neglected. Corruption has become a part of their life.

6. Lack of Administrative Responsibility. Administrative machinery is under the cloak of bureaucracy. The administrative class takes pride in keeping aloof from the people.

New Challenges to Administration

1. Violence. Developing counters are becoming arenas of violence. In some it is labour or peasant movement, in the others it is leftism or terrorism. These violent movements result in loss of life and property. The army and the police are at their wits' end.

2. Regional Economic Imbalance. These countries suffer from regional and economic imbalance. In India, Punjab, Haryana, Maharashtra, Gujarat and Tamilnadu have progressed economically, but other regions like. U.P., Bihar and Orissa have been neglected.

3. Social Tension and Instability. Due to the want of social justice, national instability has taken place. People are on the verge of poverty. Public unrest can be seen from the lower standards of living. Life of citizens is full of social tension. They are suffering from increasing population and want of amenities.

4. Increasing Population. Increase in population, the plight of public health has made these countries worse. The public is indifferent.

5. Corruption. Corruption is the most burning problem of these developing countries. Every day the newspapers are full of one or the other scandal.

6. Agriculture, Planning and Irrigation. In this direction the efforts of administrators are praiseworthy. But the prices are soaring, how to maintain equilibrium between high standard of living and dearness? Economic planning is actively helpful to it. How far plans have helped us is difficult to assess. But here also the role of administration is significant.

Questions for Exercise

1. Evaluate the importance of the study of Public Administration in modern democratic Welfare State.

2. What are the salient features of developing countries? What are their common problems? Discuss the new challenges administration is facing there?

3

Meaning and Scope of Public Administration

MEANING OF ADMINISTRATION

In common parlance, the word 'administration ' is used in four different meanings:

1. *A Synonym of the Word 'Cabinet'* or some such other body of persons in the supreme charge of affairs as, for example, when we say that the first 'Nehru Administration ' included the leaders of all the major political parties in India.

2. *The Name of a Branch of Learning* intellectual discipline, e.g., when we say that public administration is one of the social sciences.

3. *The Sum Total of the Activities Undertaken to Implement Public Policy or Policies;* or to produce some service or goods as, for example, when we speak of the Indian administration, railway administration, educational administration etc., and

4. *The Art of Management.* e.g., when we say that so and so has no capacity or aptitude for administration. These four meanings differ from one another so widely that it is difficult to combine them into a single definition of administration.

The English word 'administer' is derived from the Latin words *ad* and *ministrare,* meaning "to minister to", "to serve" or "to manage". The dictionary defines administration as the management of affairs. To administer is to manage or direct or serve. Thus, administration is characteristic of all human enterprises to achieve a purpose or objective in view.

Administrative Activities

There are two views regarding the question: what comprises administrative activities. One view is that all activities, physical, mental, and managerial which are undertaken to achieve a purpose, comprise administration. This is an all-inclusive or integral view of administration.

The other view regarding the nature of administration is known as the 'Managerial view'. It means, that administration is concerned only with the management, direction, supervision and control of human beings who are co-operating to achieve a purpose. Proper organisation and direction of men and material to achieve some desired ends is administration. Administration is concerned only with the managerial aspects of group activity.

1. *E.N. Gladden*. Administration means "...to care for or look after people, to manage affairs....is determined action taken pursuit of conscious purpose."[1]

2. *Prof. John A. Vieg*. Administration "...is the systematic ordering of affairs and the calculated use of resources, aimed at making those things happen which we want to happen and simultaneously preventing developments that fail to square with our intentions."[2]

3. *E.A. Nigro*. Administration is the organisation and use of men and materials to accomplish a purpose."[3]

4. *L.D. While*. "The art of administration is the direction, co-ordination and control of many persons to achieve some purpose or objective."[4]

5. *J.M. Pfeiffner*. Administration is defined "As the organisation and direction of human and material resources to achieve desired ends."[5]

6. *Herbert A Simon*. "In its broadest sense, administration can be defined as the activities of groups co-operating to accomplish common goals."[6]

7. *Simon, Smithburg and Thompson*. "In its broadest sense, administration can be defined as the activities of groups, co-operating to accomplish common goals [7]

8. *Ordway Tead.* "Administration is conceived as the necessary activities of individuals (executive) in an organisation who are charged with ordering, forwarding and facilitating the associated efforts of a group of individuals brought together to realize certain defined purposes"[8]

MEANING OF PUBLIC ADMINISTRATION

Thus, whenever people co-operate to achieve some ends, the activities which they have to perform, to achieve the goal in view, it is administration: Public administration is a particular area of the broader field of administration. It is administration of the governmental affairs. It includes activities like the collection of tax by the Income-tax Officer, the arrest of a criminal by the police, construction of Public roads, highways, bridges, canals, etc. It is distinguished from other forms of administration by the fact that its ultimate purpose is general interest and public good.

It is the activity of the State in the exercise of its political powers. In a narrow sense, it is the activity of the executive departments in the conduct of the Government.

The problems of administration are present in all the three branches of government, i.e., Legislature, Executive and Judiciary. All the work involved in the actual conduct of government affairs should be included in public administration. The handling of a Bill in the Legislature requires administration of a delicate character. Similarly administration of a high order is required in dealing with a case in a court of a law. Since the problems of administration are faced by all the three organs of the Government, three does not appear to be any reason why public administration should not include the 'Government in action' as a whole.

In the literal sense of the term, public administration also includes the functions of the courts—in the administration of justice—and the work of all the agencies, military as well as civilian, in the executive branch of government. An exhaustive treatise of public administration would, therefore, have to give consideration to judicial structure and procedure and likewise to the special machinery and methods employed by the armed forces in addition to legislative management.

However, in common usage and practice, the scope of the activities of public administration is restricted to the organisation and operations of the executive branch of the government. It is felt that if all the complex activities of all the three branches of the government, are studied, the subject will become unwieldy. Thus public administration includes, primarily the organisation, personnel practices, and procedures essential to the effective performance of civilian functions entrusted to the executive branch of government. It is primarily concerned with the implementation of public policy laid down by representative of political bodies. Its main task is the implementation and enforcement of public policy and the law of the State. All those activities which are undertaken to fulfil, implement or enforce public policy are included in public administration. All the activities which are performed by the different organs of government in the field of law, justice, social welfare, health, hygiene, etc. Are included in public administration. Therefore, a system of public administration is the composite of all the laws, regulations, practices, relationships, codes and customs that prevail at any time in any jurisdiction for the fulfillment or execution of public policy.

DEFINITION OF PUBLIC ADMINISTRATION

1. *W.F. Willoughby.* "In its broadest sense, it denotes the work involved in the actual conduct of governmental affairs, regardless of the particular branch of government concerned... In its narrowest sense, it denotes the operations of the administrative branch only."[9]

2. *L.D. White.* "Public administration consists of all those operations having far their purpose the fulfilment or enforcement of public policy.[10]

3. *Woodrow Wilson.* "Public administration in detailed and systematic application of law. Every particular application of law is an act of administration."[11]

4. *Luther Gulick.* "Administration had to do which getting things done, with the accomplishment of defined objectives. The science of administration is thus the system of knowledge whereby men may understand relationship, product results,

and influence outcomes in any situation where men are organised at work together for a common purpose. Public Administration is that part of the science of administration which had to do with Government, and thus concerns itself primarily with the executive branch, where the work of Government is done, though there are obviously administrative problems also in connection with the legislative and judicial branches. Public administration is thus a division of Political Science and one of the social sciences.[12]

5. *Pfiffner*. "Public Administration consists of doing the work of Government, whether it be running an X-ray machine in a health laboratory of coining money in the mint. . . administration consists of getting the work of government done by co-ordinating the efforts of people so that they can work together or accomplish their set tasks. Administration embraces activities which may be highly technical and specialised, as public health and the building of bridges . . . It also involves managing, directing, and supervising the activities of thousands, even millions of workers so that some order and efficiency may result from their efforts....."[13]

6. *Marshall Dimock*. "Administration is concerned with the 'what' and the 'how' of Government. The 'what is the subject-matter, the technical knowledge of a field which enables an administration to perform his tasks. The 'how' is the techniques of management, the principles according to which co-operative programmes are carried through to success. Each is indispensable, together they form the synthesis called the administration."[14]

7. *Waldo Dwight* Public Administrations "One phase or aspect of human co-operative", "a species belonging to the genus administration" which in turn is "a type of co-operative human effort that has a high degree of rationality."[15]

8. *Marx and Simon*. "By established usage, however, the term "Public administration" has come to signify primarily the organisation, personnel practices, and procedures essential to effective performance of the civilian functions entrusted to

the executive branch of government. We shall use the term in customary sense."[16]

9. *Simon* "By Public Administration is meant in common usage, the activities of the executive branches of the national, State and local government."[17]

10. *Pifffner and Presthus.* "In sum, Public Administration is a process concerned with carrying out public policies, encompassing innumerable skills and techniques which give order and purpose to the efforts of large numbers of people."[18]

To sum up, "Public Administration is decision-making planning the work to be done, formulating objectives and goals, working with the legislature and citizen organisation to gain public support and funds for government programmes, establishing and revising organisation, directing and supervising employees, providing leadership, communicating and receiving communications, determining work methods and procedures, appraising performance, executive controls, and other functions performed by government, executive and supervisors. It is the action part of government, the means by which the purposes and goals of government are realised."[19] Public administration is concerned with the activities carried on by government.

PROBLEMS OF PUBLIC ADMINISTRATION

Problems of public administration can be divided into five clearly distinguishable, though intimately connected, categories;

1. *General administration.* It means who is to perform the function of direction, supervision and control over administration.

2. *Organisation.* It means how are the services to be organised for the actual performance of administrative work.

3. *Personnel.* It means to the new are to manage the different services and activities?

4. *Material, supply, plant and equipment.* These are to be provided to the personnel for the discharge of their duties.

5. *Finance.* This is the crux of all the above-mentioned problems.

SCOPE OF PUBLIC ADMINISTRATION

1. Broad View. Some distinguished authors such as Prof. L.D. White and F Marx have taken a broad view regarding the scope of public administration. To them public administration is concerned with activities of all the three branches of the government i.e., legislature, executive and judiciary. The scope of public administration includes all those activities which aim at the application of public policy or their execution. Prof. White has broadly defined public administration as consisting of all those operations having for their purpose the fulfilment or enforcement of public policy. Prof. F. Marx has also broadly defined public administration by saying, "In its fullest range, public administration embraces every activity under the jurisdiction of public policy."

2. Narrow View. According to other authors the broad view of the scope of public administration is not practical, as it renders the scope public administration vague. It would, thus be better to accept the narrow view of the scope of the public administration. To them public administration is mainly concerned with the executive branch of the government, its organisation, working and method. The narrower view includes the study of the following aspects of the public administration.

3. Idealistic View or Welfare View. The supporters of this view do not differentiate between State and public administration. The State is a Welfare State today so the public administration which is not only the watch-dog of civilised life, but also a great tool of social justice and social change. Thus the scope of public administration embraces all activities undertaken for the welfare of the people.

The views of Simon and Luther Gullick are considered to be traditional outlook. Recently, some authors have tried to improve this narrow outlook. They have tried to broaden and modernise the scope of public administration. Its scope has, therefore, developed and enriched. It includes the structure, organisations, functions and methods of all types of public authority engaged in administration whether national, regional or local, and whether executive or advisory. It includes not only the central department and the local authorities, but also the known ministerial organisations, public boards and corporations. The functions of authorities include executive, legislative and judicial functions, which are the various methods appropriate to different types of functions.

4. POSDCORB view of the Public Administration. More concrete shape was given to the problems of Public Administration by Luther Gullick, in the letters called 'POSDCORB'. There letters stand for:

P Planning
O Organising
S Staffing
D Directing
Co Coordination
R Reporting
B Budgeting

1. Planning. It is the working out in broad outline the things that need to be done, the method to be adopted to accomplish the purpose set for the enterprise.

2. Organisation. It is the establishment of the formal structure of authority through which the work is sub-divided, arranged, defined and co-ordinated for the defined objective.

3. Staffing. It is the whole personnel, bringing in and training the staff, and maintenance of favourable condition of work.

4. Directing. It is the continuous task of making decisions and embodying them in specific and general orders and instructions and thus guiding the enterprise.

5. Coordinating. It is the all important duty of interrelating the various parts of the work.

6. Reporting. It is keeping those, to whom the executive is responsible, informed as to what is going on, which, thus includes keeping the agency itself and its subordinates informed through records, research and inspection.

7. Budgeting. It is all that goes with budgeting in the form of fiscal planning, accounting and control.

POSDCORB activities are common to all large-scale organisation. They are the common problems of management found in the different agencies, regardless of the peculiar nature of the work they do. These common activities are performed by public administration in military or in civil administration, in the administration of Central or State Government or in the administration of local bodies.

Critical Evaluation

The nature and character of various government agencies and the services they perform differ. There are specific administrative problems involved in different public agencies. POSDCORB view refers to activities which are common to practically all administrative positions, but it fails to take notice of the knowledge of the subject-matter involved in public administration. The substantive problems of an administrative agency are peculiar to the nature of the service it renders and the functions it performs. The knowledge of the subject-matter with which an administrative agency is concerned, is very essential for effective administration in it. The POSDCORB view gives us only the common techniques of administration, but these techniques are to be applied to plan, organize and direct something. Thus both the POSDCORB and the 'subject-matter' view, constitute the proper scope of the study of public administration. As Lewis Meriam rightly observes: "Public Administration is an instrument with two blades like a pair of scissors. One blade may be a knowledge of the fields covered by POSDCORB, the other blade is knowledge of the subject-matter in which these techniques are applied. Both blades must be good to make an effective tool."[20]

Criticism by Human Relations Approach

POSDCORB view has been further criticised by the followers of Human Relations approach to the study of administration. The

Hawthorne experiments, the first of which took place from 1927 to 1932 have been primarily responsible for the criticism of POSDCORB techniques in administration. These experiments, showed that productivity is related to the conditions of the sociological changes taking place within the work groups involved in the studies. The workers are human beings, with competitive and complex array of needs, desires, passions and prejudices, who cannot be ignored in administration. POSDCORB approach ignores this important factor in administration. Hence, it has been rejected by the believers in Human Relations approach. It is said that the modern public administrator is concerned with group process, communication, leadership skills and decision-making. He is concerned with power relationship in his agency and his government unit. Luther Gullick, the pioneer of the POSDCORB approach himself stated that the technique-oriented public administration of the 1930's and 1940's will clearly not do for the 1960's. He stated: "Some may think our greatest need in the cities is water, or sewers, or wide streets, or more schools, or housing. Fundamentally, they are wrong, the real things we need are brains, character, drive, organisation, and leadership."

Activities of Present Administrator

The inadequacy of technique-oriented or POSDCORB approach, will become more clear if the activities of the present day administration are kept in mind. The present administrator has to do following things:

1. To keep abreast of and on occasion supervise—research on the nature and the dynamics of his community, including the richly variegated political and power questions involved.
2. To do the same is his own administrative organisation, with greater emphasis here, on the political and power questions, some of which are sometimes referred to as the informal organisation which functions within every formal organisation.
3. To constantly strive to improve the communication process which his organisation, especially upward communication.
4. To provide an atmosphere in which the small groups functioning within his organisation can most effectively and expeditiously carry on their work.

5. To provide an atmosphere in which the contributions of the creative individuals in his organisation may be maximised,

6. To undertake the necessary training, education, and developmental work for himself and his subordinates, required by the delicate and demanding tasks just reviewed.

Thus administration as a process common to governments at all levels, Central, State and Local, is studied in public administration. It studies the problems of organisation, the activities of the government and the methods used by operating officers. It studies the problems of personnel and financial management. In democratic countries, public relations and public accountability of public administration are an inseparable aspect of the study. The understanding of public administration will remain incomplete if the social and cultural environment, in which the administration is working, is not studied. It is equally essential to study the behavioural problems of the human beings who constitute the 'heart' of all administrative activities. Public administration should study the techniques or tools of administration and also focus its attention on the human beings who use those techniques and tools and who work in administrative organisations. As the study of human behaviour is essential to the understanding of any social group, the study of public administration cannot ignore it, except at the cost of a right understanding of the discipline. In the traditional approach to the study of public administration, the focus of attention has been the hierarchical organisation, the chief executive's office, the departments, bureaus, sections and field offices. Now it has been realised that those who work in this hierarchy should also be studied for a clear understanding of the working of the administrative hierarchy.

Aspects of the Scope

Felix A. Nigro summarizes the various aspects of the scope of public administration as follows:

1. It is co-operative group effort in a public setting,

2. It covers all three branches—executive; legislative and judicial—and their interrelationship,

3. It has an important role in the formulation of public policy and is thus a part of the political process,

4. It is more important than, and also different in significant ways, from, private administration,

5. As a field of study and practice, if has been much influenced in recent years by the human-relations approach,

6. It is closely associated with numerous private groups and individuals in providing services to the community.

PUBLIC AND PRIVATE ADMINISTRATION

Administration is a universal activity found in every co-operative enterprise of human beings: the school, the hospital, the political party, the church, the swimming club and the family etc.

Similarities

There are some important points of similarity between public and private administration.

1. Common Techniques. Proper administration of a big enterprise, whether public or private, requires planning, organisation, command, co-ordination and control. Some general principles and procedures are to be followed to achieve the objectives. Irrespective of the fact whether administration is of public affairs, or of private business. Many techniques of management and organisation are common to both public and private administration.

2. Common Skills. Many of the skills like maintaining of files, noting, statistics, etc., are common to both types of administration. A statistician or an engineer may be doing the same kind of work in a government owned Railway Department or a private business concern. Hence many retired civil servants are re-employed by big business enterprises. The government too, sometimes borrows the services of experts from the private sector to run its industrial enterprise. Sometimes, the State takes over privately owned industries under its ownership and management. In such cases too hardly any change in the personnel of the industry is made

except for a few top employees. The same employees continue to do the same work with more or less the same procedures, in spite of the change of ownership.

3. Similarity of Employment. Increasing similarity of private and public employment is emphasised. Erwin W. Fellows states: "The similar bureaucratic structure common to most large-scale organisations, the pleasure of union activity, the passage of fair-employment legislation, and the development of a general body of knowledge concerning personnel administration, have all led to personnel practices in private industry which resemble those of the public service. This is most obvious in the use of examinations in the selection process, formal rules governing separations, systematic procedures for dealing with grievances, and pension plans for retiring employees."

Henri Fayol, L. Urwick etc., are of the opinion that the distinction between public and private administration does not exist. Henri Fayol observes: "The meaning which have given to the word administration and which has been generally adopted, broadens considerably the field of administrative science. It embraces not only the public service, but enterprises of every size and description, of every form and every purpose. All undertakings require planning, organisation, command, co-ordination and control, and in order to function properly, all must observe the same general principles. We are no longer confronted with several administrative sciences, but with one which can be applied equally well to public and private affairs."[21] In the same tone Urwick says: "It is difficult to contemplate seriously a biochemistry of bankers, a physiology of professors, or a psychopathology of politicians. The attempts to sub-divide study of management or administration in accordance with the purpose of particular forms of undertaking seems to many authorities . . . equally misdirected."[22] Thus Urwick is also opposed to the distinction between public and private administration.

Distinctions

1. Basic Differences. In spite of the abovementioned similarities, there are some basic differences of approach,

attitude, and the scope of activities, performed by public and private administration.

2. Range. The range of activities of even the biggest private business enterprise cannot compete with the range of government activities.

3. Accountability. No private business concern is accountable to the public in the way the government departments are. Public administration has to face the criticism of the public, press and political parties. The searching eyes of public criticism are directed towards administration. Administration have to think carefully about possible public reactions before taking any particular step. Every government employee lives and moves in the midst of 'Public dynamite.' As Paul H. Appleby rightly observes "Government administration differs from all other administrative work to a degree not even fairly realised outside, by virtue of its public nature, the way in which it is subject to public scrutiny and public outcry. An administrator coming into government is struck at once, and continually thereafter, by the press and public interest in every detail of his life, personality, and conduct. This interest often runs to details of administrative action that in private business would never be of concern other than inside the organisation. Each employee hired, each one demoted, transferred or discharged, every efficiency rating, every assignment of responsibility, each change in administrative structure; each conversation, each letter, has to be thought about in terms of possible public agitation, investigation, or judgement."[23] Public accountability and public scrutiny is one of the most important characteristics of public administration, a feature which is absent in private administration, Public administration is subject to legislative criticsm and investigation, and judicial review. "Unfortunately, there is a need for all these checks, and for counterchecks as well; inspectors must not only inspect, but also be inspected. The civil servant must be ready at all times to meet criticism; he must be prepared to produce documents showing the exact instructions issued to a certain official on a certain day; he

must be able to show that the one rule has been consistently followed, and that Tom Jones has been given no privileges and no different treatment than Joseph Andrews."[22]

4. Politics and People's Aspirations. There have a great influence over the activities of public administration. Public administration has to take care of the reaction of the people to a particular activity. This political character of public administration, differentiates it from private administration.

5. Importance. The activities of public administration are 'essential' for the existence of civilisation. The basic and important needs of the community are satisfied by public administration.

6. Objectives. Private business primarily furthers its private ends, whereas public administration is expected to serve public interest. Thus, private profit tends to become the driving force for private administration, while service to the community and not private profit is the motive of the services rendered by public and administration. Public administration undertakes many services which may result in financial loss to the exchequer: still these services are performed because they are essential to the life of the community. Private administration will abandon any project if there is the slightest hint of financial loss or little possibility of enough profit. Private profit is the measuring rod of the efficiency and success of private business. This, however, cannot be applied to measure the efficiency of the services of public administration. "Private business, for example, is almost invariably conducted for profit, and this forms an automatic measure of its efficiency. It can declare a dividend, it succeeds; if not, is a failure, and disappears from the commercial world. While the same test might be applied to certain activities of the Government (such as the postal services, for example), to do so would be the emphasize a quite secondary aspect of its function. The administrative departments exist primarily to render a service to the community, and the price that they charge.... does not necessarily represent the money equivalent of the work which

they perform ...In short, there is little or no effort made to estimate the success of a department by its credit balance at the end of the year, not is it desirable that any such effort should be made.[25]

7. Absence of Preferential Treatment. Absence of any preferential treatment in the provision of services is another important characteristic of public administration. It is controlled and regulated by the law of the land. Its duties, responsibilities, mode of work, area of activity and such other factors are determined by the law of the land.

8. Anonymity of the Official and Uniformity of Treatment. Anonymity of the official and uniformity of treatment is another important feature of the activities of public administration. Due to these reasons, the attitude of government officials towards the public is very different from that of private business. Public interest and public-service attitude are essential for any public servant. Through rules and regulations an attempt is made to free public administration from likes and dislikes, favoritism, hatred and all other personal, irrational, and emotional factors.

9. Monopolistic Nature of Services. Another difference between public and private administration is, that many services provided by the former, to the community, are of a monopolistic character.

10. Need of Legislative Control. On account of the monopolistic character of services, and the divorce between finance and administration, the necessity of legislative control over public administration assumes great importance.

Public responsibility, uniformity of treatment, impartiality and public-spiritedness distinguish public from private administration. But the difference between the two is one of degree and not of kind. Private business is also regulated and controlled by the law of the land, and profit is not its sole aim. Moreover, both have some common techniques of work and employ some common skills. One comes across many common basic problems, whether one is studying the administration of private business or of public affairs. There is a feeling that a 'general theory of administration' can be developed to study both public or private kinds of organisations

FUNCTIONS OF PUBLIC ADMINISTRATION

Prof. Walker had based applied public administration upon 10 functions chiefly, viz., political, legislative, financial, defence, educational, social, economic, external, colonial and local self-government.

1. Political functions. Relationship between executive and the legislature, administrative functions of the Council of the Ministers or Cabinet, relations between ministers and civil servants.

2. Legislative Functions. Delegated legislation, law making process, and the part played by the administrative officials therein.

3. Financial Functions. These include functions from preparation of budget, its execution, accounting and auditing management to treasury etc.

4. Defence Functions. All functions relating to soldiers are included among the defence activities.

5. Educational Functions. In the broad sense under educational administration all educational activities are included.

6. Social Functions. The social administration comprises food, building construction, social security, employment etc.

7. Economic Functions. The economic administration aims at the establishment of prosperous and stable economy, encouragement to foreign trade and commerce, regulations of industries in the interest of consumers.

8. External Functions. The external administration deals with the management of external affairs, diplomacy, international cooperation and administration of various international organisations and agencies.

9. Colonial Functions. Under colonial administration we deai with those problems and techniques which arise from the rule of one nation over the other.

10. Local Self-Government Functions. These are concerned with the working of local self-government.

THE MODERN VIEW

According to modern view about public administration, it is government in action. The concept of Welfare State becoming more and more popular, modern State is increasingly undertaking more and more responsibilities. This tendency has widened the scope of public administrator. It is usually agreed that the functions of public administrator are similar to those of the State. The administrator infuses a sense of practicability in the abstracat notion of the State. A public administrator is supposed to be an ex ecutive, legislator and judicial officer. He is expected to know the administrative systems and constitutional set-ups of other countries. A good public administrator should possess up-to-date comparative data about basic aspects with which he is frequently concerned. He should appreciate cultural and historical background as well as religious sentiments of the people of other countries in order to the establish healthy relations with them. There is no aspect of human life which public administrator today does not touch. A public administration is supposed to make his nation dynamic, progressively establishing relations with national and international organisations and associations. It can be achieved by improving means of transportation and communication and encouraging constructive initiative of the individuals. Development of education is also one such method. As the functions of public administration are ever widening, its scope has immensely increased. Thus, "A system of public administration is the composite of all laws, regulations, practices, relationships, codes and customs that prevail at any time in any juridiction for the fulfilment or execution of public policy."

Questions for Exercise

1. Public Administration consists of all those operations having for their purpose the fulfilment or enforcement or Public Policy—(White L.D.) Is this a satisfactory definition of Public Administration?

2. Discuss the proposition that 'administration begins where policy making ends'.

3. The administration gets things done and just as the science of politics is an enquiry into the best means whereby the will of the people may be organised for the formulation of policy so the science of public administration is an enquiry as to how the policies may best be carried into operations (Mersom). Explain this definition of public administration and point out any deficiencies it may have.

4. Administration is at once the marshal of techniques and lieutenant of policy.' Discuss.

5. "Today Public Administration is concerned not merely with the routine executive business of the government, it is also an instrument of social justice and social change." Discuss the scope of Public Administration in a modern State in the light of the above statement.

6. Account for the expanding scope of the Public Administration in the modern society.

7. Define Public Administration and distinguish it from Private Administration.' The gap between Private and Public Administration is narrowing.' Comment.

8. Indicate the areas where Private and Public Administrations are borrowing from each other. How does the administration of public enterprise illustrate this development.

References

1. E.N. Gladeen, *An Introduction to Public Administration,* Staples Press, London, p. 17.

2. F.M. Marx (Ed.) *Elements of Public Administration,* Prentice-Hall, New York, 1946, p.

3. E.A. Nigro *Public Administration: Readings and Documents,* New York, Rinehart and Co. Inc., 1951.

4. L.D. White, *Introduction to the Study of Public Administration,* The Macmillan Co. 1955, p. 4.

5. J.M. Pfiffner and Presthus, *Public Administration,* The Ronald Press Co., New York, 1960, p. 3.

6. Simon, Smithburg and Thompson, *Public Administration,* Alfred A. Knopf, New York, 1955, p. 3.

7. Simon, Smithburg and Thompson, *Public Administration,* Alfred A. Knopf, New York, 1956. p. 3.

8. Ordway Tead, *Art of Administration,* McGraw-Hill Book Co., New York, 1951, p. 4.

9. W.F. Willoughby, *Principles of Public Administration,* Indian Edition, p. 1.

10. L.D. White, *Introduction to the Study of Public Administration,* Macmillan Company, N.Y. 1948, p.3.

11. Woodrow Wilson, *The Study of Administration,* Political Science Quarterly 1941, pp. 481-566. Also in the Political Science Quarterly, Vol. 2, pp. 197-222, June 1887.

12. Luther Gulick, "Science, Values and Public Administration" in Luther Gulick and L. Urwick (Education.) *Papers on the Science of Public Administration.* Institute of Public Administration, N.Y., 1937, p. 191.

13. Pfiffner *Public Administration:* The Ronald Press Company, N.Y. 1946, pp. 4-6.

14. Marshall E. Dimock, "The Study of Administration', *American Political Science Review,* XXX, No. 1 (February), 1937, pp. 31-32.

15. Dwight Waldo, *The Administrative State,* Ronald Press, (New York), 1948, pp. 5-6, *The Study of Public Administration* (Doubleday); *Short Studies in Political Science* (Garden City, New York), 1955: *Ideas and Issues in Public Administration,* McGraw –Hill (N.Y.), 1953.

16. Morstein Marx (Ed.) *Elements of Public Administration.* New York, 1946, Prentice Hall, Inco. p. 6.

17. Simon and others, *Public Administration,* Alfred A. Knopf, New York, 1950, p. 7.

18. Pfiffner and Presthus, *op. cit.,* p. 6.

19. John J. Corsen and Joseph P. Harris: *Public Administration in Modern Sciences,* McGraw Hill Book Co. U.S.A. 1963, p. 21.

20. Lewis Meriam, *Public Service and Special Training* (1946), p. 267.

21. Address to the Second International Congress of Administrative Science quoted in L. Urwick's Foreword to Fayol's 'General and Industrial Management', p. XV.

22. *Ibid.*, p. XVI.

23. Paul H. Appleby, *Big. Democracy*, Alfred A. Knopf, N.Y., 1945, p. 7.

24. MacGregor Dawson, "The Civil Service is Different", from "*The Civil Service of Canada", pp. 220-23*, Copywright 1929 by Oxford University Press, London, Reproduced by Donald C. Rowat, *Basic Issues in Public Administration*, The Macmillan Co. N.Y. 1961, p. 25.

25. Robert MacGregor Dawson, *The Civil Service of Canada*, quoted by Donald C. Rowat, *Basic Issues in Public Administration*, The Macmillian Co., N.Y., 1961, pp. 23-24.

4

Nature and Role of Public Administration

The question whether public administration is science or art or both or even a philosophy, has assumed much more importance with the passage of time. There are conflicting views and opinions on this issue and each appears to be justified in its own way. Modern thinkers hold extreme views on the subject. Jacob Winer says, "No one knows better than the occupants of the Social Science chairs that their discipline is so fallible and erratic that to persist in the term scientific, is an open invitation of ridicule." But Prof. Beard says, "Now if Science means conceptual scheme of things in which every phenomenon, particularity covered, may be assigned a mathematical value, then administration is not a Science. If on the other hand, we may rightly use the term Science, in connection with a body of exact knowledge, derived from experience and observation, and a body of rules of axioms which experience has demonstrated to be applicable in concrete practice, and to work out in practice approximately as forecast, then we may, if we please, approximately and for convenience speak of science of administration."

PUBLIC ADMINISTRATION AS AN ART

The following arguments have been given to prove that public administration is an art:

1. It can be Acquired. A school of thought believes that public administration is definitely an art. According to them to think that only music, dance, drama or painting are covered in the category of art, is only giving it a narrow interpretation. Public Administration is not only an art but a fine art. Art is

a natural gift. A natural or born poet or artist is a only gifted artist. Art can be acquired. The natural gifts can find their best exposition by proper training, without which even the best artists will die unknown. Similarly, art of public administration can be acquired. The talented become the best administrators under proper training. Like other arts, art of public administration can be well acquired.

2. It can de Wonders. A true artist is one who with his skill and application of knowledge, can make wonders by combining and bringing together available material so that it becomes appealing an useful. A painter contributes to art by mixing colours. A sculptor does his job with the aid of sand and dust. Similarly, public administrator too have done useful wonders. Kautilya Bismark and Machiaveli were skilful artists who changed the very fate of their nations with their skill. Today success of every programme depends on how a public administrator performs his job.

3. Practical Application of Knowledge. Art is a practical application or systematic knowledge. It is not merely theory but putting that into actual practice. Similarly, public administration is not merely theory but practice. It is more a practical aspect rather than mere theoretical discussion. A public administrator cannot be a success by merely being a theorist. The best knowledge can be gained by practice alone. Urwick has said "Administrative skill cannot be bought. There are no hints and tips and short cuts. It has to be paid for in the only currency which is sound in this market-hard study and harder thinking mastery of intellectual principles reinforced by genuine reflection on actual problems. For which the individual has real responsibility" Thus public administration is both an art as well as fine art. In his '*Art of Public Administration*'. Ordway Tead has gone to the extent of saying that it is the art of the highest order. In his own words," If the works with paints or clay with combination of words and ideas in literature... if these are fine arts, we are certainly entitled to call that labour a fine art which would bring closer together in purpose the organised relationship of individuals and group to each other.

PUBLIC ADMINISTRATION AS A SCIENCE

Some thinkers have argued that public administration is not merely an art but also a science. In the simplest way science is a systematic study of knowledge. Those who believe that public administration is a science point out that there are certain very specific and clear principles on which day-to-day administration of states is being run and managed. They also argue that these principles are very sound and rational an can be obtained as well as considered with uniformity. Pfiffner has said that, "Specialists in public administration have achieved a considerable degree of uniformity in their thinking on those problems of administration which tend to exist irrespective of the subject-matter of the service being performed." Public Administration has already obtained considerable perfection to claim a place in the family of physical sciences. It has well defined field and sufficient data for application to arrive at facts. There is also a fair degree of certainty in the principles of public administration. Others believe that public administration is not an exact science but one of the social sciences. Yet other thinkers believe that though public administration is not at present a perfect science yet with more development, it will become a science. The modern writers have subjected these views to critical analysis, Public Administration is not exact. It has no universally applicable principles. However, the following arguments have been given to prove that public administration is a science.

1. Application of Scientific Method. The claim of a discipline to be called a science depends on whether the scientific method of study is applicable to it. Public Administration is a science, because the scientific method of study is applicable to it. The 'facts' of public administration can be studied scientifically. The building of a hypothesis and collection of facts to verify it, is the essence of the scientific method and this method is applicable to the study of Public Administration. Its facts can be observed, analysed, correlated and co-ordinated: hypothesis can be built and facts can be collected to verify it.

2. Critical Examination. Critical examination and study of evidence is the prime requisite of any scientific study. This

is possible in public administration. This position is explained well by Morris R. Cohen. He observes. "The man who has an eye for facts, whether it be about human being, stones or anything else, the man who asks. 'It is so? And "Can it be verified?' has the essence of all sciences provided he follows the critical methods of proof and verfication."[1]

3. Universal Principles. Some argue that public administration, cannot be called a science because the scientific method of study is inapplicable to the study of administrative phenomenon as 'values' cannot be studied scientifically. As Waldo observes: "Administrative study, an any 'social science' is concerned primarily with human being, a type of being characterised by thinking and valuing. Thinking implies creativeness, free will. Valuing implies morality, conceptions of right and wrong. It is submitted that the established techniques of science are inapplicable to thinking and valuing human beings."[2] Again "Many administrative matters simply are not, by their nature, amenable to the methods of physical sciences."[3] Robert A. Dahl raised a controversy in the Public Administration Review (USA 1947) regarding the question: Whether public administration is a science? His position can be summarised as follows:

As long as the study of Public Administration is not comparative, claims for "a science of public administration sound rather hollow" Generalisations derived from the operation of public administration in the environment of one nation-state cannot be universalised and applied to public administration in a different environment. A principle may be applicable in a different framework, but its applicability can be determined only after a study of that particular framework. There can be no truly universal generalisations about public administration without a profound study of varying national and social characteristics impinging on public administration, to determine what aspects of administration, if any, are truly independent of the national and social setting. Are those discoverable principles of universal validity, or are all principles valid only in terms of a special environment? Dahl concludes: "We are a long way from a science of public administration. No science of public administration is possible unless: (a) the place of normative values is made clear; (b) the nature of man in the area of public administration is better understood and his conduct is more predictable; (c) there is a body of comparative studies from which it may be possible to discover principle and generalities that transcend national boundaries and peculiar historical experience."

L. Urwick joins issue with Dahl on the question of whether there is any principles of public administration of universal validity. His reply is contained in Public Administration Review USA, 1957. He points out that principles of public administration are 'approximate or probable anticipations'. He illustrates it with the principle of 'Span of control.' Span of control comes into conflict with the principle of reducing administrative levels to a minimum. Urwick's reply to this objection is that: "Men have an appetite for power and self importance... It is an appetite which feeds on having rows of subordinate waiting on their doormat. And where it is not retained by recognition of the limits imposed by the span of control, there will always be some managers in every kind of undertaking driving their subordinates scatty and themselves into the ground by ignoring the human limitation of a restricted span of attention."

4. Comparative Studies. Comparative studies in public administration are gaining popularity. Cross-cultural studies conducted by Fred W. Riggs would open a new vista of understanding the science of public administration.

5. Scientific Study of Facts. Scientific study of the 'facts' of administration is possible and therefore, to this extent public administration is a science. An objective understanding of administrative Phenomena are certainly possible. Simon rightly observes: "The emphasis on the factual does not mean that we discount the importance of values. It simply reflects our belief that the competent practitioner reaches his desired ends—whatever they may be—through a mastery of the phenomena he is dealing with and a clear, objective understanding of their behaviour."[4] It is argued, that to

understand or to practice administration of any kind, one should devote himself to the examination of administration in several of its forms. As a writer observes: "Now, instead of a universally valid theory of administration is a growing variety of part theories—of business administration, public administration, hospital administration and other administration... Administrative science is establishing an identity and is gaining momentum. We firmly believe that there is in the making, a rigorous science of administration, which can account for events in particular times and place and for the ethical or normative content of those events without itself incorporating the particular conditions and values of those events."

APPROACHES TO THE STUDY OF PUBLIC ADMINISTRATION

The earliest writers on public administration concentrated their attention on the question of achieving efficiency. The so-called 'principles' of public administration, which were developed in the earlier period, were nothing more than devices suggested to achieve efficiency. A leading authority wrote in 1937: "In the science of administration, whether public or private, the basic 'good' is efficiency. The fundamental objective of the science of administration is, least expenditure of manpower and materials. Efficiency is thus axiom number one in the values scale of administration."[5] Woodrow Wilson observes, "The field of administration is a field to business. It is removed from the hurry and strife on politics, ... that administration lies outside the proper sphere of politics. Administrative questions are not political questions. Although politics sets the tasks for administration. It should not be suffered to manipulate its offices."[6]

DANGERS OF PUBLIC ADMINISTRATION BEING CALLED A SCIENCE

Even if it is believed that public administration, is a perfect science, it is not its, interest to place it in the family of exact sciences. It is rather dangerous for it to do so. Sciences being exact, a public administration might take his results as final and thus attempt at generalising them. This will result in untold miseries for the people who become the victim of his policy of generalisation. It will kill the initiative of the people who are at present trying to make new searches and researches, which always enrich the subject. It will bring premature rigidity in the subject making it most outdated. It is absolutely dangerous to take its hypothesis as final.

PUBLIC ADMINISTRATION AS A PHILOSOPHY

Some thinkers have tried to establish that public administration is neither an art not science but a philosophy. As philosophy deals with human beings, similarly public administration also deals with human beings. Both have the same subject of their study and both also have more or less the same field to cover. But, this does not entitle public administration to claim the status of a philosophy. There are various other subjects as well which deal with human beings but all those cannot claim the status of philosophy and Public Administration cannot be an exception to this rule.

To conclude, public administration has characteristics of both science and art. It is neither a perfect science nor complete art. It is one of the social sciences and has a place in that family. In the words of Mr. Merson, "The science on public administration offers even greater difficulties, but observation and experience have particularly during the last fifty years, provided a mass exercise of deductive faculties, and the statistician is constantly providing him with materials for fresh deductions or for the verification of general propositions previously advanced." Wallace B. Donham says, "Administration is a social science with its own abstractions, clustering around the concept of action through human organisations, and its own problems of theory. It is vitally concerned in integrating other sciences, physical, biological, psychological and social, at the point where action is involved."

SOCIAL ROLE OF PUBLIC ADMINISTRATION

1. Maintenance of Law and Order. Public Administration maintains law and order. The survival of human beings in society depends on protection provided by public administrators who have to enforce law and maintain order. Human beings can make progress only if their life is protected

against attacks from law-breakers. Hence proper enforcement of laws becomes a primary responsibility of public functionaries. Human behaviour should be regulated, and conduct of human beings should be based on norms acceptable by the people. The most important norm of social living is that man should not kill a man and law of jungle should not prevail in human society. Every human being needs protection of life before he can perform any other role in society. Such a protection of human life is provided by public administration. Thus the maintenance of law and order is the most primary and crucial role of public administration.

2. Promotion of Human Welfare. Public administration promotes human welfare. Human beings enter into cooperative relations to fulfil their basic social needs. Any cooperative human activity demands the creation of institution and organisations for achieving goals. In early simple societies, family or tribal organisations were created to help human beings to promote their welfare and produce wealth for consumption and survival.

As societies became more complex, impersonal and formal organisations were needed to promote collective human welfare. Public administration in modern societies is concerned with activities of human welfare. All essential welfare services are provided by organisations and agencies managed by public administrators.

3. Solution of Complex Social Problem. Public Administration in advanced industrial societies of the West, deals with complex social problems with the help of advanced technological techniques. The foundations of complex industrial societies are based on the application of science and technology for human welfare. Its consequence is that public administration in the western industrial societies grapples with situations which demand complex solutions. Public administration of the industrialised countries is influenced by developments of science and technology. Public administrators have to familiarise with scientific discoveries for managing human affairs. Thus it is always considered

relevant to differentiate between the roles of public administration in the industrialised societies and the developing societies.

4. Economic Development and Social Change. Public administration in the developing countries has to act as an instrument of economic development and social change. Public administration is the locomotive of development in the poor countries of Asia, Africa and Latin America. It is recognised that public administration plays crucial role in all societies, but the specific roles played by it differ in various societies. Hence a relevant distinction is made between the industrialised countries and the developing countries. The developing countries depend on their governments for all crucial decisions regarding economic development. The developing countries have limited material and human resources for development. Because of scarcity of resources, governments of the developing countries intervene in social life by laying down major priorities and goals of development. Further, agencies and organisations have to be established by governments of the developing countries for rendering social welfare services. While the challenge of development faced by the developing countries are multiple and quite complex, resources available to governments of these countries are limited. Public administration in the countries of Asia, Africa and Latin America is concerned with the development of agriculture, management of industry, and many other welfare programmes. With the proliferation of tasks of administration in the developing countries, the questions of administrative capability have emerged on the scene. Is Public Administration equipped to perform multiple tasks of development?

PRACTICAL PROBLEMS OF PUBLIC ADMINISTRATION

1. Context of Public Administration. In the contemporary literature on public administration, a great emphasis is attached to the study of context of public administration. Fred W. Reggs and many other scholars have made a distinction between the developed and the developing societies, and their

arrangements of administration. Problems of the study of public administration would vary from society to society depending on the context of societies. Public administration in the industrialised countries, has developed capacity of implementing laws of the land. In the developing countries, many laws enacted by legislatures remain on paper because administration does not have capability of implementing them. Corruption in public administration of the developed countries. In the developing countries, is marginal, it is all pervasive in the developing countries, Public administration fear to violate law in the developed countries. In the developing countries, while implementing the law, the public administrators do not hesitate to violate them. The violation of law by the law enforcement agencies is observed everyday in the developing countries. Thus it is maintained that in the study of public administration, emphasis should be laid on the context of administration. If the specific context of administration is ignored, the study of public administration would lead to irrelevant generalisations. While the scientific study of public administration should be concerned with generalisation it should not ignore the specific and concrete the context of administration. Public administration is a concrete, and observable activity. Corruption in Public administration in the developing countries is a concrete thing. Its explanation can be found by identifying the problem in the context of society in which problem of corruption exists. Many scholars of public administration maintain that public administration deals with concrete social problems, and in the study of public administration proper social context of problems should be understood for arriving activity valid and relevant Scientific explanations.

2. Role of Tradition and Values. Many contemporary scholars of public administration have argued that public administration as an activity in society deals with social traditions and values of community. A family planning programme in any society confronts itself with traditional values of society. The acceptance or non-acceptance of any public administration programmes depends on traditions of

a society. Many programmes and policies of public administration are resisted by the people because of their social order, traditions and social values.

The activity of public administration has to confront with traditions and social values everyday, the study of public administration cannot be valueless and normless. Public administration cannot be a pure science like physics or mathematics. The scientific study of public administration should recognise the existence of values in society. Public administrators cannot be value-free and neutral between right and wrong. Similarly the study of public administration cannot be value-free and value-neutral.

3. Contribution of Private Management. The study of public administration should interact with the study of business management and private factory management culture. A very important debate in the literature of public administration evolves round a belief that studies of public and business management have many things in common, and scholars of public administration can learn much from the practice and theories of management. A good and efficient management categories faces problems similar to that of public administration. It is suggested that public administration and private factory management are involved in decision-making, coordination, communication, and leadership. It is further argued that after a particular stage, public administration tends to become management of human affairs, and the techniques of management are common in a government office or a big Ford Car Factory or Tata Steel Plant. It is maintained that a Tata Steel manager, or the manager of Ford Car Factory or a senior administrative official of a big government department have to undertake some steps for managing human affairs. The dichotomy between the science of public administration and the science of private factory management has been proved harmful because both of them have many common things to share. The science of public administration would become rich if it interacts with management experts, and utilises their studies to improve efficiency. Management studies are result-oriented and problem solving. The orientation of management

scholars is towards concrete problems of efficiency and performance. Management studies want to find out causes of inefficiency and mechanism of removal of bottlenecks in the factory organisation Public administration is also concerned with the removal of bottlenecks in organisation. In spite of differences between public administration and private management, the studies of private management would enrich the studies of public administration because at one level both public and private management are seeking to improve efficiency and cut red-tape and unnecessary administrative delays. Public administration has much to learn from private management and *vice versa,* and they have harmed each other maintaining a distance. The scientific study of management has sharply focused attention on the role of human psychology and human behaviour in the functioning of organisations. Public administration should use insights provided by science of management and human psychology in dealing with human problems.

4. Differential Levels of Efficiency and Performance of Various Government Departments. Leadership, decision-making and communication are central in the scientific study of public administration. Some administrative departments are more efficient than others. They respond quickly and promptly. They show initiative and spirit of public enterprise. They are able to cut red-tape and deal with problems of emergency and crisis. Other administrative departments collapse under the weight of challenge and crisis. Thus, departments of the government do not work on the same levels of efficiency. Some departments of government are more efficient and performance-oriented than others.

5. Lack of Administrative Leadership. It makes a department or an organisation what it is. If a leader is competent and enterprising, the organisation reflects it and shows performance. If the head of the organisation is a pessimist or a cynic, procedure-oriented and rule-oriented, cautious bureaucrat, the organisation reflects his personality traits. A forward looking leader would take his administrative

organization along with himself. A timid leader would make everyone timid in the organisation. Efficient organisation has to be created by the leader of the organisation. Thus in the study of public administration scholars attach great importance to the role of leadership and personality traits of the leader. The study of leadership in an organisation is central in public administration.

6. Problems in Decision-making. Decisions have to be made at every step in public administration. The exercise of decision-making has become very complex. A decision-maker has to deal with many options. He has to pick and chose from the given options depending on the situation. A decision-maker has to respond to a situation, make his choice and face the consequences.

However, all decisions in public administration are not made under the stress of emergency situations. A decision-maker has to weigh properly the pros and cons of an option picked up by him. More complex is the situation greater are the options of a decision-maker. Again, options before a decision-maker are of a conflicting and contradictory nature. Many a time he is helped by past precedents of the office, but he has to work on a clean state. Hence in the contemporary literature on public administration great emphasis is laid on the techniques of decision-making. Statistical data and computers are used in decision-making in modern complex administrative organisations. An effort is made to minimize errors of judgement or subjective feelings in decision-making. Objectivity in decision-making in public administration is a goal worth achieving though it is not always possible to be objective. Many subjective factors and irrational feelings and calculations enter human decision-making in administration. Administration is a human activity, and no computers can replace human judgement and human feelings. The best results in public administration are obtained through participating decision-making.

IMPEDIMENTS IN PARTICIPATORY DECISION-MAKING

In decision-making in public administration many theorists have identified many difficulties of participatory and democratic system of decision-making.

1. Principle of Hierarchy. Public administration establishes its offices an organisations on the principle of hierarchy and superior-subordinate relationships. If the principle of hierarchy is central in public administration, opinions and views of the superiors always prevail over the subordinate. On the other hand, participatory or democratic decision-making in administration assumes a level of equality among the decision-making.

2. Social Culture. The actual functioning of administrative hierarchy is bound by cultural traditions of society. An egalitarian and democratic culture has emerged in many advanced countries of the West. It has developed a feeling of equality among participants in administrative decision-making. A subordinate does not fear to express his difference of opinion with his superior on an administrative problem. If a meeting has been called to discuss various aspects of organisational problem, participants express their views and opinions quite frankly because of strong traditions of democracy and equality. In traditional societies which are hierarchical, the opinions of superior cannot be questioned and challenged. Administrative culture of traditional societies reflects values of those societies. Participatory decision-making is confronted with many obstacles in societies where hierarcy is taken very seriously. The subordinates are not expected to question the views and opinions of the superiors. The conference method of decision-making in public administration in developing societies sometimes tends to be formal because many of these societies are hierarchical. Theories of administration have to make cross national and cross-cultural generalisations though they cannot ignore that administration is culture bound. If a society glorifies hierarchical relationship, democratic decision-making is a mere formality. Thus the first impediment in democratic decision-making is hierarchy. Participatory decision-making requires frankness on the basis of equality, while hierarchy assumes respect for opinions of the superiors in administration. Hierarchical rigidity and participatory decision-making do not go together.

3. **Generalist Specialist Confrontations.** In the developing societies, specialists in public administration are late extrants. With the increasing application of science and technology for economic development, many specialists and technically trained personnel are being appointed in public administration. A participatory decision-making involves some common level of knowledge and understanding among the participants. The generalist administrator feels that specialists have an understanding of a narrow field of their speciality. The specialist feels that generalist administrator cannot comprehend the technical aspects of administrative decision. The generalist feels that broad implications of a decision cannot be appreciated by a specialist who has a narrow view of problems. Participatory decision-making requires participation of personnel with common background and common perspectives. But a generalist administrator and specialist are brought from different backgrounds.

4. **Influence of Politics.** As differentiated from decisions in a private firm or a factory decisions in public administration cannot be insulated from the influence of politics and various pressure group in a society. All decisions in private firm are evaluated on the basis of the goal of earning private profit. In public administration decisions do not have any one goal. Decision-makers have to achieve multiple goal of efficiency social service, and welfare of various sections of society. Political considerations play crucial role in decision-making in public administration. A general law of decision-making in public administration is: more important the decision in the role of politics in it.

Democratic governments are elected to the countries on the basis of programmes and promises made by political leaders. Political leaders in a democracy are accountable to the people for their performance. Public administrator has to implement many decisions about whose merits he may not be convinced. Further, political leaders have many sectional interests to satisfy. Decision-making in public administration has to reconcile demands of politics and efficiency of implementation. Politicians do not lay down the broad framework of policies alone, they are also interested in details of implementation. They define goals of administration and also supervise it. Public administration has to recognise the role of political factor in decision-making. A conference of administrators may arrive at a particular decision on rational consideration, but they may be over-ruled by political leaders on political considerations.

5. Sectional Pressures. Decision-making in public administration is subjected to sectional pressure of organised groups like, Trade Unions, Employers organisations, Journalists Associations or Farmers organisations. Many sectional demands have to be accommodated by decision-makers in public administration. As a process, decision-making has to make many adjustments and compromises with various sections of society. Many pressures are built by regional or sectional leaders to influence governmental decision-making. Thus location of factory or budgetary allocations for developmental purposes cannot be decided by the government on the basis of rationality or considerations of administrative propriety alone. The governmental decision-making process is subjected to all sorts of pressures by various groups in a society.

6. Lack of Communications. Some contemporary theorists have highlighted the central role of communications in public administration. Communication is a network of information system. Which must flow upwards and downwards from Headquarters to the field offices. The spirit and meaning of a decision should be properly communicated by decision-makers. An efficient implementation of decision depends on the clarity of communication. Bottlenecks developing while implementing a decision, should be highlighted, and decisions should be revised. Administrative communication links decision-makers with implementation process. Any failure in this process creates difficulties in administration.

Communication in public administration is a broader concept than information. In includes the totality of steps involved in decision-making and their implementation. The rationale of a decision and the need for proper implementation are an integral part of an administrative communication system. The mechanism and the style of communication are matters of detail. A developed society utilises many technologically evolved mechanisms to communicate while an under-developed society lacks in sophisticated mechanisms of communication. As public administration has become a very complex activity both in developed and developing societies, has to act as 'monitoring' of implementation.

QUESTIONS FOR EXERCISE

1. Explain the statement that public administration is both an art and science.
2. Define and discuss public administration whether it is a science or an art, or both.
3. Discuss the view that unless the study of public administration is made comparative, claim for the science of public administration will remain hollow?
4. Explain the social role of public administration.
5. Explain the practical problems of public administration.
6. Discuss impediments in participatory decision-making.

References

1. Cohen, M.R. *Studies in Philosophy and Science* (N.Y.) Henry Holt & Co., Inc., 1949 p. 86.
2. Dwight Waldo, *The Administrative State,* The Ronald Press Company, N.Y., 1948, p. 18.
3. *Op. cit.,* p. 191.
4. Simon and others, *Public Administration.* Alfred A. Know: N.Y. 1956, p. 20.
5. L. Urwick, *op. cit.,* p. 192.
6. Woodrow Wilson "The Study of Administration, *Political Science Quarterly,* Vol. 2 (June 1887), pp. 1972-22.

5

Problems of Administration

I am afraid that for years to come India would be engaged in passing legislation in order to raise the downtrodden, the fallen, of the mire into which they have been sunk by the capitalists, by the landlords, by the so-called higher classes, and then, subsequently and scientifically, by the British rulers. If we are to lift these people from the mire, then it would be the bounden duty of the National Government of India, in order to set its house in order, continually to give preference to these people and even free them from the burdens under which they are being crushed. And, if the landlords, zamindars, moneyed men and those who are today enjoying privileges—I do not care whether they are Europeans or Indians-if they find that they are discriminated against, I shall sympathize with them, but I will not be able to help them, even if I could possibly do so, because I would seek their assistance in that process, and without their assistance it would not be possible to raise these people out of the mire.

It will, therefore be a battle between the haves and the have-nots: and if that is what is feared, I am afraid the National Government will not be able to come into being if all the classes hold the pistol at the head of the dumb millions and say: 'You shall not have a Government of your own unless you guarantee our possessions and our rights.'

The Nation's Voice, p. 71

Governors

...Much as I would like to spare every piece of the public treasury, it would be bad economy to do away with provincial

Governors and regard Chief Ministers as a perfect equivalent. Whilst I would resent much power of interference to be given to Governors, I do not think that they should be mere figure-heads. They should have enough power enabling them to influence ministerial policy for the better. In their detached position they would be able to see things in their proper perspective and thus prevent mistakes by their Cabinets. Theirs must be an all-pervasive moral influence in their provinces.

Harijan, 21-12-'47

Ministers

If the Congress wants to continue as a people's organisation, the Ministers cannot live as *sahib log* nor use for private work facilities provided by Government for official duties.

Harijan, 29-9-'46

Nepotism

This office-holding is a step towards either greater prestige or its total loss. If it is not to be a total loss, the ministers and the legislators have to be watchful of their own personal and public conduct. They have to be, like Caesar's wife, above suspicion in everything. They may not make private gains either for themselves or for their relatives or friends. If the relatives or friends get any appointment, it must be only because they are the best among the candidates, and their market value is always greater than what they get under the Government. The ministers and the legislators of the Congress ticket have to be fearless in the performance of their duty. They must always be ready to risk the loss of their seats or offices. Offices and seats in the legislatures have no merit outside their ability to raise the prestige and power of the Congress. And since both depend wholly upon the possession of morals, both public and private, any moral lapse means a blow to the Congress.

Harijan, 23-4'38

Taxes

A popular ministry is responsible to the legislatures and cannot do anything without their consent. Every elected member in a popular legislature is responsible to his voters. Therefore, the voter who represents the public should ponder well before embarking on any criticism of the government of his creation. Moreover, one bad habit of the people should be borne in mind. They do not like any tax whatsoever. Where there is good government, the tax-payer gets full return for his money as, for example, the water tax in cities. No tax-payer could get water on his own for the same payment. But even so, and in spite of the fact that the tax is levied by the popular will, tax-payers always resent even paying such taxes. It is, of course, true that one cannot prove the benefit of all taxes as easily as the one I have cited as an example. But as society growe in size and complexity and the field of service also grows, it is difficult to explain to the individual tax-payer, how he gets his return for any particular tax. This much, however, is clear that taxes as a whole should stand for the general benefit of society. If this were not so, the argument that the taxes were levied by popular will would not hold.

Harijan, 8-9-'46

Crime and Its Punishment

In independent India of the non-violent type, there will be crime but no criminals. They will not be punished. Crime is a disease like any other malady and is a product of the prevalent social system. Therefore, all crime including murder will be treated as a disease. Whether such an India will ever come into being is another question.

Harijan, 5-5-'46

What should our jails be like in free India? All criminals should be treated as patients and the jails should be hospitals admitting this class of patients for treatment and cure. No one commits crime for the fun of it. It is a sign of a diseased mind. The causes of a particular disease should be investigated and removed. They need not have palatial buildings when their jails become hospitals. No country can afford that, much less can a poor country like India. But the outlook of the jail staff should be that of physicians and nurses in a hospital. The prisoners should feel that the officials are their friends. They are there to help them to regain their mental health and not to harass them in any way. The popular governments have to issue necessary orders, but meanwhile the jail staff can do not a little to humanize their administration. What is the duty of the prisoners?....They should behave as ideal prisoners. They should avoid breach of jail discipline. They should put their heart and soul into whatever work is entrusted to them. For instance, the prisoners' food is cooked by themselves. They should clean the rice, *dal* or whatever cereal is used so that there are no stones and grit or weevils in them. Whatever complaints the prisoners might have should be brought to the notice of the authorities in a becoming manner. They should so behave in their little community as to become better men when they leave the jail than when they entered it.

Delhi Diary, pp. . 113-14

Adult Suffrage

I am wedded to adult suffrage.... Adult suffrage is necessary for more reasons than one, and one of the decisive reasons to me is that it enables me to satisfy all the reasonable aspirations, not only of the Musalmans, but also of the so-called untouchables, of Christians, of labourers and all kinds of classes. I cannot possibly bear the idea that a man who has got character but no wealth or literacy should have no vote, or that a man who works honestly by the sweat of his brow day in and day out should not have the vote for the crime of being a poor man.

Young India, 8-10-'31

Death Duties

In this of all countries in the world possession of inordinate wealth by individuals should be held as a crime against Indian humanity. Therefore the maximum limit of taxation of riches beyond a certain margin can never be reached. In England, I understand, they have already gone as far as 70 per cent of the earnings beyond a prescribed figure. There is no reason why India should not go to a much higher figure. Why should there not be death duties? Those sons of millionaires who are of age and yet inherit their parents' wealth, are losers for the very inheritance. The nation thus becomes a double loser. For the inheritance should rightly belong to the nation. And the nation loses again in that the full faculties of the heirs are not drawn out, being crushed under the load of riches.

Harijan, 31-7-'37

Reform by Legislation

People seem to think, that when a law is passed against any evil, it will die without any further effort. There never was a greater self-deception. Legislation is intended and is effective against an ignorant or a small evil-minded minority; but no legislation which is opposed by an intelligent and organised public opinion, or under cover of religion by a fanatical majority, can ever succeed.

Young India, 30-6-'27

The first thing is to avoid the slightest shadow of compulsion or untruth. No reform worth the name has yet, in my humble opinion, been achieved by compulsion. For whilst compulsion may lead to apparent success, it gives rise to so many other evils which are worse than the original evil itself.

Young India, 8-12-'27

Trials by Jury

Trials by jury often result, all over the world, in defeating justice. But people everywhere gladly submit to the drawback for the sake of the more important result of the cultivation of an independent spirit among people and the justifiable sentiment of being judged by one's own peers.

Young India, 12-8-'26

I am unconvinced of the advantages of jury trials over those by judges....We must not slavishly copy all that is English. In matters where absolute impartiality, calmness and ability to sift evidence and understand human nature are required, we may not replace trained judges by untrained men brought together by chance. What we must aim at is an incorruptible, impartial and able judiciary right from the bottom.

Young India, 27-8-'31

Law Courts

If we were not under the spell of lawyers and law-courts, and if there were no touts to tempt us into the quagmire of the courts and to appeal to our basest passions we would be leading a much happier life than we do. Let those who frequent the law-courts—the best of them—bear witness to the fact that the atmosphere about them is foetid. Perjured witnesses are ranged on either side, ready to sell their very souls for money or for friendship's sake.

Young India, 6-10-'26

The first thing which you must always bear in mind, if you would spiritualize the practice of law, is not to make your profession subservient to the interests of your purse, as is unfortunately but too often the case at present, but to use your profession for the service of your country. There are instance of eminent lawyers in all countries who led a life of self-sacrifice, who devoted their brilliant legal talents entirely to the service of their country, although it meant almost pauperism to them....You can follow Ruskin's precept given in his book *Unto This Last.* 'Why should a lawyer charge fifteen pounds for his work', he asks, 'whilst a carpenter for instance hardly gets as many shillings for his work?' The fees charged by lawyers are unconscionable everywhere. In England, in South Africa, almost everywhere I have found that in the practice of their profession lawyers are consciously or unconsciously led into untruth for the sake of their clients. An eminent lawyer has gone so far as to say that it may even be the duty of a lawyer to defined a client whom he knows to be guilty. There I disagree. The duty of a lawyer is always to place before the judges, and to help them to arrive, at the truth, never to prove the guilty as innocent.

Young India, 22-12-'27

Communal Representation

Independent India cannot afford to have communal representation and yet it must placate all communities, if the rule of independents is not based on coercion of minorities.

Young India, 19-1-'30

Military Expenditure

Our statesmen have for over two generations declaimed against the heavy expenditure an armaments under the British regime, but now that freedom from political serfdom has come, our military expenditure has increased and still threatens to increase and of this we are proud! There is not a voice raised against it in our legislative chambers. In spite, however, of the madness and the vain imitation of the tinsel of the West, the hope lingers in me and many others that India shall survive this death dance and occupy the moral height that should belong to her after the training, however imperfect, in non-violence for an unbroken period of thirty-two years since 1915.

Harijan, 7-12-'47

Navy

I do not know of the navy but I do know that the army of India of the future will not consist of hirelings to be utilised for keeping India under subjection and for depriving other nations of their liberty, but it would be largely cut down, will consist largely of volunteers and will be utilised for policing India.

Young India, 9-3-'22

6

Personnel and Personnel Administration

However necessary and useful organisation and machinery may be in administration, the importance of the manning of the administration is greater, for it is men that work the machine. From the top to the bottom, from the centre to the circumference and in between, it is men that make the machinery of administration work. The political philosophy of a great and long-lived people the Chinese and of their Empire was that the services of wise and capable men are indispensable to good government. And Bacon, philosopher and administrator, said a thousand years later "it is vain for princes to take council concerning matters if they take no council likewise concerning persons; for all matters are as dead images; and the life of the execution of the affairs lies in the good choice of persons." And he went on to say that the greatest errors are committed and the worst judgement is shown in the choice of persons. "Regner, c'est choisir" was the maxim of a great ruler, Louis XIV of France. "The due arrangement of men in the active part of the State" and Burke "far from being foreign to the purposes of a wise Government ought to be among its very first and dearest objects." In any study of public administration therefore the placing of men in administration in its various parts and grades and the means used to get the best out of them must be among the more important questions. First, comes the question how to get proper and suitable men into administration, that is the question of recruitment.

Before we consider the best way or ways of recruitment we must first know what kind of men are wanted in administration. The preliminary question to be considered is that of the qualifications of good administrators or what are the qualities, natural or acquired, and what is the equipment, moral, intellectual, and physical, required of men that can be serviceable in administration. Some qualities and qualifications are general and expected of all those that are to serve their fellowmen. Truthfulness, honesty, trustworthiness, conformity to the moral standards of civilised society, psychology soundness, a fair measure of education are required of every man that is to work in and for society. But there are certain special qualities and qualifications that are expected of men that are to succeed in the business of administration. And it is with these that we are concerned.

QUALITIES AND QUALIFICATIONS REQUIRED OF ADMINISTRATORS

They may be classified under the heads Intellectual, Moral, Social and Physical

INTELLECTUAL

1. *Love of knowledge:* An administrator must have the general knowledge of an educated man and the special knowledge that will be useful to him in administration in general and the department in which he works in particular. A wide intellectual horizon with the foreground of special knowledge makes for enlightened administration. "A statesman must be avid of facts" said Talleyrand. He need not be a Chadband a gatherer of facts for the sake of gathering them, a slave of facts indeed. The gathering of knowledge and information might be overdone as it was by Herr Abeuker of the German Chancellery in Bismarck's time who according to Bismarck was "so much of a sponge soaked in ink that one had only to touch it to be inundated." And this knowledge is to be acquired not only from books, official documents, learned reviews and newspapers and other printed work but from conversation with all kinds and classes of people and from travel which is the finishing governess of a statesman's education.

2. *Devotion to detail*—Mastery of detail is necessary, for the successful administrator must pursue every question that

comes before him in all its chief aspects and down to its lowest roots; otherwise his decisions might be rendered null and of no effect. Huxley's description of a scientific tragedy "as a beautiful theory killed by an ugly fact" might be realised often in his career. A famous devotee to hard work and detail was Philip the II of Spain of whom a historian has said that "he would retire to the Escorial with masses of papers, reading and noting on the journey; he would study the despatches of ambassadors, covering the margins of reports with his remarks, calling for explanations, raising doubts and difficulties; when he found anything interesting he would write *ajo* (attention) against it; when his secretaries sent him their replies and drafts he would re-draft them and his orders and drafts were characterised by precision and decision in contrast to the sterile abundance and vague phraseology of the Spanish Chancellery; he revelled in detail; he knew the names of the distinguished persons of every town, he knew which cleric was fit for which benefice; he had catalogued in his brain the men and the things of his empire". Louis the XIV of France was another great lover of detail. Saint Simon a hostile witness says that his taste for low details drown him in the petty. Napoleon was a still greater master of detail, with an insatiable activity in detail, said Mollien of him, a restlessness of mind always eager for new cases; he not only reigned and governed, he continued to administer not only as Prime Minister but more minutely than each Minister.

But this hard work and love of detail should not lead to slowness and indecision. Philip the II would in the most critical times spend six months in studying a question without sending an order to his officers; he would often lose occasion which of course would not wait for him, and the obstinacy which is the obverse of indecision often baffled him. The wise administrator must not lose himself in the details of administration; the superior administrator has to supervise and superintend. "It is not his business to be all day long engaged in seeing what other people are doing and can do" an English Minister told Helps. Rather, a successful Minister or Head of a Department is one who gets things done rather than does everything himself. The power of selection is necessary for decision in administration, the power of selecting the one crucial point from a multitude of relevant facts and arguments. Inability to combine and co-ordinate is often a defect of those who amass knowledge. It was the fault detected in Gladstone by a civil service contemporary of his who said that "although Gladstone had an immense mass of knowledge, it was not methodically arranged but the separate items had to be looked for in their separate boxes and did not float about and combine; the consequence was not merely want of play but that crotchety, one-sided narrowish mode of treating a matter uncorrected by the necessary comparisons and considerations which people called ingenious, subtle, and Gladstonian; he looked at the details and the aspects of the subject and mastered it by pursuing it hither and thither from one starting point not by walking round it; this mode of treatment was more suited to financial subjects than any other".

3. Accuracy—is necessary to and a concomitant of detail; accuracy is one of the cardinal official virtues, it is tolerated even if it is combined with slowness.

4. Reason and objectivity—The service of the State requires that the interests of the State rather than the interests of the administrator or his family or his class or community should be his pre-occupation and the motive of all his decisions. Reason, therefore should inform the thought and conduct of the administrator. Emotion and sentiment will divert him from the general interests to the interests of family or class or fashion or the crowd. "Reason" said Richelieu "ought to animate and cause the action of those that are in employment of public affairs." He wanted to exclude the women of his time from public affairs solely for the cause that they allowed their conduct to be governed by emotion rather than by reason. Balance and matter-of-factness are aids to this objectivity. The Earl of Cromer's success as British proconsul in Egypt was attributed to his disinterestedness and his poise of mind.

5. Ability to anticipate events—Of the Emperor Charles V an Italian contemporary said he hesitated till things became

dangerous; it was no wonder therefore that finding events like the Reformation and the disunion of Europe too much for him he abdicated and retired into a monastery. Far different was the behaviour of Richlieu who would pare short the nails of those he had to guard against so that their ill-will might be ineffective and attributed his failure in his dealings with the Queen Marie De Medicis to the fact that he did not nip cabals in the bud. If one wishes to save oneself, he said, one must make the counter-stroke; it is better to do too much than too little, for by too little we run the risk of losing.

6. Mastery of the art of expression—Modern administration which has to do so much talking and writing requires the cultivation of the art of expression. Ability to write clearly, intelligently, precisely and economically is expected of everybody in an office from the clerk to the Head. Outdoor workers and expected to write clear and intelligible reports. And as in modern administrative work, conferences, discussions, and interviews are frequent, the art of vocal expression is also required of the modern administrator. Lord Kitchener's failure as a War Minister in the First World War was due to his being tongue-tied in the Cabinet while Winston Churchill and Lloyd George could always persuade their colleagues to accept their proposals.

MORAL

Moral qualities are of the last importance in an administrator. "There is greater need of character in administration than in war" said Napoleon. The chief moral qualities required in the administrator are:

1. Honesty—It should not be necessary to insist on it but it has to be at a time when morality has become fluid and elastic when the great sin is the sin of being found out. Honesty is the best policy in administration as in business. Dishonesty costs the of the State a mint of money beside bringing the administration into contempt. Honesty is required not only in money matters but in speech and writing and includes honesty of purpose. It calls for integrity, that is what makes

the whole of a man, what makes a man whole, not a thing of shreds and patches. Richelieu the rationalist and the realist in politics, adjured the statesman to be true to God, to the State, to men and to himself.

2. Self control—is absolutely necessary to officials in high position. Restraint is necessary to authority as to liberty. It is only officials drest in a little brief authority that

   Play such fantastic tricks before high heaven
   As makes the angels weep.

3. Application—Is more a moral than an intellectual quality. It belongs to character rather than to mind. Voltaire said of Francis I of France "with great knowledge; great perspicuity, he lacked *esprit development suite* (the ability to follow a thing through to the end); everything in his reign happened in jerks". Perseverance was lacking in Emperor Maxmillian I of Germany, whereas of Richeleu the French historian Mignet said that "he always possessed the will to push through to success all that he undertook". Not incessant work but attachment to one's work in spirit, in thought, in affection was what Richeleu meant by application. Zeal which comes from belief in the goodness of the work one does is a consequence. *Pas de zele* was the advice of Talleyrand given to ambassadors only.

4. Decision—After long and mature deliberations, and it must be only as long as it is necessary to mature the thought on the business in hand, the administrator must decide quickly and promptly. Turenne, the famous general of Louis XIV, had learnt never to decide except out of much deliberation but execute his designs with hardihood and perseverance. Decision is easy with resolute characters. Government, said Richelieu, requires "male virtues and unbreakable firmness in use of them."

5. Courage—To ensure decision, courage is necessary. Richelieu called courage the heat and the fire of a ruler. Courage does not mean courting danger but to meet and support danger or adversity when it confronts one.

6. Prudence—The biblical injunction to be as simple as a dove and as wily as a serpent is applicable to the ruler of men and events. To speak little and listen much was the advice of Richelieu to statesman and administrator and his own adviser Pere Joseph, known in history as the Grey Eminence, advised his master not to rely so much on his fourteen and goodness but on his conduct and prudence.

7. Moderation—is part of prudence. Pascal said "one steps out of humanity when one leaves the middle way". Presumption is a vice in a ruler, according to Richeleu, and although humility may not be necessary in government, modesty is.

8. Ability to use discretion—In administration much has to be left to the individual's decision. Not all of his conduct can be provided for beforehand in rules and regulations. Especially, in the higher grades and in executive work as apart from office work, is this capacity for making up one's mind and acting without aid from rules or other persons, in other words, the use of discretion is necessary. "Is he good at taking corners" Bismarck would always ask of anyone that was suggested for a leading position in Government. And this discretion, of course, must be exercised, as Burke advised, "on public principles and national grounds not on likings or prejudices, intrigues or policy".

9. Elasticity of conduct—A ruler of men must ever adjust himself to changing conditions and circumstances; "govern" comes from a French word meaning to steer and a governor's work is allied to that of a pilot or a captain of a ship who has to take it through a storm as well as a calm. The rigidity of the ordinary bureaucrat makes for failure in administration. "The German Empire" said Bismarck "could stand any kind of chancellor but a bureaucrat". Ability to change course was the quality required from his diplomats. The art of adjustment of *combinazione* as the Italians call it, is very necessary to an administrator. Lord Cromer's complaint of some of the English civil servants in Egypt in that "although excellent public servants they were wanting in elasticity of mind" should not be reported of the good administrator. Elasticity

however cannot go to the point of immorality. The end cannot justify the means in administration.

10. Imagination and foresight—More than ever before does the modern self-conscious, progressive State require men that "look before and after and pine for what is not." As great administrator like Lord Beveridge and Lord Stamp have insisted, modern needs require long range, constructive, co-ordinated thinking "Anticipate agitation" was Admiral Fisher's advice to statesmen.

Physical and Social

1. Sound Health—*Mens sana in corpore sano*—the mind of an administrator can work only in a sound body. Modern administrators whether Ministers (with long hours of attendance and work in the legislature in addition to work in their offices) or officials have so much work to do that sound health and physical strength are essential qualifications. The qualification of bodily strength is becoming every day more indispensable to public business, said Taylor, and he wrote nearly one hundred years ago. Age is a physical factor to be reckoned with. Adults are wanted in the public service not old men to enter it. In the lower grades the middle years of adolescence 18 and for the higher grade the loater years of adolescence 21 to 25 seem to be indicated as the age of entry.

2. Sociability:—Administration is the rule of men by men and it cannot be done without the possession of a number of social qualities. Ability to move with others and to establish personal contacts and relationship is necessary. Especially necessary is it to emphasize this need in these days when administration has become so mechanical and formal and impersonal. One cannot go far in the government of men without moving with and treating men as men. It was the lack of these personal contacts that proved the undoing of Woodrow Wilson who used to correspond with his ministers instead of conferring with them and used to carry his typewriter to and from his room when he attended the Peace Conference of Versailles.

Knowledge of men, derived from intercourse with men is more useful than knowledge from books. Let us remember the successes of illiterate rulers like Charlemagne and Akbar. "In administration" says Masaryk, the maker of Czechoslovakia, "one has to know men, select them and assign to them suitable tasks." At an early stage he had acquired the habit of observing the people with whom he had to deal or who were prominent in public life as though he intended to write a book about them; he would collect all possible data upon friend or foe and gathered biographical matter about them; before meeting statesmen and public men he would read their writings or speeches and get as much information as he could about them. Ministers and other administrators should miss no opportunity of learning from men in every walk of life. They must act like men in a world of men and women. "Knowing how to take people" was according to Bismarck the quality that told in diplomacy.

3. Tact—is the greatest of the social qualities required of an administrator. The art of listening must be specially cultivated by administrators. Louis XIV in his audiences would listen with patience, with kindness, moved by the desire to instruct and enlighten himself.

4. Sympathy with all, pity for the lowly:—Administrative decisions must be based on the knowledge of the views and opinions and wants of all classes of people specially of those that cannot help themselves and have to be helped. An inspiring motive of this knowledge is sympathy and pity. The late Lord Morley thought that pity was the mark of the great statesman. It certainly inspired, the work of the greatest statesman like Asoka, Louis IX, Burke (in his great work for India), Gladstone. Especially does the modern welfare State require training in this social feeling and imagination.

Education for Administration

These qualities intellectual, moral, physical and social being necessary in persons that are to enter administration, how are we to ensure that the candidates for admission to the administrative services shall possess them. It is not necessary that there should be special institutions for obtaining the kind of persons required in administration. For, apart from the cost to Government, they would be superfluous for any sound system of general education would produce the required number of men in possession of the qualities required. For the large number of clerks required the ordinary school or college education would be sufficient. For the physical social and moral qualities required for the higher and executive grades of administration, schools and colleges provided with playing grounds and equipped with boarding houses or hostels would be enough. As for the intellectual equipment required of candidates for the administrative services the courses of study and examination that obtain in the high school and university college serve the purpose. No longer is the complaint that Bacon made in the *Advancement of Learning* valid that "there is no education collegiate designed to this end (education for the service of the state) where such as are formed and fitted by nature there to might give themselves chiefly to histories, modern languages, books and discussions of policy that so they might become more able and better furnished to the service of the State." And it is all to the good of administration that its services are manned by persons that have had the best general education the country can offer and possess the broad culture that men educated specifically for administration may not possess. But as school and university education has in these latter days tended to narrowing specialisation it is necessary that administration should make sure of getting persons that have been taught those special subjects that are specially useful in the making of the mind of the administrator.

Among such subjects pride of place must be given to History. It comes first in Bacon's enumeration. "From this source" advised Burke "much political wisdom can be learnt and this not by way of giving hints and suggestions for conduct in present circumstances but as an exercise to strengthen the mind and as furnishing materials to enlarge and enrich it, not as a repertory of cases and precedents as for a lawyer." For, as Richelieu observed, there is nothing more dangerous to the State than those who wish to govern States by measures they derive from books, "for the past is not altogether related to the present and the constitution of places and times is different." Richelieu does not repudiate a general knowledge of history for his ruler. Napoleon who had read a whole library of history taking down notes and making comments, has warned us that "history furnishes us not with models but with lessons." But even so, it is still considered the fittest study for a statesman. A detailed study of particular epochs or persons is more useful for persons aspiring to the higher grades of administration than summary histories of whole countries, especially if it is accompanied by the study of original documents, as it would be in a good Honours course at a University, for this would train them in the handling of documents and large masses of detail as they would have to do in an administrative office. Next to history would come political economy; it would not be necessary to canvass support for this subject in an economic age such as ours. Law, especially, general jurisprudence, political science including public administration, international law would also be useful studies for the modern administrator. A lawyer's training is not to be despised for the modern administrator who has to attend conferences or meetings of ministers must know how to debate and hold his own. The art of dissecting a brief, finding out its telling points, and going to the core of the matter would be useful to the administrator who has to deal with large masses of information.

Since University courses of study do not make the study of these subjects compulsory the authority charged with the duty of recruiting persons for the administrative services should test the possession of knowledge of these subjects.

CLASSIFICATION OF SERVICES

But before such a body can proceed to do its work, something that lies at the very threshold of any recruitment to the services is a condition precedent. That condition precedent is classification. "We must class services; we must, as far as their nature admits, appropriate funds or everything however refined will fall into the old confusion" said Burke recommending his great scheme of economical reform of the administration in the England of his time. Appropriation, we have dealt with when we described the duties and work of the Finance Department. We have now to see how classification is necessary to the organisation of the services. Services have to be classified because of the variety of work and the different grades and kinds of equipment required for the different varieties and kinds or grades of work. The peon or the messenger, the clerk, the manager, the superintendent, the inspector, the Head of a Department, the secretary, are all members of the services but each of them does a different kind of work and starts with difference in equipment. "Every man" said Napoleon "must be suited to his work" and he added "the greatest of immoralities is to take up work for which one is not fit." Classing them all together will serve neither the interests of the several and different members or promote the efficiency, of the services. The organisation of the civil service in any country begins with classification. Division of labour calls for classification of the services. Classification was done for the first time in England in the middle of the 19th century when the foundations of the organisation of the modern British Civil Service were laid. Every reform of the civil services concerns itself with classification to some extent or other.

The division of work between a higher and a lower grade or class is the key to every scheme of civil service organisation. The principle of this division is based on difference of work; there is work of a routine character which does not require a high grade of intelligence, and there is work which requires responsibility, discretion, power to direct others. And the people doing these different kinds of work must be put into different classes. Division of work leads to division into classes.

This division of labour calls for different scales of remuneration. They call for different sets of tests or examinations to regulate admission to the services; any one single system of examination or education leading to admission to the civil services of a State is out of the question. Separate schemes of examination for admission to the public service and two or more sets of such examinations or tests are therefore used. It would be a great waste of power and money to require that all candidates for the services including those that are to do routine inferior work most of that time, should submit themselves to the same examination as those that may be called on to do the highest grade of work.

The two broadly divided classes are (1) the Clerical and (2) the Administrative. These in English practice have been each divided into two sections or grades. The clerical grade has a lower sub-division called the writing assistant class employed in mechanical work like punching, labelling or hand-copying or transcribing work, writing out acknowledgements, filling up forms, bills, addressing letters, and simple routine work of a similar character. The upper clerical grade would be entrusted with superior clerical duties like dealing with cases in accordance with well-defined regulations, instructions or general practice, scrutinising, checking and cross-checking, straight-forward accounts claims, returns under well-defined instructions, preparation of materials for accounts, statistics in prescribed forms, simple drafting and precis work, collection and statement of material on which judgement can be formed.

The Administrative class may also be divided as is the English practice, into a lower sub-class, dealing with the examination of particular cases of lesser importance, initial investigation into matters of higher importance, the higher work of finance and accounting and supply, also with examination work like that of inspection, supervision, etc., and a higher sub-class being concerned with the formulation of policy, the supervision and co-ordination of the sections. In the Administrative class differentiation may be made between office-workers and field workers like Inspectors, Collectors of custom and excise duties, and others.

In the U.S.A. also classification was consolidated by the classification Act of 1923 which provided a five-fold division of positions in the federal service namely professional, sub-professional, C.A.F. (Clerical Administrative Fiscal) C.P.A. (Crafts, Protective, Custodial) and clerical-mechanical.

A sound classification has been considered necessary to ensure efficiency of recruitment especially if that recruitment is to be based on qualification and merit. A good classification system should therefore include a clear statement of the duties of the positions in each class and the qualifications necessary for entrance into it. The analysis of the duties and the requirements of the positions to be occupied by recruits to the public services lays the foundation for the development and perfection of the tests to be applied in order to discover the possession of the requisite qualifications by candidates. Classification according to duties, responsibilities and qualification is also necessary for the establishment of a sound system of remuneration and for the testing of efficiency in the members during their service. Remuneration and efficiency testing systems that are not based on an analysis of duties are not based upon facts and therefore their value is doubtful. Classification is also useful in determining promotions within the services.

In the determining of salary systems and salary grades, classification is eminently useful. If duties are not classified, it may often happen that the salary paid a civil servant has no relationship to the value of the work he does. Wide variations in pay for similar duties may arise if the principles that ought to govern remuneration of public service, equal pay for equal work, and salaries fair alike to the public servants and the tax-payers are not observed. A classification of duties and positions according to duties is absolutely necessary. Classification would thus introduce into public service the maximum possible incentive to efficiency both by furnishing definite rewards for efficient performance of unchanged duties and by the maximum development of opportunities for advancement.

Classification is also useful in promoting economy in the cost of administration. Classification helps in bringing the great cost of administration under control. Salary standardisation prevents paying too much for the individual post or paying so little that an employee with the proper qualifications cannot be secured. When positions in the civil service are given their proper place by classification the makers of the budget will get real information about the cost of administration and will be in a position to make enquiries that may lead to economy. Classification also may reveal defects in organisation. When posts and the men occupying these posts are classified, it would be easy to discover which men and which posts are required where and when and it would be easy to determine whether these men and these posts are essential or superfluous. The uses of classification have been summed up thus.

1. It makes morale in the services possible, by making the principle of "equal pay for equal work" operate, thus making for better work and happier workers."

2. Fair promotion is possible because there is a comparable basis for selection.

3. A proper selection of employees for every job is possible as every job has been analysed.

4. The tex-payer gets better service at lower costs.

5. Checks on public expenditure on the services are possible; errors in increasing number of personnel or favouritism could be prevented.

Classification therefore is found useful not only for recruitment but for the promotion of efficiency, economy, and improved organisation but it is especially for recruitment that it is the condition precedent. That is why it has been said with justification "that personnel classification or re-classification is one of the major reforms instituted, when Governments, National, State, County or Municipal endeavour to put their houses in order."

RECRUITMENT

Examination

In these days of democracy and progress the old method of recruitment to the public services of nomination by Monarch, Ministers, or Heads of Departments, or sale of offices, or popular election are deemed to be out of date. Submission to tests which seek to discover the possession of qualities and qualifications needed in administration is required of candidates for appointment. Written examinations to regulate admission to public services were probably invented by the Chinese among whom written examinations to test the possession of high standards in literary education have held pride of place in the public administration of that great people. Among no people, ancient or modern, have written examinations as doors of admission to the public service been held in such high esteem. After them it was Prussia of the 17th and 18th centuries that pinned its faith on written examinations as tests for admission to the public service. It was not till after the French Revolution whose results in the field of government were organised by Napoleon who threw open careers to talent that examination came to be used generally for this purpose. But in England it was not till the middle of the 19th century that examination or "open competition" as opposed to the closed system of nomination, as it was described, came to be the normal method of admission, first to the civil services and then later to the military services where the purchase of commissions continued till Gladstone abolished it in 1870 and that only by royal warrant after a legislative attempt to abolish it had been foiled by the House of Lords.

After a trial of more than 50 years it has been found that written examinations tested only one kind or set of qualities and gave no clue to the possession of other qualities just as necessary for success in administration especially in the higher grades of the services. Written examinations could test the possession of knowledge, memory, application, industry. But they could not discover whether the candidates possessed judgement, discretion, tact, sociability, capacity for working with others in a team, *savoir faire*—not to speak of physique and personality. Therefore they may be the only tests for recruiting candidates to the clerical services. And they must be of a standard expected of the candidates for these services, i.e., of the High School Leaving Certificate. The encyclopaedic range of information required of the candidates for clerical posts in the French civil service would be entirely out of place in the scheme of such an examination.

No examination, it was the decisive opinion of Lord Haldane (who according to his own confession had been concerned with examinations or tests during a good length of his life) that does not take account of record of work done prior to it is at all valuable. It is not, he says, by questions put by an external examiner to a candidate who has anticipated the kind of questions and has crammed up answers that a real test of fitness can be made. And so the old method which was being used frequently in business administration—the Interview and the Examination of Records has been used extensively in recent years.

Interview and Records

Experience has shown that observation and examination of the behaviour and answers of a candidate in half-an-hour or a quarter of an hour conversation by competent and experienced selectors can test the possession of the moral and social qualities required of candidates required for the higher or executive services. Men experienced in recruiting to the civil services of England have testified to the value of the interview in the selection of candidates for the higher administrative services. Some of them would even use it to exclude unsuitable candidates as is done in England in examinations for the diplomatic service. Men and women of affairs that have come to the study of the method of interview with suspicions of the bias, class, sex or national that are said to play in these interviews have ended by enthusiastic advocacy of this method of selection.

It is obvious that as the interview is an examination conducted by men of men, all extraneous and vitiating influences like personal likes and dislikes, class or community partialities or hostilities must be eliminated. But when it is remembered that even written examinations are not perfect as they have been found to give strange and unwarranted results, it may be that they have to be corrected by the interview and other oral examinations.

This interview, if it is preceded and helped by an examination of the school and college records and certificates of the candidates, has been found eminently useful wherever and whenever it has been used. The interview which is the normal method of recruitment in business combined with the competitive written examination has been justified by experience. It alone is used for selection to the technical posts for which technical examinations and diplomas or degrees have already presented the evidence of basic qualifications.

The interview therefore is of four kinds:

1. The Specialist Post interview.

2. The *viva voce* test interview to supplement the evidence of written examinations. It is an additional examination.
3. The personality interview to assess personality of candidates and is used side by side and in addition to written examinations.
4. The Weeding-out interview which comes before the written examination and is used in selecting candidates for such special services like the diplomatic where personality counts first and more than any other qualification.

Group Tests—Army selection boards have introduced the use of combination or group tests that may be employed in the selection of candidates for the administrative services. Psychological tests, psychiatric, prolonged observation of candidates for two or three days are the principal stages in the tests. Such a system of selection was tried for the selection of the officers of the Army in U.S.A., England, Germany, Soviet Russia. The system as it was practised in India towards the close of the last war is thus described.

The group tests consist of the following tests:

1. A general summing up of personality, behaviour and basic intellectual equipment.
2. Various psychological tests to judge the quickness and adaptability of the candidate's mind, his complexes and his potential capabilities. Cases which are more difficult to analyse are tackled personally by highly-trained psychiatrists, who play an important part but are certainly not the deciding factor.
3. Practical tests to discover candidates that possess powers of leadership, who can take sober decisions in times of emergency and act accordingly, men who, in short, can inspire confidence.

All these tests are carried out under the watchful eyes of specially trained Group Testing Officers. Each officer-examiner works independently of his colleagues, taking notes on the characteristics shown by individual candidates. Not once during the period of selection do these officers compare notes. When these scientifically-planned tests are completed, then the full Board meets under the chairmanship of the President. Candidates are graded by each Group Testing Officer (GT.), listed from A to DD (very doubtful) and those rejected get a U (Unfit) or NY (not yet). At the Board meeting officers read out their opinions of each candidate who is known throughout the period of selection by a special number. Candidates sent to the O.S.B. at Lonavla were made to feel at home. A number of comforts including a reading room and a bar were provided. They spent four days at the centre. On arrival, they were issued uniforms and formed into sections. On the first day close contact was established between the officers and candidates, many of whom come straight from the village: picnics and walks were organised to create confidence among them. Intelligence tests to gauge the basic intelligence of the candidates, began on the second day. These were simple and did not require elaborate answers. Then followed a psychological inquiry designed to show the candidate's aptitude not his learning. Tests included simple commonsense problems that any intelligent person should be able to answer. Other tests threw light on the candidates' basic make-up. It was a general complaint among candidates that they were not given enough time to answer questions. The psychological examination, however, is designed to get immediate reactions and not considered, deliberate answers. After the written tests were completed, the President of the Board interviewed the candidates to get some idea of their personality and interests. A civilian member who was attached to the Board, also interviewed the candidates. Practical tests began on the third day. These include, discussions on topical problems and the planning and carrying out of actual tasks. In addition to all this, was the role of the psychiatrist, who tried to find an explanation for any conflicting tendencies noticed in the candidate. In order words, no effort was spared to give the candidates a fair chance. The full Board meeting on the last day provided compelling proof of the accuracy of the system, for the opinions of all testing officers usually tallied.

Such a system is tried in England for recruitment to the higher grades of the administrative and foreign service. It is used as an alternative to the open competitive written examination and interview. Those choosing this kind of selection sit for a qualifying examination and then undergo a series of tests for personal qualities as guests in a country house at Stoke D' Abernon in Surrey followed by a final selection board at which their fate is finally determined. It is in an experimental stage, it is costly, it costs the country £26 for each candidate; its results are worth watching.

THE RECRUITMENT AUTHORITY—CIVIL OR PUBLIC SERVICE COMMISSIONS

To ensure efficient recruitment, at all times and in all places, and whenever and wherever democracy obtains as it is necessary to keep recruitment to the public services out of the vitiating and corrupting influence of political, especially party influences, the institution of a special, permanent, independent, impartial and competent body charged with the important duty of recruitment to the public services has been found necessary. In English speaking countries this authority is known as the Civil or Public Service Commission. Civil Service Commissions were established as soon as it was realised that a progressive democratic Government required recruitment to its civil services to be based on merit and equality. In English it was established 25 years after the Reform Act of 1830. In the U.S.A. only after the Spoils system had been found to serve ill the ends of democracy and progress, were Civil Service Commission established. It was the assassination of President Garfield in 1881 by a disappointed office-seeker that brought the campaign against the Spoils system to a head. The first Civil Service Commission in America was appointed in 1883. Commencing with Massachusetts, New York and the Federal Government, Civil Service Commissions have steadily grown in number and there is hardly a large State or city which has not its Civil Service Commission. But the battle for the Civil Service Commission system is not yet over in the U.S.A. There are still important sets of posts like the Collectorships of Internal Revenue which last year secured world-wide notoriety on account of the charges of corruption framed despite them and which are still patronage plums in politics despite the recommendation of the Hoover Commission on reorganisation of the Federal government.

Entrusted, as it is, with the duty of recruiting to all civil services of the State the constitution of a Civil or Public Service Commission and its working must conform to standards that will ensure not only its own efficiency but public confidence and esteem. The following principles are the chief of those that ought to govern the constitution and working of a Civil or Public Service Commission.

1. It must be composed of men of the highest education and competence; although they have to be appointed by the Government of the day, they must be appointed with the same sense of duty and responsibility as are used in the appointment to the highest courts of the country. "In our opinion" said the Macdonell Commission on the Civil Service, of England "the aim which should be kept in view in the selection of Civil Service Commissioners as to ensure the appointment of men possessing wide experience both of school and university education to work under the chairmanship of a man of affairs possessing official experience as well as sympathy with academic studies."

2. Its number must not be too low to command a variety of competence nor too high to ensure unity and unanimity; three to five has been proved to be about the right number. As most of the work has to deal with education and examination a member of the teaching profession should always be one of the members of a Civil or Public Service Commission.

3. Their emoluments must be high, as high as that of the highest paid public servants on account of the responsible work they have to do.

4. To ensure independence and impartiality permanence of tenure is necessary; they would be removable only as Judges of the High Court are removable by special vote or petition of the Legislature.

5. Except for the few exceptional or temporary offices the Commission must be the sole recruiting authority; the police being in most countries a quasi-military force has its own recruiting system and officers.

6. Although for state reasons asserted and proved in public certain classes of posts may be excluded from the purview of the Commission yet as regards posts within its purview appointments must be made by the Government department only from the lists compiled by it.

Its Duties

1. Its main duty is to organize the recruitment to the civil services of the country especially in regard to classification and the admission of candidates of the civil services.

2. To this end it has to hold examinations, written, oral and by interview and record, competitive or qualifying; to appoint examiners for these purposes and fix their rates of remuneration and other conditions of tenure.

3. To make such rules and regulations as may be necessary for this purpose.

4. To draw up the qualifications and requirements of age, education, etc. Expected for the several classes and grades of the civil services; it must relate age and education to the grade and class of services to be filled; a lower age (say 18) and lower stage of education (high school) would be required for entrance to the clerical services so as to prevent economic and educational wastage.

5. In consultation with educational authorities and keeping in touch with educational institutions, it has to relate its examinations and tests to the educational system of the country.

More Than a Recruiting Body

In addition to the original function of conducting examinations for admission to the civil service, Civl Service Commission have in some concering general personnel administration like:

1. Preparing classification and salary rules and schedules.

2. Making efficiency and promotion lists of persons already in the service, conducting promotion examinations and tests.

3. Organising and administering post-entry training.
4. Advising departments on rules concerning transfer, suspensions, retirement, reinstatement and even administering these rules. In India Public Service Commission have also been given the work of advising Governments on disciplinary cases against civil servants and on appeals to Government or the Head of the State against decisions in such cases of Heads of Departments.

Its Modus Operandi

1. As soon as the Government or Department informs it that eligible lists are required for particular classes or positions in its service the Commission prepares a public notice giving the dates of the examinations, the last date for applications, the details of the examination, the qualifications required of the candidates and the nature of the posts to be filled up.
2. Notices are published on the notice board of the Commission and sent to the principal newspapers of the State.
3. The examination is conducted by an examining staff composed of examiners appointed for each examination; in interview and record examinations the Board of Examiners consists of one or more members of the Commission assisted by outside examiners.
4. The results of the examination are published in the form of eligible lists for class of post, either exactly the number required or twice or thrice the number from which the Government or Department is to choose its nominees, but all in the order of merit.

If a Civil Service Commission is to play its part in administration it is necessary that:

1. Its independence should be guaranteed against interference and influence from Government and its Departments.
2. Its lists should be operated without any deviation.
3. Its jurisdiction should be co-extensive with the civil service. The number of posts taken away from its jurisdiction should

be limited to a low minimum laid down once for all and not changed from time to time; temporary appointments should be temporary and must be replaced from among the Commission's lists as early as possible.

Training After Recruitment

Is any special training required to fit recruits to the civil services for work in administration? In the clerical services where the work is of a routine character the best training was till recently held to be immediate introduction to the routine work. The old method of learning by having to tackle the work somehow from the start with papers thrown at recruits with the vague and unhelpful injunction to get on with it has been found to be ineffective. If only of eliminate waste of energy and time, not to speak of scientific management and rationalisation and planning, even routine work requires some kind of training as the raw recruit may not know, nor have practiced the normal clerical processes. Especially during war when energy and time and men have to be economically used aducate training of the available staff was found necessary in the English Civil Service and the report and recommendations of a Committee laid down the methods of training. Trained officers have been appointed in most departments of the English Civil Service whose responsibility it is to train new recruits of all grades, typists, shorthand writers and ordinary clerks. Refresher courses for the higher staff are run. Training in the art of dealing with the public is given. Background training helping the civil servant to realize the significance of his work and his relations to the other departments and the public is also found. Educational visits to field operation of the departments widen the mind of the officials and the office. Discussion, films, broadcasts, departmental journals are freely used.

For those that are recruited into the higher administrative services a higher and broader kind of training has been found useful. Especially for the Departments of Social and Economic Welfare it has been suggested that recruits to the higher administrative classes of the department might undergo special training in social science and social service and in administration.

They might acquire this training either in a special training college or at universities which provide such facilities for learning social science subjects and for training in social service. One section of them might be recruited at a higher age, say 30 years, when they would have had some practical experience in social service in actual field conditions. Wherever there are universities or other institutions which provide this training candidates for admission may be asked to enter them for such training, or recruits in the services may be seconded to them. But in their absence, this training may be provided at a Civil Service College that may have to be established and maintained. It may be modelled on the Metropolitan Police College of England. The college is a residential college. It is situated at Hendon in delightful surroundings, the grounds being about 60 acres in extent. There is ample accommodation for all kinds of sports and recreation, including Association and Rugby football, squash rackets, hockey, cricket, and tennis. Games and athletics are an important part of the training. One of the objects of the college is to enable men selected for their special qualifications to attain the highest police efficiency by means of intensive training. Thus it is estimated that at the end of a course of 15 months, followed by a year of actual police duties a student will have acquired as much practical experience as if he had service in the force for 10 years under the present system. Every department of police activity is represented at the institution. Where residential universities and residential colleges to which civil servants may be sent for post-entry training are not to be found it may be necessary that such special Civil Service College should be established where not only post-entry training can be obtained but which would also allow that *esprit de corps,* so necessary for the maintenance of the highest standards of honour, integrity and service, to be imbibed. In this Civil Service College the recruits would live and learn through social life as in an Oxford or Cambride College.

Refresher courses in the social studies and service may also help older but not too old civil servants. In America a National Institute of Public Affairs provides for such training for candidates for the public service and the School of public affairs of the

American University, Washington, provides for such training of servants of the Federal Government. For the administrative class in England the Ashetion Committee proposed a course of three months in such subjects as administration, public relations, machinery of government, relationship with Parliament and the public. A library and lecture room were also suggested. A beginning has been made in this direction under Treasury auspices and a Director of training and education has been appointed. The Committee also recommended period of sabbatical leave up to a maximum of 12 months for travel and study of public administration in other countries.

Special training seems required for the officials of Local Government. As we have seen, the bulk of them are technical men. But they also should posses and practice, tact, courtesy the art of persuasion, for party, caucus, faction, local, class, family influences play a greater part in local than in central national administration. For the Local Government official post-entry training is perhaps more necessary if only to liberalise his technical and specialist tendencies.

Universities can help a great deal in providing such post-entry training or refresher courses. An example to be followed is the Summer School in Colonial Administration organised in 1937 by Oxford University with the encouragement and help of a number of colonial Governments and which dealt in detail with problems of native administration including lectures by foreign experts in native administration outside the British Empire, lectures on local Government, co-operation, education which might throw light on these problems in the colonial dependencies but also lectures on general political and economic trends. Another example to be followed is that of the London North-Eastern Railway which some years ago arranged with all the universities of the country on their system for a series of lectures to be given covering a cycle of four years and covering subjects of knowledge which would be useful to railway servants like geography, railway law, railway economics. Such provision would help forward the movement of adult education of the educated with which the honoured name of Sir Richard Livingstone is associated.

Pay

Speaking of the limitations on any attempt at the reform of the administration with a view of economy, Burke in his famous speech on economical reform said his limits were "the rules of law, the rules of policy and the service of the State". The rules of policy and the service of the Stete require that the best talent should be attracted to it, hence service of the public "is a thing which cannot be put to auction and struck down to those who will agree to execute it at the cheapest." He also reminded would-be cheeseparers that "in all offices of duty there is almost necessarily a great neglect of domestic affairs and therefore, if the public servant is to see that the State take no detriment, the State must see that his affairs take as little." The public servant is a wholetime servant of the State, he cannot resort to side occupations nor can he supplement his income by speculation on the stock exchange or gambling on the turf. Burke went so far as to say that "if men where willing to serve in such stations without salary they ought not to be permitted to do so, for ordinary service must be secured by the motives to ordinary integrity and an honourable and fair profit is the best security against avarice and rapacity."

Work in Government offices cannot be governed by the law of supply and demand that prevails in the business world though here also the principle in practice of the living wage has made headway. Work in Government offices cannot stand the strain of frequent changes nor can Government afford to pay competitive price for services rendered. Lower scales of remuneration than those offered and taken in business may be offered and taken in Government service on account of the security, the dignity and esteem of Government service. Government service offers continuous employment, it does not depend on changes and chances as does employment in business. Government services is one of the learned professions. For these reasons, the scales and rates of pay are settled by laws peculiar to the public service. The factors to be considered in the fixing of salaries to men in Government service are not only market rates, supply and demand, cost of living, but the ability of the Government to pay. But these cannot be decisive factors for the State may not get the best material and there are imponderables to be considered like the dignity of public service and public esteem. If the State is to get the best it must offer employment, which when pay, conditions of service, security, hours of work, leave, sick leave and pensions are taken together, compares favourably with similar service elsewhere.

All these things considered, the sound doctrine on payment in Government service is that enunciated by a British Civil Service Committee which laid down that there is only one principle in which all the factors of responsibility cost of living, marriage, children, social position are included. And that is Government should pay what is necessary to recruit and retain an efficient staff. It went on to expand the principle when it said, on the one hand the State should hold the scales even between its own servants and those through whose enterprise its servants are paid; on the other hand, employees of Government would have a real ground for complaint if their pay were related to wages in industry only in the sense of low wages; if they do not get pay relative to the boom, they must be spared the full severity of the slump. Thus adequate remuneration of its employee is required not only in justice to the employed but in the interests of the State. "I do not hesitate to say" said Burke "that the State which lays its foundations in rare and heroic virtue will soon have its superstructure in the basest profligacy and corruption."

The State offers security, a dignified service and moderate remuneration in the place of the excitement and possibilities of employment in business. But the civil servant also is worthy of his hire, he must be paid the remuneration that will enable him and his family to live a life decency. The decisive principle that regulates that rates of remuneration to the civil servant as of every other part of his employment is that efficiency should be controlled by interest, that is to say he must be made to see that it is to his interest to be efficient and that to make him efficient his interests should be safeguarded. Burke laid down as one of the principal of administration "the engaging with those who shall have an immediate and direct interest in the proper execution of the business."

A good system of salaries would provide for previously laid down rates of pay, for annual or other periodical increments, and a maximum for each grade of service leading up to the highest to which the public servant can aspire. In some systems of administration increments are a matter of course and are payable, unless a decision is taken to the contrary by the Head of the Department before the time the increment is due. Increments in the U.S.A. Civil Service are not granted as a matter of course but are subject to the wishes of the Head of the Department. Rigid appropriations ruthlessly scrutinised by Congress are said to be the cause.

Promotion

By promotion is meant the raising of a member of the civil service from a lower to a higher grade. It does not ordinarily mean the improvement in the civil servant's financial position by the operation of the rule of increment and by his passage along the time scale. Promotion in the real sense of the term is governed by the general principle that only those that deserve it by their merit and record of service can be raised from a lower grade to a higher grade in the service. It is an incentive to good work. It might have been otherwise in the antique, world according to old Orlando "when service sweat for duty nor for need" but in these materialistic times" none will sweat save for promotion and having that do choke their services up even with the having." Fitness for the higher grade is the governing consideration. The general principle governing promotion is the promotion of the efficiency of the department. Promotion is not only a reward for efficient and conscientious service in a grade but it is intended to ensure the most efficient and economical performance of public duties by seeing that every post is filled by the officers most suitable by character and ability to fill it. Seniority can never by itself be a claim to promotion. Other things being there, seniority would be considered; but then if the other things were there, there would be no need to consider seniority. No efficient civil service can be built on mere seniority. "The British Empire would be lost one day" said Admiral Fisher "because it is Buggin's turn." It is not only by efficient service in the lower grade but by possession of intellectual, moral and physical and social qualities that will make him suitable for a higher grade, that promotion is earned, Promotion is a selective process.

Within a grade also promotion must not be automatic as the result of the passage of time; supervising posts like that of superintendent or manager of a section cannot be filled except by selection on merit. Excellence in the performance of routine work, although a factor, is not the determining factor in promotion to posts which require qualities of a good manager or supervisor. Although the prospect of promotion is a strong incentive to efficient service in one's grade, it cannot and ought not to be the only incentive for there is not enough room at the top, as the saying goes; the efficiency in one's own grade is incentive and reward enough for most.

By whom is the promotion to be made? The normal practice is for the Head of the Department to have a decisive voice in the matter of promotion. But as selection in modern circumstances is a difficult matter, if only because the Head of the Department in the midst of other duties is not able to give his whole mind and time to this business, he is generally helped by a Selection or Promotion Board consisting of senior officials of the department. In England, posts over £900 (i.e., in the higher grade of the administrative class) are left to the discretion of the Head of the Department. In regard to posts falling below them the principle has been accepted in England that the staff is entitled to make representations through their representative councils. Promotion and promotion work are an important part of the work of the Establishment section in each Department in England. But it has been contended that promotion outside a grade should not be in the hands of an Establishment Section but should be given to a higher Appointment Board that would be able to take a much wider view both from the educational and the official angle than would a mere Establishment Section. In large departments where it is impossible for the Head of the Department to be familiar with the qualifications and work of every member it has been the practice in the British Civil Service for the Head to appoint Promotion Boards cosisting of the principle establishment officer, the head of a section or branch in which the vacancy occurs and one or more other departmental officers of experience and standing, representative of the staff being allowed to attend before the promotion board to make representations on matter of principle and procedure. The Head of Department has the final say in promotion.

Evidence in Promotion

General impressions not committed to writing of Heas of Departments even of officials under whom the candidate for promotion has directly worked being evanescent and fallible, written records and reports on the work of each member of the services are kept. These to be of use, must be written up year after year. Systematised, the information is arranged under several heads like those used in British Civil Service Reports.

1. Knowledge of branch or section or department.
2. Personality and force of character.
3. Judgement.
4. Power of taking responsibility.
5. Initiative.
6. Accuracy.
7. Address and Tact.
8. Power of supervising staff.
9. Zeal.
10. Official conduct.

Against each of these particulars an official judgement as to standard, whether above average, or average or below average of achievement must be recorded. And the whole report must be signed by the officer under whom the candidate has immediately and directly worked and also by the Head of the Department.

The evil to be avoided in the making of these reports is to make them too detailed, calling for information on a number of minor matters and for minute marking on each of these matters to the point of according marks and fraction of marks for the possession of the qualification required and adding them up.

Promotion Machinery

Promotion tests are tried in some administrations. The interview has also been used to test the qualities required of candidates to higher grade posts than those to which they had been recruited. Not merely to help out the aggrieved persons left out of promotion who appeal against decisions of the Head of the Department, but to help the Head of the Department of decide on promotion the interview has been used by the Head. When a Department is large and the head cannot be expected to know the work of all the officials Promotion Boards are indicated. Such interviews are a correction of the annual reports which cannot be altogether dependable, for, prejudice, temporary hostility, temperamental differences, communal prejudices (as in India) may have gone to the making of these reports. It is a conviction of an experienced English official that the promotion of officers to posts calling for qualities of leadership, fair-mindedness, good relations with the staff and the public from written reports alone has resulted in the advancement of many people in the civil service to posts which they were quite unfit to hold.

Transfer

Now that it is a rule in most administrations to establish a system of grades or divisions applicable to the whole service with more or less uniform scales of salary for the same, or approximately the same, duties in the several Departments, transfers from one department to another on account of superior attractions do not happen. Moreover the differing work of the several departments leads to specialisation and within certain limits efficiency and economy alike demand the separate organisation of each department. Moreover, the practical difficulties in transferring public servants from one office to another are great. Heads of Departments naturally prefer the men trained in them; if for any reason, like diminution in the amount of work in them, the departments become over manned the man they are willing to part will always be the least efficient. But, on the other hand, the decision to retain useful men should not be pushed to the extent of barring their promotion to better-paid posts in other Departments. The interest of the administration as a whole are paramount.

The problem of transfer becomes especially acute when retrenchment or reduction in numbers takes place for some reason or other. If men are found too many in one Department or found inefficient it would be profitable to the State that places suitable for their capacity should be found for them as vacancies occur in other Departments. If they are inefficient it would be false economy to force them upon offices and into work for which they are not qualified. A British Commission on Civil Services speaking on this point remarked that it would after all be cheaper to pension off redundant clerks, appointing new clerks in the lowest grade in the offices in which vacancies exist than to transfer the redundants from one office to another with their old rates of salary and something like their old chances of promotion. The dilemma, another Commission, says is a serious one, such pensions to unwanted men, "abolition terms" and the conferring of them practically amounts to giving a pension to comparative incompetency. This is a consequence of past action and for sometime to come the State has to continue to pay more than it should until a new order of things will be set up for certain classes of work.

Transfer may be found necessary in the interest of the administration. Staleness may be cured by transfer of an efficient official. Change of work and environment such as caused by transfers from the centre to its circumference and from outdoor executive work to the office or *vice versa* may improve the work of an official. In the Foreign and Colonial offices in England such transfers are tried: it would improve all officials to be transferred from one post to another, form one kind of work to another; the work of the official, the needs of the department, above all the interests of the administration as a whole are decisive. Transfers in India, as we shall see, are an unduly frequent feature of administration.

Leave and Leave Rules

Apllo's bow may not be stretched tight the whole time. Most administrative systems provide for leave for members of the civil service to recoup their strength and health, lowered or impaired by continuous work in an office, especially if it is sedentary work. Annual leave of about one month to six weeks or raised to nine weeks in case of unhealthy spots which may be accumulated up to three months is usual. Leave for odd contingencies is also given up to a small maximum of about 15 days. Sick or Medical leave needs no arguments. In the U.S.A. annual leave with pay has been standardised at 26 days working days per calendar year, and may be accumulated up to a total of 60 days. Sick leave with pay is granted at the rate of 1¼ days per month cumulative to a maximum of 90 working days although in exceptional cases an additional 30 days may be granted by the Head of the Department. In England annual leave varies between 21 and 36 days a year. Sick leave on full pay is granted for six months a year and for higher periods on reduced pay. In India on account of the climate leave for long periods, 6 months to 18 months, for a portion on full pay and for a longer portion on half pay is granted. Insistence on provision for leave and leave rules is not superfluous as there are still some State in the U.S.A. where vacation and sick leave is left largely to the discretion of the administrative head.

Some enlightened administrations as in the U.S.A. provide concession in regard to health services, insurance, recreation and the like.

Although civil service is wholetime service the working hours are limited. In England the hours are 45½ hours a week. Overtime is paid for in the lower salary groups and a temporary extra duty allowance to some of the higher. The higher administrative officers get no extra allowance for such work. The jest that the British Civil Servant was like the fountains in Trafalgar Square, playing from 10 to 4 has no point now if it ever had.

Punishment in the Civil Service

Punishment is a concomitant of law and order. Anybody that infringes the rules and regulation of a body corporate whether it is a social club or a State has to be punished; otherwise it cannot survive. An unpunished course of misconduct of members of that body would lead to disorder and if general would lead to its dissolution. The good order of administration also requires punishment to sustain it. These punishment are not of the kind prescribed for offences against the law of the State, especially those classed as crime. But the object of punishment in the civil service is as in the State threefold, retributive (punishments as a consequence of the crime), preventive (deterrent of further crime) and educative or reformative. The consequence of offences against the rules and regulation and the good order and efficiency of an administrative department not being so serious as offences against the laws of the State, the punishments are of a lighter kind. They are in the ascending order of gravity.

1. Fines.
2. Suspension from office for temporary periods with total or partial loss or reduction of salary.
3. Compulsory retirement with or without pension or with reduced pension.
4. Dismissal with the loss of pension rights.

Disciplinary action or punishment is visited upon members of the civil service for negligence of various degress in the performance of their chief duties and obligations which are:

1. Obedience to the laws and orders pertaining to his work and the orders of his superiors in regard to his work.
2. Efficiency accompanied by whole-heartedness and probity in the performance of the duties of the office.
3. Punctuality in regard to hours of work.
4. Truthfulness in all official dealings; they must not keep back relevant information in their possession, *suggestio falsi* is as reprehensible as *suppressio veri.*
5. Courtesy not only to superiors but to equals, inferiors, and the public.
6. Maintenance of the dignity, respect, and honour of the service in and outside the office; their conduct in private life must not bring them or the service into comtempt.

Machinery of Punishment

In the interest of the discipline of the Department the Head of the Department must be the authority to award punishment to delinquents. And in regard to major offences and punishments the accused official should be given opportunities for answering charges which should be delivered to him in writing with particularisation of the offence. In some countries, to ensure greater security for officials, independent and impartial bodies like administrative tribunals have been invested with the right of hearing cases on appeal from aggrieved officials. In countries where the rule of law obtain and the ordinary courts of law have jurisdiction over the acts of officials serious offences may be taken to courts of law or aggrieved officials may sue their superiors for unjust punishment in such courts of law.

Mode of Punishment

The effectiveness of punishment in the civil service depends on the rapidity with which it is dealt out. A regulation in an English office manual runs "it is of the utmost importance that disciplinary cases should be dealt with expeditiously so that if punishment is inflicted it may follow the offence as rapidly as possible. The offender should not be left uncertain and uneasy and he and his fellows should not fancy he is escaping. The association of penalty with offence must be close and immediate if efficiency in the civil service is to be maintained. And the punishing officer need not be as impartial or impersonal as Rhadaman-thus thus: he must convey a sense of his personal and the departmennt's indignation at the offence and the offender. An offence against discipline is an offence against loyalty to the department and to the service. It is not a mere cash nexus that binds an official to his department and to the service.

Discipline in the civil service is necessary for its very efficiency. Especially in democratic times when the people or their representatives in the Legislature may, out of a false interpretation of democracy, try to intervene directly in the activities of members of the services their loyalty to the services must be maintained by enforcement of discipline. The stronger the influence of Parliament in the State, observed Bismarck, the more necessary it is to maintain a stern discipline in the civil services.

Partnership in the Civil Service

In the administrative services the principle and practice of partnership that have characterised the relations in recent times between employees and employed, between superiors and subordinates in the industrial sphere, have come to regulate the relations between the Heads of Departments and Sections and their subordinates. Democracy is essentially a government by partnership and the administration in a democratic State cannot long keep this principle out of its system. Under the democratic impulse not long could the old principle and practice last, of orders and directions issuing from the tip of the services to be blindly and silently carried out by those at the bottom and in between, theirs not being to reason why, theirs being but to do and lie low, Consultation, negotiation, conciliation, arbitration are now the practice in most systems of administration in democracies. In England, as in industrial factories, Whitley Councils (so called after Whitley once Speaker of the House of Commons who suggested it in a Report of a Committee on the relations between employees and employed in 1927) have been established in the civil service. At first (in 1919) there was a National Whitley Council for the national civil service which was soon after supplemented by about 70 Whitley Councils for as many departments. These Whitley Councils are joint councils composed of representatives of the Government and of its servants. They are essentially joint conciliation boards.

The objects of the Whitley Councils are to secure the greatest measure of co-operation between the State in its capacity as employer and the general body of civil servants in matters affecting the civil service with a view to increased efficiency in the public service combined with the well-being of those employed; also to provide machinery for dealing with grievances and generally to bring together the experience and different points of view of the administration clerical, and manipulative services.

The functions of Whitley Councils are:

1. Provision of the best means for using the ideas and experience of the staff.

2. Securing to the staff a greater share in the responsibility for the determination and observance of the conditions under which their duties are carried out.

3. Determination of the general principles governing conditions of service like recruitment, hours of work, promotion, discipline, tenure of service, remuneration, superannuation, etc.; it is obvious that in regard to promotion only the general aspects of the matter and the principles upon which promotion in general should rest, not individual cases can be the subject of such discussion; so also in regard to disciplinary action only the general principles underlying discrinary action, not individual cases can be considered.

4. Provision for the further education of civil servants and their training in higher administration and organisation.

5. Improvement of office machinery and organisation and the provision of opportunities for the full consideration of suggestions by the staff on this subject.

6. Consideration of proposals of legislation as far as it has a bearing on the position of civil servants in relations to their employment.

Composition of Whitley Councils

To these ends the National Whitley Councils is composed of about 27 members drawn from the superior grade (what may be called the directing officials) and 27 from the staff. The Chairman of the Council is a superior official of the Treasury, the Vice-Chairman being a representative of the staff elected by it. Decisions are effective only if they are reached by agreement, the representatives of the two sides acting as a cement, individual voting being excluded. Standing and *ad hoc* committees are freely used. Corresponding to the National Whitley Council each Department has its own Whitley council composed in a similar manner and having the same objectives and employing the same methods of procedure on a departmental scale.

These Whitley Council have justified their invention. and, now that major issues have been settled, the departmental Whitley

Councils are more active and vigorous than the National. But while they have done much to promote harmonious and therefore efficient working of the departments, they cannot relieve the Government of its responsibility to the Legislature, nor Ministers and Heads of Departments of their executive responsibility. Whitley Councils are essentially organs of discussion, conference, and conciliation, they are not organs of executive administration. Even so, they are one of the beneficial inventions of modern administration.

Superannuation and Retirement

Men cannot go on working at exacting jobs all their lives. A time cones even to the strongest of men when they can no longer give of their best to their lifework. Most systems of administration have fixed a period beyond which public servants will not be employed in the public services. The age of retirement varies from country to country depending mostly on the climate of the country. For instance it is 60 in England and 55 in India. It may vary from Department to Department. Some departments are more exacting than others. Teachers can work longer, judges even longer, than officials of the Finance Department. Every department would be all the better for letting in fresh blood. To make room for it there must be letting of old blood. That there must be a Superannuation period is easily allowed. Superannuation Acts have been passed in England at the same time as Classification Acts. But whether there should be any Superannuation allowances has been debated. It is argued by some that the only duty of Government should be to pay adequate salaries and leave its servants to make proper provision for their own future wants and those of their families. But as the British Commissioners of 1857 pointed out the arguments against this contention are overwhelming.

Those arugments are:

1. The incapacity caused by illness may come on at any period life and cannot readily be provided against by means of insurance as in the case of death.

2. It is desirable that the public servant should feel himself in a safe an independent position and not be harassed by anxiety as regards the future.

3. Men that have grown old in the service of the State or who have become incapacitated by infirmity should not starve even though such starvation was the result of their own improvidence.

4. It is an insurance against irregular methods of public servants enriching themselves, against bribery and corruption in the service.

5. Otherwise, if there were not a system of Superannuation, incompetent men or men who had survived their competence would be retained in the service and heads of departments would find it hard and therefore unjust to remove such men.

Pensions

Pensions in Government services have been justified by Burke on the ground that "no man knows, when he cuts off the incitements to a virtuous ambition and the just rewards of public service, what infinite mischief he may do his country through all generations". And a pension has been the subject of one of the great pieces of prose in Burke's Letter to the Duke of Bedford.

They are peculiar and normal in Government service. They are not based on the contributory principles, whereas other forms of remuneration at the end of service like bonuses or gratuities or provident funds are made up partly of contributions made by the beneficiaries in the course of their employment in business. The pension is calculated at varying rates and on proportions of salaries at the enf of the service. Generally, there is a mximum placed beyond which no pension goes. Few Governments can afford the rates granted in certain Indian States like Hyderabad before the integration of States when some exceptionally favoured officials enjoyed a pension of the same amount as the last salary they received. Pension is payment for service rendered and cannot be denied to any officials except for activities subversive of the State and not merely critical of the Government of the day. Pensions and gratuities are in England not claimable as rights and English Courts of law have decided that the Treasury is the final court of appeal on such matters. In Germany on the other hand the civil servant has a code of economic rights enforceable in courts of law.

The general rules governing the grant of pensions in England are:

1. The claimant must have been one who was appointed in accordance with the rules governing admission to the service to which he belongs.
2. He has given his whole time to the public service.
3. He has drawn the emoluments on which he is pensionable from the public funds exclusively.
4. Has served for upwards of a minimum number of years usually 10.
5. Has been certified to have served with diligence and fidelity to the satisfaction of the Head of his Department.
6. If the claimant is under the age of superannuiation he has been certified to be permanently incapacitated from infirmity of mind or body from discharging his official duties or has been removed from his office on its cessation.

The rates of pension may vary. In England implementation is 1/80 of the annual salary for each year's service with the maximum of 40/80.

In England gratuities amounting to three times the annual pension is also given on retirement. Earlier retirement on account of ill-health earns a proportionate pension. A widow's and children's pension scheme was introduced by the Superannuation Act of 1948.

Women in Administration

Women in the civil service constitute a modern phenomenon in administration. Although the accident of birth has put women into the position of rulers of heads of states, it is conscious and deliberate policy that has brought women into the administrative services in modern times. The growth of spinsterhood in communities among whom the obligation of women to marry does not obtain, the spread of the influence of the doctrine of equality of sexes, the aspiration of women to economic independence, the comparative cheapness of their employment, the services of women in administration during wars when the man power of the country was led into other channels have brought women in the administration in increasing numbers in the last 25 years. Even in such a socially conservative country as India these forces have operated. Their special aptitude for subordinate work like that of typists, telephone and telegraph operations, post office work and the womanly qualities of gentleness and courtesy and their special competence in the welfare and social services have ensured their stay. In England to-day about 1/3 of the total number of civil servants are women. They fill about 1/2 the number of clerical posts, nearly 20 per cent of the executive and about 14 per cent of the higher administrative services. They have risen to the position of Assistant Secretary in England and the corresponding position of Under Secretary in India.

In most countries women work on the same conditions as men, though the principle of equal pay in equal work although accepted has not been operated on in England, probably on account of the cost. In England women are not required to resign on marriage but if they choose to do so after serving not less than 6 years they secure a gratuity on marriage rising according to length of services up to a maximum of one year's salary.

Department of Personnel Management

Personnel, filling such a large place, and playing such an important part in administration, it is necessary that its management should be put under a special Department with a specially qualified person as its head. For the administration of such matters as those of the fixation of salary for each grade of work, the rates of increments in pay, assignment to work after recruitment, promotion, efficiency, leave and leave rules, retirement and retirement rules—in fact all the questions dealt with in this chapter except that of recruitment, a special department is necessary. It has to devise means and methods of getting the best out of the personnel in administration. It has to see to the development and improvement of standards of work and conduct of workers of all grades of the civil service. One has only to remember the high cost of administration in order to be convinced that it would be wise economy training set up a special department to see that the country gets value for the money spent on its civil services. In the USA the civil service pay roll amounts to 700 million dollars for the Federal Government alone. And no other department which has work or enough work of its own can be allotted to it—not even the Civil or Public Service Commission because its work of recruitment is big enough and specialised enough for it. And the qualities and qualifications of members of the Civil Service Commission are not those required of the officials of a department of personnel management who must have had more personal and intimate experience of the work of Government Departments. And the independence and impartiality of a Civil Service Commission may become impaired if it were to enter into discussion and decision over the questions that have to do with personnel management. And no agency entirely independent of the departments and establishments of the civil service can successfully deal with and recommend personnel policies and practices with any prospect of acceptance. Although each Department may have its own Establishment Section looking after the personnel problems of each department there is need for a general personnel Department that should be able to take a general, broad, and liberal view of the problems and difficulties of personnel in the services. The Cabinet Secretariat to which such a duty of supervision of personnel was attributed earlier would assume this as only one of its subjects and its supervision would be of an over-all ultimate character, and not all Cabinet Secretariats would have the time or the energy for such work left after its main function had been performed.

As for the constitution of such a Department of personnel management the USA offers a model in the Federal Personnel Board established under an executive order of the President in December, 1921. Under this order the duties of the Board were to formulate policies and plans designed to place the personnel administration of the Federal Government abreast of the best practice in private enterprise, with due regard to the peculiarities of the public service. In the prosecution of its activities the Board was directed to consider, among other things, closer relations between the Civil Service Commission and the several Departments; the character of the personnel problems in the various departments and establishments, the development of an adequate system of personnel records, to furnish a medium for effective control of personnel administration, and to provide basic statistics, the formulation of recommendations for so using employees in the various departments as to take care of the maximum load of work, the development of a personnel inventory system to facilitate the assignment of specially qualified employees to offices and duties in which their services would be of the greatest value, the question of training with the object of reducing the period before an employee becomes an effective worker, the possibilities of adopting the principle of promotion from within in filling the higher positions, the development of a system for the more careful review of selections for increased compensation, and the formulation of plans regarding hours of service, leave of absence, privileges under the Retirement Act, and other matters designed to increase the effectiveness of the public service.

The work of such a department of personnel management would also consist in putting into effect reforms in administration such as those proposed by the Hoover Committee on the reorganisation of the Executive branch of the Government of the USA. If only by putting through some of these reforms such a department could effect a great saving in the cost of administration as has been done in the U.S.A. where some of the reforms suggested by the Hoover Committee have already resulted in a saving of 2 million dollars such reforms would conduce to the health and progress of administration.

The Rights of Members of the Civil Service

In common with all other citizens the members of the Civil Services have the right to all the rights of citizenship. But there are certain limitations placed on the exercise of some of these rights by the nature of their work. They can exercise most of the rights of citizenship including the right to vote at elections to all public bodies. But it is obvious they may not stand for parliamentary election as Parliament sits in judgement on their work. But recently it has been held in England that subordinate civil servants mainly of the industrial and non-industrial, manipulative grades which have nothing to do with the formulation of policy activity any stage could stand for election. To election to local bodies members of the higher administrative class may stand subject to certain limitations.

The right of association is also open to the civil service. As workers in the industrial sphere, workers in the civil service in obedience to modern trends have also formed themselves into association for the defense and promotion of their interests. Associations or unions of civil service employees were formed in England as early as 1890. At the close of the First World War in 1918 the Union of post office workers had a membership of about 100,000 and the Civil Service Confederation 65,000 Smaller groups also have been formed like the Civil Service Clerical Association with about 20,000 members. Introduction of the principle of Whitley Councils stimulated the formation of such Civil Service Associations.

Into the methods of working of the civil service association the trade union spirit has crept in. Since 1920 these associations have tried the industrial weapon of strike culminating in their participation in the general strike of 1926 which however was broken by the action of the general public. But the danger to the State of resort to strike by the civil services was realised soon after when by the enactment of the Trade Disputes and Trade Unions Acts, civil service organisations cannot affiliate themselves with a political party or a labour organisation. Although mass movements or agitation by the civil service to secure redress of grievances is not precluded, resort to strikes is presumably excluded. Tardieu, once Prime Minister of Franc was of the opinion that civil servants, although they are full citizens have ceased to be so when of their own accord they agreed to enter the hierarchy of Government servants, and have lost the right to fight its hierarchy; the State cannot allow itself to be broken or betrayed by those whom it has recruited and paid.

In France there are Syndicalist Civil service staff association affiliated to the *Confederation generale du travail* which had established by struggle and victory the rights of French civil servants. Administrative law and the Conseil d'etat protect the rights of civil servants in France. In Germany under the Weimar Constitution the rights of civil servants were secured by law.

The value of Civil Service Associations has been realised by Governments themselves. This realisation finds expression in a British Treasury official hand-book for new servants which says "You are not only allowed but encouraged to belong to a staff association. Beside being a good thing for individual civil servant, it is also a good thing for departments and for a civil service as a whole that civil servants should be strongly organised in representative bodies."

The Civil Servant's Code of Conduct

All the personnel management and civil service associations will not produce good civil servants if they are not society minded. It is they, that in the last resort and as individuals in their individual conduct have the making and unmaking of themselves as civil servants and of the civil service. Implementation is their standards of conduct that can promote high standards of work and achievement. Personal religioin, conscience and morality must keep them to the straight and narrow path of duty. But religion does not always produce moral conduct in the public servant. It was a shrewd observation of Cardinal Richelieu that "there are many who would die rather than go against their conscience, but nevertheless do not serve the public for they are not capable of resisting the importunities or appeals of those they love." For those on whom religion has lot its hold some code of social conduct like the Japanese Bushido or the Chinese Jen or English form must act as an influence. It must be a tradition, that is, it must be handed down from one civil servant to another, from one generation of civil servants to the next. Tradition has been a salutary influence in public school, college, university and the public services in England. The irreverent H.G. Wells spoke of "the tradition of honour and devotion of honour and devotion to duty that animated the civil service in England". Lord Hewart who criticised its new despotsm called it the best civil service in the world. But only two Acts have been found necessary for maintaining the integrity of the British Civil Service, the Official Secrets Act of 1911 and the Prevention of Corruption Act of 1906. It has survived, with its honour untarnished, two inquests, one the enquiry instituted by the Prime Minister in 1928 into certain allegations against the conduct of civil servants and the enquiry of the Lynsky Tribunal. The former laid down the code of conduct of civil servants in the following words: "A civil servant is not to subordinate his duty to his private interest; but neither is he to put himself in a position where his duty and his interests conflict. He is not to make use of his official position to further those interests; but neither is he to order his private affairs so, as to allow the suspicion to arise that a trust has been abused or a confidence betrayed... His position clearly imposes on his restrictions in matters of commerce and business from which the ordinarily citizen is free..." "Practical rules for the guidance of social conduct depend also as much upon the instinct and perception of the individuals as upon cast-iron formulas; and the surest guide will, we hope, always be found in the nice and jealous honour of civil servants themselves. The public expects from them a standard of integrity and conduct not only inflexible but fastidious and has not been disappointed in the past. We are confident that we are expressing the view of the service when we say that the public have a right to expect that standard, and it is the duty of the service to see that the expectation is fulfilled"

The code of conduct of civil servant includes all those ideas and practices of conduct which makes for efficient administration—devotion to duty, care of public money and public property, preference of public interests to private interests, tact, courtesy. It may be summed up in the one word which is used in its name and title—service.

7

Promotion and Performance Appraisal

The word 'promote' is derived from the Latin expression '*promovere,*' meaning 'to move forward'. The dictionry defines 'to promote' as: "1. To exalt in station, rank or honour; to elevate; to advance. 2. To contribute to the growth or prosperity of (something in course); to futher the progress of, to promote learning. 3. To advance from a given grade of class as qualified for one higher." Indeed, promotion refers to advancement in rank and status, usually (not necessarily immediately) accompanied by increase in emoluments.

Civil service is a career service and persons who join it expect to spend their lifetime in it. This emphasizes that the public personnel work their way up the organisational hierarchy with the flux of time. Promotion is, thus, an intnegral part of a career service.

The need for promotion arises from a variety of factors. An organisation is enabled to retain the services of its personnel by the device of promotions. Man is a growing creature and if his need for recognition and advancement is not adequately staisfied by his organisation, he is apt to seek change, thereby causing a large turnover of staff. Secondlly, lower positions in an organisation would be able to attract competent persons if it holds out a promise that these persons would move to higher levels in course of time. Flowing from this is the third advantage of no mean significance. A sound policy of promotion fosters a feeling of belongingness in the personnel, contributes to a measure of continuity in policies and practices and leads to building up of traditions and conventions. All these add to the goodwill of the organisation.

Recruitment is undoubtedly, the most vital process in personnel administration, and all other processes, such as, in-service training and promotion cannot undo the harm which can be caused by unsound recruitment. Yet, in a sense, promotion is a much more sensitive device. Recruitment makes the unsuccessful vanish from the scene; and thus the employers has no subsequent dealings with them. Not so in the case of promotion, especially in societies characterised by less than full employment. If promotion get governed by favouritism, nepotism, etc., the 'left outs' will in all probability continue floating in the same organisation nursing grievances against employers. The consequent low morale cannot but affect organisations productivity.

HISTORY OF PROMOTION POLICIES IN THE CIVIL SERVICES IN INDIA

In India the question of promotion in the civil service was first discussed in the year 1669 when the principle of seniority was announced by the East India Company. The Company decided, in 1669, that "none should be sent out from here (London) to step over the head of others." Despite this resolve, the Court of Directors of the East India Company continued to send to India, "Factors' until 1765, thereby ignoring the claims of "Writers'. In 1771, when the Company took over administrative functions, the principle of seniority was modified to make allowance for merit. The Court wrote: "However desirous we are that our servants should succeed to superior stations according to priority in service (which means seniority) in all cases where the same can be observed without prejudice to the interests of the Company, it is not our meaning that seniority alone should entitle them to enjoy such posts as require not only an undoubted integrity but also a competent degree of ability and attention...." But the principle of seniority was sanctified by the Charter Act of 1793. "....for establishing a just principle of promotion amongst the covenanted servants...and preventing all undue supersessions, be it further enacted, that all the civil servants....under the rank or degree of members of the Council, shall have and be entitled to precedence in the service...at their respective stations according to their seniority of appointment." This principle remained in force till its repeal by the Indian Civil Service Act, 1861. The Charter Act of 1793 further provided that there was to be no advancement or promotion to any higher station, rank or degree in the service, any law or usage to the contrary notwithstanding." Vacancies in the higher posts were to be filled up from among covenanted servants belonging to the same Presidency. Each Presidency had its own separate civil service although in respect of appointment and general conditions of service the covenanted servants in the three Presidencies were subject to more or less uniform rules.

Coming to Independent India this matter received attention in 1947 itself. The (First) Central Pay Commission (1947) recommended a judicious blending of both direct recruitment and promotion for filling up positions in all the four Classes in the Civil service. The case for promotion was particularly strong for, as the Commission pointed out, the civil service in India attracts 'overqualified' staff. According to it, administrative positions in respect of which long familiarity with office work is itself adequate training, the principle of seniority was to be adopted and merit was to be the overriding consideration for tip positions while for middle-level positions the principle of seniority-cum-merit was the most appropriate. It also stressed the need for improving the prevalent mechanism for assessing merit. The First Pay Commission observed:

"We are not prepared to throw any doubt on the expediency of making direct recruitment to each of the four Classes of the public service; but we should nevertheless like to see the claims of those already in service recognised in an increasing measure by affording to the deserving amongst them abundant opportunities for promotion. In recent years, candidates who enter the lower grade of the services, frequently possess much higher educational qualifications than are prescribed as the minimum requirements for these grades. It often happens that persons who sit for competitive examinations for recruitment to the highest grades just miss selection and they accordingly enter grades next below. Few first-class men will be tempted to enter service in these ways, if they are likely to be permanently excluded by outsiders. Without going the length of endorsing the claim for reservation of high percentage of posts for promotion, we would recommend that the claims of competent men already in the service should be recognised and satisfied to the fullest extent possible. If such men are promoted to responsible posts fairly early in their career, they will bring all the benefits of practical experience without the disadvantages entailed by a prolonged course of routine work. We would also recommend that even when direct recruitment to particular posts is decided on, deserving men already in service should be enabled to compete for such recruitment, by a reasonable relaxation of the rule relating to age limit and other restrictive conditions."[1]

The Commission continued: "As to the principles to be adopted in making promotions, the familiar controversy between seniority and merit has been revived before us. The general formula of seniority-cum-merit was formally accepted by all; but the advocates of seniority interpreted it to mean that seniority should prevail except when a person has been declared to be unfit. We do not think implementation right to put such a limited interpretation on the principle. The purpose of promotion is not merely to give the public servant more pay, but also to give him a more responsible position and more extensive authority. The question must, therefore, be judged both from the public interest, and from the interest of the individual concerned. The principle of seniority assumes that all members of a particular grade are equally fit for promotion. Such an assumption may not do much harm in the lower grades of the service; but it cannot be generally accepted when dealing with promotion in or to the top grades. The principle of seniority has no doubt, the advantage that its operation is very nearly automatic and implementation avoids the need for making invidious distinctions between one person and another and the embarrassment of placing a young officer over the head of an older one. For many situations, especially those in respect of which long familiarity with office work is itself adequate training, the rule of seniority may be generally followed. But, even in this category of posts, occasional instances of exceptional promotion of deserving persons would be an inducement to greater endeavour, provided, of course, that care is taken to guard against all suspicions of nepotism. In the higher grades of the service considerations of fitness must have precedence over the claim of seniority. The task of selection may not always be easy or agreeable and the possibility of mistake, unfairness or injustice cannot be wholly excluded, but the situation has to be faced. The efficiency of such a promotion system will largely turn upon the means adopted to determine the relative merits of the candidates.

The Second Pay Commission, called the Commission of Enquiry on the Emoluments and Conditions of Service of Central Government Employees (1959), give its attention to how promotions should be made in the civil service. It recommended the principle of merit for filling higher level posts and the principle of seniority-cum-fitness for lower levels in administration. It observed: "Merit should continue to be the criterion in making promotion activity at higher levels. At lower levels where the work is essentially of a routine nature, and it is extremely difficult to make a distinction between the performance of two men doing the same standard work with reasonable efficiency, the principle of seniority-cum-fitness is appropriate. But fitness in such cases, as in others, should be judged mainly with reference to the post to which promotion is to be made."[3]

The Second Pay Commission (1959) visualised a broadening of the base of recruitment to the All-India Central (Class I) services by recommending that the members of Class II and Class III services should be permitted to qualify for those higher services through a limited competitive examination open only to Class II and Class III. This scheme was expected to provide a much-needed incentive to the members of these lower classes in government and also to make available brighter persons in these services for manning the All-India and Central (Class I) services. The Commission explained the outlines of the proposed scheme in this way: "We suggest the introduction of a system of promotion, by a special competitive examination that would provide to young officers in the Class II and Class III services an additional opportunity to enter any of the Class I services to which their is recruitment by a competitive examination. At present, those who fail to enter a particular service, or class of service, on the result of the normal competitive examinations, 'miss the bus' for many years, or even for good. It is well known that there is an element of chance in examinations; administration even apart from that a person's mental development does not stop activity the stage when he appears at the competitive examinations open to those within the age limits of 20-24 years. It may well be that a person who had failed to get into a higher service may, after some years, develop mental and personal qualities which would make him eminently fit for that service. Moreover, there is at present hardly any scope of promotion from a lower service in one functional group of services to a higher service in another group.....The Union Public Service Commission holds a combined competitive examination every year for recruitment to the all-India and Class I and also some Class II central services. A proportion of the vacancies—perhaps about ten per cent in those services—may be set apart to be filled by another examination to be conducted by the Commission for serving civil servants. The age limits may be between 24-30, and the qualifying service may be five years. It should be an essential part of the schemé that only those who are nominated by their departments should be permitted to take the examination; and the criteria for the departmental nominations should be not only good work and good conduct but also exceptional promise. A university degree need not, however, be essential. Whatever, safeguards are considered necessary to ensure fair nomination, such as selection by a committee, may be adopted. The examination may be open not only to central government employees, but also to those working under the state government, public corporations and other undertakings in the public sector.....The scheme would permit some amount of lateral mobility which would bring into the higher services a very valuable new element; and it might also reduce, to howsoever small an extent it may be, the barriers which divide the services in one department from those in others. It would, in a measure, equalize as well as add to the chances of promotion to the higher service of young officers of outstanding merit in the different Class II and Class III services to all of which the proposed limited competition would be open. We have felt called upon to suggest this scheme partly because we believe that its incentive value would be far greater than the number of promotions permissible under it might suggest."[4] This scheme as visualised by the Commission is but a system of promotion, but the promotion is to be gained by a competitive examination.

It should also be noted that the Estimates Committee (First Lok Sabha) in its Ninth Report on Administrative, Financial and other Reforms examined, among others, the promotion policies in the Government. The Committee expressed itself against a diversity of practices governing promotion of personnel and laid down the following system which 'is now an accepted principle in all the modern countries and business concerns':

(i) Promotion should be solely on the basis of merit regardless of the seniority of the persons concerned in service;

(ii) Persons should be judged for promotion by the people who have watched their work and conduct over a period;

(iii) Promotions should be made on the recommendation of a committee consisting of not less than three officers, one of whom at least is acquainted with the work of the person concerned. In each case, the committee should record in writing the grounds on which claims of persons, if any, senior to the person selected, were overlooked;

(iv) In judging the person on the basis of the confidential report on him, it should be seen that he was warned in time of the defects noticed in his work and conduct and that if he did not show improvement he was warned again; and

(v) If no warning has been given to a person, it should not be presumed that the reports on him are so good as to justify his promotion.

PRINCIPLES OF PROMOTION

Promotions is based on one of the following principles:

(i) Seniority,

(ii) Merit, and

(iii) Seniority-cum-fitness (or, seniority subject to fitness).

Promotion in public services is governed by seniority and/ or merit. In the case of non-selection posts, by and large, in class III and Class IV, promotion is made on the basis of seniority subject to the rejection of the unfit. For selection posts, largely in Class II and Class I, criterion is merit, the officers considered for promotion, limited, arranged in order of seniority, to 3 to 5 times of the number of vacancies available for promotion.

Traditionally, the principles governing promotion have been seniority at lower levels, seniority-cum-merit at middle level an at senior levels.

Performance Appraisal

To adopt a system of promotion by merit calls for an efficient performance appraisal system. The true purpose of a performance appraisal system is primarily to assess the capabilities of a person in terms of his contribution towards the achievement of organisational goals. It, thus, serves a short-term purpose of assessing the usefulness of an employee to the organisation and in the long run determines his potential for elevation to higher levels. Conversely, implementation pinpoints the shortcomings of an employee and by pointing these out to him, the superior officers can manage better utilisation of the services of that employee through either correction or position-change.

The existing performance appraisal system in India consists of an annual appraisal given by the superior about the subordinate in the shape of a form which carries entries to determine the adequacy and quality of work done and the general personality and integrity of the officer reported upon. Besides, his fitness for promotion or otherwise is also commented upon. To reduce the ambiguities in relative grading by different officers, a common gradation of 'outstanding', 'above average', 'fair', 'below average' is prescribed to judge each item in that from. This report is written by the reporting officer in a narrative from, evaluated by the reviewing officer and finally endorsed—or countersigned—by the next higher officer. This constitutes the Annual Confidential Roll, better known by its abbreviated name, A.C.R. To give an example, the A.C.R. of an under-secretary is written or initiated by the deputy secretary under whom he is working; the deputy secretary is the reporting officer in this case. The A.C.R. will then be reviewed by the joint secretary and countersigned by the additional secretary/secretary, depending upon the hierarchy. This is observed for all the classes of civil servants.

The present procedure is that if the A.C.R. contains any adverse remarks as finally confirmed by the reviewing officer and the next higher officer, they are required to be communicated to the officer concerned, the intention being that he would correct himself. Also, he is given an opportunity to represent to the authorities against the adverse remarks, such representation being considered in consultation with the reporting and reviewing officer, a final decision being taken to expunge, modify or retain the adverse remarks. The communication of adverse remarks to the person concerned is based on the principle of natural justice, *viz.*, none should be punished without being heard. It is equally true that this practice may spoil the superior-subordinate relationship in the organisation and drive both the persons into rigid postures. An awareness of adverse remarks being communicated to the 'reported' officer and a likely challenge by him inclines the reporting officer generally to shun giving adverse comments: sneaky, disguised, unfavourable observations or colourless entries are more common in such cases. This can be remedied to an extent by making the A.C.R. forms more scientific. Equally necessary is the creation of an awareness among public personnel activity all the levels of the hierarchy that the business of writing A.C.Rs should be taken seriously.

The present system of performance appraisal leaves many flaws. In the evaluation form the qualities required of an officer are often not defined nor is there any report on the results and performance of special nature. Besides, the interpretations of the language of the proforma may vary and have subjective elements. Secondly, invariably the yardsticks are not commonly accepted and different superior officers attach different values to these terms. As a result, surprising though it may appear, the same subordinate may earn different gradings from different officers. This points up to a need for more explicit definition of the yardsticks, and even their possible qualifications, where necessary.

Thirdly, both the reviewing and the countersigning officers may or, as more often happens, may not have any direct or intimate knowledge about the work of the officer reported upon. Further, as the reports are written either at the end of the calendar year or the financial year, they are far too many and the reporting and the reviewing officers may not have the time or patience to do justice. Invariably, therefore, the judgement is faulty, or, at best, sketchy and follows the safe middle course of treating everyone as 'average' to aviod the later risk of being called upon to substantiate one's remarks through documentary evidence. There have been suggestions of staggering the writing of A.C.Rs. Still, it may not very much improve the practice.

Fourthly, the biggest factor against the present arrangement is the element of subjectivity which is built into it. Since it is a case of one individual passing a judgement on the other, an element of subjectivity cannot be completely ruled out. The reporting officer is free to compliment a dutiful drudge an be lukewarm to a person with independent mind who does not desist from occasional disagreements.

The appraisal blank needs to be so designed as to reduce to the irreducible minimum the element of subjectivity. A scientific method of framing the Annual Confidential Roll (A.C.R.) with in-built checks to curb loose reporting should be employed.

As the civil servant writing the A.C.R. may—often does—run short of words to describe, it would be better to give a scale with points so that the total can be struck to indicate how many points are scored. There should also be a separate column for general assessment. But for appraisal it is very wrong to go by the few words written under general comments and omit the weight of the points scored.

There is presently little uniformity or consistency in the method of appraisal. The reporting officer may commend the clear thinking of one person and the drive of another one—that is, traits commented upon do not run through a common or standard chain.

Curiously, there have been cases of adverse remarks not getting communicated to the reported officer. In 1973, the Supreme

Court held that it would not intervene in such cases of non-communication. It is, therefore, essential that the present arrangement should specifically provide for a certificate by the reviewing officer to the effect that the adverse remarks had been communicated to the official concerned.

At present, merit speaks only in the 'zone of promotion' which is a multiple of 3 or 5 of number of vacancies existing at a time. This precludes younger and talented civil servants further down from getting an opportunity of advancement. In order that such deserving people may also get out-of-turn promotions, internal competitive examinations may be organised, as recommended by the Second Pay Commission, as well as the Administrative Reforms Commission (1966-1970).

There is often a plea to do away with the ACR altogether. This must not be done. Otherwise the basis of evaluation will be still more subjective. This is tantamount to throwing away the baby along with bath-water. What is needed is the mending of the system of performance appraisal, not its ending.

The Administrative Reforms Commission examined the matter of performance appraisal. It recommended:

"1. At the end of each year the official reported upon should submit a brief resume, not exceeding three hundred words, of the work done by him, bringing out any special achievement of his. The resume should be submitted to the reporting officer and should form a part of the confidential record. In giving his own assessment, the reporting officer should take due note of the resume and after making his own comments and assessment submit the entries record to the next higher officer, namely, the reviewing officer. The reviewing officer should give his own comments, if any, and also do the grading.

"2. The Second Pay Commission limited the field of choice for promotion to those who were 'outstanding', 'very good' and 'good', thus excluding those who were assessed as 'fair' and 'poor'. The Government has recently revised the instructions regarding these gradations to a few categories. According to the latest government instructions only three gradations, namely, 'fit for promotion', 'not yet fit for promotion', and 'unfit for promotion' are to be made when writing the confidential reports for secretariat officers of the level of Under-secretary and above. Further, it has to be indicated whether the officer reported upon has any outstanding qualities which entitled him for promotion out of turn. In effect, therefore, the number of gradings have been reduced to four from the earlier five. We are glad to find, the Government, has taken action on these lines which appears to be, more or less in consonance with the recommendations made by our Study Team (N) which had recommended that the system of five gradings should be replaced by only three gradings, namely, (i) fit for promotion out of turn; (ii) fit for promotion; and (iii) not yet fit for promotion. The grading 'unfit for promotion' is likely to carry the impression that the officer concerned is unsuitable for promotion for all times. We feel that no one should be left with the feeling that he has permanently been branded as unfit for promotion. The grading 'not yet fit for promotion' will take care of cases who are unsuitable for promotion on the basis of their performance during the year under review. We, therefore, recommend the adoption of the three gradings proposed by the Study Team (N), *viz*., (i) fit for promotion out of turn; (ii) fit for promotion; and (iii) not yet fit for promotion.

"3. In the new system of grading, it is only those who are graded in the first two categories, *viz*., 'fit for promotion out of turn; and 'fit for promotion' that will have to be considered for promotion. The parentage of personnel in any group of civil servants working at the same level who are really outstanding and deserve out-of-turn promotion cannot but be small. We have feeling that at present 'outstanding' gradings are being given too liberally and not unoften undeservedly. We would suggest that as a rough guideline only five to ten per cent of officials engaged in work of a similar nature and at the same level in any office or organisation should be graded 'fit for promotion' out of turn'. (There would, of course, have to be exceptions to this in special circumstances). The grading 'fit for promotion out of turn' should be supported by specific mention of outstanding work that has been done.

"4. Good work done during the year should receive prompt appreciation either on a file, or in a tour or inspection note. The concerned official should be allowed to quote these in his resume.

"5. The suggestions made above will ensure that an individual's own estimate of his performance will get a place in his confidential report. It is equally important that his superior officer's assessment made frankly and faithfully is also available in it. There has been, however, a noticeable disinclination on the part of the reporting officers to record adverse remarks against those working under them, because such remarks are required to be communicated to the individual concerned and on his representation they are called upon to justify them. Moreover, the communication of adverse remarks quite often becomes a source of grievance aganist the reporting officer. To aviod this unpleasant contingency, the reporting officer quite often fails to record adverse remarks even when they are justified. This appears to be particularly true of headquarters offices than of field offices. This defect needs to be remedied in the larger interests of the efficiency of the civil service.

"We feel that when an opportunity is afforded as suggested by us to the official himself to write out an account of his performance and provision is made for a prompt review of the adverse remarks by a reviewing officer, it should not be necessary to communicate the adverse remarks. The reviewing officer will have to go through the adverse remarks and after discussing them with the reporting officer as well as; if necessary, the officer reported upon, either confirm the remarks or suitably modify them, as the case may be. To our mind, this procedure will ensure that both favourable and unfavourable remarks about a government servant are available at the time of assessment of his performance and subsequently when his performance over the years is assessed for purposes of promotion. It should also eliminate chances of any unfair or prejudiced treatment of government servant by the reporting officer, a circumstance against which government servant has a right to be safeguarded.

"6. In view of our new approach to the annual reports as a document spotlighting the performance of an official during the course of the year, we recommend that this report should be called 'performance report' instead of 'confidential report'.

"7. While considering the suitability of an officer for promotion, a realistic view needs to be taken of the adverse remarks recorded in his confidential reports. An adverse remark bearing on deficiencies in character or moral turpitude would certainly render an officer unfit for promotion. So would a series of remarks indicating inefficiency, indolence, etc. But if the records of an official are otherwise so good as to merit promotion, a stray adverse remark other than the one bearing on character and moral turpitude should not be made a ground for supersession. Needless to say, where merit is equal, seniority will be decisive for promotion.

This recommendation has been accepted since 1977. Yet we cannot say that performance appraisal has since become objective. Personal factors do affect the writing of the annual character roll, thereby vitiating the system of promotion in the civil service.

References

1. *Report of the Central Pay Commission*, Delhi, Manager of Publications, Government of India, 1947, p. 63.
2. *Report of the Central Pay Commission*, p. 64.
3. *Report of the Commission of Enquiry on the Emoluments and Conditions of Service of Central Government Employees*, New Delhi, Manager of Publications, Government of India, 1959, pp. 505-06.
4. *Report of the Second Pay Commission*, pp. 507-08.

8

Education and Training

Education and training of public servants form essential aids to the overall efficient operation of the public services. The problem of training is particularly acquiring an overwhelming significance in the face of the recruitment policy, which prefers general abilities, and in the context of an expanding government, the functions of which are becoming highly technical, specialised and complex. Basic to training is a well-articulated determination to prepare the public employees for these tasks. It is, however, true that the training must not confine itself to a mere inculcation of occupational skill and knowledge: it must set 'a wider goal, and be set against a wider background. The importance of training is, thus, quite apparent. Indeed, it is increasingly becoming an integral part of the contemporary administrative beliefs. Indicative of this growing realisation is the setting up of training institutions and devising of suitable training programmes in most countries.

Yet, the training of public servants has been until recently a much neglected field almost everywhere, India being no exception. "Even now it is still generally considered one of the lesser developed areas of public personnel administration—one in which much remains to be done.[1]

It is proper to note the distinction between education and training. Training is more specific and has a narrower scope. Education is, on the other hand, identified with "the complete upbringing of the individual from the childhood, the formation of character and of habits and manners, and of mental and physical aptitude."[2] The two are, however, closely interrelated and even overlap each other.

OBJECTIVES OF TRAINING

Training has been defined by William G. Torpey as "the process of developing skills, habits, knowledge, and aptitudes in employees for the purpose of increasing the effectiveness of employees in their present government positions as well as preparing employees for future government positions."[3] It is a well-articulated effort to provide for increased competence in the public services, by imparting professional knowledge, broader vision, and correct patterns of behaviour, habits and aptitudes. It is, or should be, a continuous process in response to a continuously felt need. It should not be restricted to the new entrants to public services only. The initial training should be supplemented by special courses and refresher courses to which those who are already in the service should be frequently invited. The role of training has been brilliantly analysed in the Report of the Committee on the Training of Civil Servants (popularly known as the Assheton Committee Report, after the name of its Chairman, Ralph Assheton), submitted to the British Chancellor of the Exchequer in 1944:

"At the outset we asked ourselves the question: 'What is the object of training?' If the answer is to attain the greatest possible degree of efficiency, then the word 'efficiency' seems to need some closer definition. In any large scale organisation, efficiency depends on two elements—the technical efficiency of the individual to do the particular work allotted to him, and the less tangible efficiency of the organisation as a corporate body derived from the collective spirit and outlook of the individuals of which the body is composed. Training must have regard to both elements.

Five main aims present themselves:

First, training should endeavour to produce a civil servant whose precision and clarity in the transaction of business can be taken for granted.

In the second place, the civil servant must be attuned to the task which he will be called upon to perform in a changing world. The Civil Service must continuously and boldly adjust its outlook and its methods to the new needs of the new times.

Thirdly, there is a need to develop resistance to the danger of the civil servants becoming mechanised by the machine; whilst we must aim at the highest possible standard of efficiency, our purpose is not to produce a robotlike, mechanically-perfect Civil Service. The recruit from the first should be made aware of his work to the service rendered by his Department to the community. The capacity to see what he is doing in a wider setting will make the work not only more valuable to his Department but more stimulating to himself. In addition, therefore, to purely vocational training directed to the proper performance of his day-to-day work, he should receive instruction on a broader basis as well as encouragement to persevere with his own educational development.

Fourthly, even as regards vocational training it is not sufficient to train solely for the job which lies immediately at hand. Training must be directed not only to enabling an individual to perform his current work more efficiently, but also to fitting him for other duties and, where appropriate, developing his capacity for higher work and greater responsibilities.

Fifthly, even these needs are not in themselves enough. Large numbers of people have inevitably to spend most of their working lives upon tasks of a routine character, and with this human problem ever in the background, training plans, to the successful, must pay substantial regard to staff morale."[4]

This is a brilliant exposition of the main aims of training in a democratic country. These aims hold good for imparting training to civil servants in any democratic country, and, therefore, have been reproduced verbatim.

It will do well to analyse a bit more closely the objectives and aims of a training programme for civil servants. For the sake of brevity, these are summarised below:

1. Training helps the entrant by inculcating occupational skill and knowledge, making him familiar with the objectives of the department to which he belongs, and his potential contribution in the furtherance of the department's goal.

2. There are constant changes in the goals and techniques of departments. The broad goals are defined by legislation and

are, therefore, occasionally modified and revised. Training adjusts the employees to the new environments.

3. Training makes up for any deficiencies of the recruits. The public services have to meet their personnel requirements from the existing supply. Training forges and shapes the existing material into the desired instruments of a good administration. Thus, the deficiencies of the new appointees may be corrected by imparting them necessary training.

4. The Government must impart training in activities and occupations which are peculiar to it and have no parallel in the private enterprise. The familiar examples are the specific skills of firemen, policemen, food inspectors, etc. The Government must train the appointees in these skills.

5. In an era marked by spectacular advances in the fields of knowledge, training helps keep the employee informed of latest development in his special field and, thus, keep his knowledge up-to-date.

6. Training helps employees become people-oriented. One of the objectives of training is, or should be, inculcation of respect and regard for the general public. They should be emotionally integrated with the community. It is pertinent to recall the following observation of the Assheton Committee (1944): "Nothing could be more disastrous than that the Civil Service and the public should think of themselves as in two separate camps. The inculcation of the right attitude towards the public and towards business should, therefore, be one of the principal aims of Civil Service Training"[5]

7. Training helps broaden the vision and outlook of the appointees by constantly holding out to them wider, national objectives and their potential contribution towards the realisation of the same. As Nigro puts if, "...the function of training is to help employees grow, not only from the standpoint of mechanical efficiency but also in terms of the broad outlook and perspective which public servants need."[6] "Training must aim at broadening the mind."[7]

8. Training equips those who are already in the public services for higher positions and greater responsibilities that inevitably

devolve upon the existing personnel in view of the expanding functions of the modern government and the demand for increased competence in the public services.

9. Training is vital to a career service, which provides for the recruitment of persons of young age and their subsequent promotions. It makes them fit for such advancement. It is, indeed, implicit in the idea of the career service that efforts would be incessantly made to develop the capacities of the recruits.

10. Training sets the tone and equality of the organisations. As it enhances the efficiency of the employees, by developing their capacities, the efficiency and prestige of the department go up. Work is not only well done, but also quickly done and to the satisfaction of the people.

11. Training helps build integrity and morale in the public employees by inculcating right mental attitudes to questions of personal and public conduct. It is imperative that the Civil Services should build up a higher standard of integrity than that generally prevailing in the Community.

12. Training fosters homogeneity of outlook and *esprit de corps* in the employees. It is conducive to cohesion in regard to method of work, and approach to problems.

TYPES OF TRAINING

Training may be informal or formal. Informal training is training by doing the work, and learning from mistakes, thus, leading to the acquisition of administrative skill through practice. Imparted imperceptibly, it leaves profound impressions upon the mind of its recipient. This training "occurs in the day-to-day relationships of employee and superior, in conferences and staff meetings, in employee, newspapers and organisation publications, at meetings of professional associations, and in the reading and study that the employee undertakes at his own volition or at his supervisor's suggestions. Because such training is connected with the regular tasks of the employee, he can best integrate with his own experience and thereby profit from it. Since there is no compulsion, connected with it, his motivation is positive. Its influence, whether good or bad, is profound."[8] It was this type of training which was adopted by the Britishers in India. The newly joined civilian was encouraged to often walk into the Collector's house and develop personal contacts. The young official used to go and live with the Collector for a few days at the beginning of his service, to accompany a senior officer during the touring season, and to participate in revenue settlement cases under the immediate guidance of a senior settlement officer. He was, thus, enable to imbibe the art of administration by actually practising it as well as by seeing how it is practised. Almost unconsciously he imbibed suitable habits and standards. Indeed, the Collector was his precepter. "A good Collector's house was often a second home to the young Assistant Collector," in Gorwala's words. These personal contacts helped to stimulate qualities of initiative and administrative leadership as well as capacity to feel responsibility and rise to it. Commending such a system of training, Trevelyan, whose name is indelibly associated with the evolution and rise of the Indian Civil Service, observed: "The real education of the civil servant (in India) consists in the responsibility that devolves on him at an early age which brings out whatever good there is in a man; the obligation to do nothing that can reflect dishonour on the service; the varied and attractive character of his duties and the example and precept of his superior who regards him rather as a younger brother than a subordinate official."

The ultimate success of informal training, however, depends upon the experience and seniority of the senior officer, and his interest in the new entrant. As a result of the phenomenal increase in the governmental tasks, the senior officers now find themselves too busy to devote time and attention on the young official sent out for field training. The latter are consequently not in a position to draw on their senior colleagues' experience; they are left to learn through trial and error method. This situation is unpromising. We agree with Gorwala's suggestion that "suitable senior officers should be posted to some districts, despite their seniority with a view to make these districts a training-ground for the young."[9]

Formal training purports to inculcate administrative skill by well-defined courses at proper stage in the man's career. It is, of late, receiving increasing attention, as the need for increasing the number of administrators as well as for improving their quality is felt so crying. Informal training must consequently be supplemented by formal training. Training schemes need be multiplied by instituting formal instruction by lecture and group discussion, specialised in personnel administration, financial management, etc., conference, workshops and seminars.

Formal training may be divided into the following four categories: (i) Pre-entry training, (ii) Orientation training, (iii) Inservice training, and (iv) Post-entry training.

1. *Pre-entry Training.* It prepares a prospective candidate for entrance into the public service. Viewed in this light, even education imparted in schools and universities in pre-entry training, as it seeks to fit its recipient for all sorts of jobs including jobs in the government. The term 'pre-entry training' is, however, restricted to refer to vocational or professional instruction. In India, there is hardly any pre-entry training scheme in existence. A striking example of pre-entry training is, however, provided by the Rajasthan Government, which decided, in 1960, that candidates securing 65 per cent or more marks in the Junior Diploma Course in Secretariat and Business Training, started in July 1959 in collaboration with the Rajasthan University, would be taken straightway as upper division clerks.

The United States has developed a rather comprehensive system of pre-entry training for administrative and managerial positions in the forms of internship and apprenticeship. "An internship programme is an educational method providing specially selected and specially supervised trainees with preparation for administrative and policy careers in public affairs by (i) encouraging these trainees to apply previous academic and employment experience to new concrete job situations through direct participation, on a systematically planned and scheduled basis, in the work of organisations appropriate to the particular interest of trainees and sponsor; (ii) providing, if appropriate, for trainees' participation in supplementary, academic, and professional activities that will contribute further to their development."[10] The internship has thrown quite a good number of outstanding young persons into the public service, and he brought the educational institutes and the Government closer. Apprenticeship training differs from internship in that it is concerned with trade or craft skills whereas the latter is related to administrative or professional work.[11]

2. *Orientation Training.* The object of orientation training is to introduce an appointee to the basic concepts of his job, new work environment, organisation and its goal. The importance of orientation is highlighted by Marx in the following words: "It is clear that significant advances in the functional efficiency of the 'administrative state' cannot be expected without corresponding changes in the working style of the administrative system. In this respect, perhaps, the most important thing is the acceptance within the higher civil service of a reorientation towards its role. The men of the top cadre must shift their attention from watching 'processes' to measuring their impact, from 'getting things done' to give each citizen his due, from the technology of administration to its effect upon the general public, from utility to ethics. Not what is being said but what is being done, will decide whether the 'administrative state' will stand out eventually as a benefactor or as a destroyer. It is for the civil servant to realize that much of what can be done must be his doing."[12] Orientation training is becoming important in India in order to keep bureaucracy, particularly the fast emerging rural bureaucracy, attuned to the new tasks. The National Institute of Rural Development, Hyderabad (formerly called the Central Institute of Study and Research in Community Development) is particularly seized with this problem.

3. *In-service Training.* In-service training has the twin aims of stimulating the employee to make his best effort, and helping him to improve his performance. The recruitment system in India under which young persons possessing general abilities are selected for the public services, envisages a comprehensive scheme of in-service training for the higher

services. And, indeed, over a period of years, a network of training programmes for higher service had evolved.

4. *Post-entry Training.* The distinction between post-entry training and service training is indistinct, and is, thus, described by Milton M. Mandell: "Post-entry training, while for the most part not directly related to the work of the employee, is definitely of help to an organisation. An example would be training in engineering for a personnel specialist in a public works of highway department. Training in personnel work of public administration in this instance would be considered in service training; yet training in engineering, in our example, might be as valuable to the employee as the more closely related work in personnel administration."[13] Though not directly concerned with the immediate work of the employee, the post-entry training is of much use to the organisation. There seems to be a growing realisation of the need for post-entry training in India; and a broad indication of the feeling is provided by the liberalisation of provisions relating to study leave for the Central Government employees. In 1961, the Central Government decided that study leave may be granted for studies which may not be closely and directly linked with the Government servant's work, but improve his abilities as a civil servant, and to equip him better to collaborate with those employed in other branches of the public service.

The above analysis abundantly highlights the importance of the training of public servant, in any effort to make the public service competent and responsive to the aspirations of the people. Training should be imparted to the new entrants. In addition to this, those who are already in the services should be occasionally required to attend refresher courses and special courses. It is not impracticable to suggest that such courses should be properly spaced throughout the length of the service. It is well to bear in mind that the ultimate success of a training programme rests upon a wise recruitment policy for training cannot rectify the original error. Nor can training endow its recipient with the flair for administration, which is something inborn. This flair may be stimulated, but it cannot be artificially acquired. These are, then, some of the limitations of training. Despite these limitations, training is a paramount need of public administration today. Having convinced ourselves of the necessity of evolving programmes, we should ask ourselves a few questions and try to answer them.

WHO SHOULD BE THE TRAINERS?

This is an important consideration in devising a suitable training programme for the employees. Should trainers be the practitioners of administration or university professors? So far as training in social sciences and other allied subjects is concerned, the university professors may well teach these subjects with greater depth and comprehension than others whose main sphere of interest lies elsewhere. Their teaching, however, may not reveal intimacy with the realities of the situation. For this task, the seasoned administrators are indispensable. Indeed, it is stimulating for the trainees to be placed under the direct tuition of the latter. The satisfactory solution lies in selecting both the university professors and the seasoned administrators. Attempt should also be made to provide the academician with opportunities for acquainting himself directly with administrative problems. This may be done by giving him short *ad hoc* assignments in administration and appointing him to advisory and consultative committees, commissions of inquiry, etc.

WHAT SHOULD BE THE 'CONTENT' OF TRAINING?

A well-devised training programme must be multi-dimensional. It should cater to different requirements listed out earlier in this chapter. In countries like India where there is an avowed preference for the generalist administrators, the training programme must inculcate adequate knowledge and understanding of the work of specialist. All the varied requirements must be articulated in the training programme. Supremely important, however, is the adequate provision of social sciences in the training programme. A sufficient grounding in social science is an essential equipment of the administrator, who has rightly been called 'the social scientist in action'. He (the administrator) needs ideas; and the disciplines dealing with ideas should be ranked important. One writer correctly points out: "Now that the range is widening for management problems, we shall do well to demand that the traditional disciplines, which have dealt in ideas as they interact, in situations as wide as the artist's view of life, become a major part of education for managers. The greater this range of resource for the minds of management, the more and better will be the ideas that emerge."[14] Bernard Baruch similarly writes "I also believe it a mistake that Greek and Latin are no longer subjects that all students must take, At C.C.N.Y., I read most of the Greek and Latin classics in the original and could carry on a conversation in Latin. My study of both languages gave me an appreciation of the cultural background of our civilisation which I never would have had otherwise."[15] Transplanted into Indian context, it means familiarity with Indian history, culture, traditions, mores, customs, etc. Knowledge of History, Sanskrit and Indian social problems would help realize these aims. Further, the training of administrators would be incomplete without their grounding in the basic concepts of public administration. In the end, it may also be emphasised that training for recruits to different services must be different as the nature of work varies from service to service. Also it must be related to the post-entry qualifications as well as to the duties the appointees are to perform.

The case for a system of training for public servants is unassailable, particularly in a system of recruitment, which selects young persons, and prefers general abilities to "being possessed of any special requirements." Yet, training has been a neglected aspect in the personnel administration. It is only recently that increasing attention is being given to it, though the overall situation still seems to be not too satisfactory. In 1968, a Training Division was set up in the Ministry of Home Affairs to deal with training policies and programmes of the Government of India in the field of administration; the Division which is headed by a director of the rank of a joint secretary sponsors training programmes for officers at the various training institutions.

TRAINING IN BRITAIN

The British approach to training was conditioned until recently by their belief in the principle of 'training by doing' and in 'learning from mistake'. It was widely held that the administrative skill had an essential empiricity, and was amenable to acquisition more through practice than by training whether theoretical or otherwise. This question was first explored by the Assheton Committee in 1944. In accordance with the recommendation made by this Committee, a Division of Training and Education was constituted in the Treasury, which co-ordinated training, ran central courses for members of administrative, professional and scientific classes at different stages of their public careers, and finally, trained the departmental instructors, and few other groups. For the rest training was undertaken within the departments, which could, it was believed, better assess their special needs and requirements. Each of the bigger departments had a training officer and some instructors, who organised technical as well as general courses.

In 1945, a school was established to impart training to new entrants to the administrative class. It was, however, abolished in 1951 on grounds of economy.

TRAINING IN INDIA

The problems of education and training of civil servants have assumed special significance in India today. With expanding machinery of Government necessitating the constitution of fresh services and the change in the nature of governmental work following in the wake of Independence, it has become imperative for government to plan suitable training and education courses in Public Administration. It is well to recall the following observation of the Planning Commission in this respect "Next to recruitment the training of personnel has considerable bearing on administrative efficiency. Each type of work in the government requires a programme of training suited to it. In general, in all branches of administration, it is necessary to provide for the training of personnel at the commencement of service as well as at appropriate intervals in later years. In this connection, we would emphasize the importance of careful grounding in revenue and development administration for recruits to the Indian administrative service and the State administrative services."[16] Training for civil servants in India must be attuned to the following goals in addition to making its recipients competent and efficient.

1. Training must inculcate in the recruits respect for the traditions of parliamentary democracy which India has adopted. This point needs emphasis in view of the authoritarian basis of the Indian administration in the past. A seasoned administrator has rightly pointed out; "For a country like India, with a tradition of thousands of years of authoritative paternal administration, the transition to Parliamentary Democracy has involved a revolutionary change in the physiology of the body politic. It calls for a radical adjustment of attitude on the part of its operative organs, viz., the higher administrative personnel."[17] To recall the relevant part of the German Civil Service Act 1953, "By the entire conduct the civil servant must profess his attachment to the free democratic order in the sense of the Basic Law and exert himself for its preservation."

2. Training should aim at fostering an essentially national outlook, combating, in the process, the feelings of regionalism, communalism, casteism, etc.

3. It should foster emotional integration with the people. This point is of enormous importance in view of the wide gulf between the 'governors' and the 'governed'.

4. As civil services are mostly manned by urban people, having little knowledge and appreciation of rural life and problems, training programme should take special note of this factor, so that the employees may not ignore the realities of situation in rural areas. Training must provide rural bias to the employees.

5. India's destiny is linked up with the successful implementation of the successive Five Year Plans. It should be an important aim of training to make the employees 'programme-oriented'.

The British thinking largely conditioned the Indian approach to the problem of training of civil servants. This approach has been to make, the young official learn the job by doing it under the supervision of a superior officer. This approach did not look deficient, as the functions of the Government were severely limited to the maintenance of law and order, and the collection of revenue. It, however, looked untenable and unworkable when the Indian administration was, after 1947, attuned to new goals and objectives, and rapid expansion of governmental activities followed. Training of civil servants, is, thus, essentially a post-independence phenomenon. Not only is it receiving greater attention but also attempts are being made to make it broad-based. The Planning Commission recognised the need for such training when it recommended the conversion of the I.A.S. Training School into a sort of Staff College for a combined training of officers of different services. The Commission also proposed the appointment of a director of Training charged with the responsibility of "organizing systematic training programmes and refresher course for different grades of employees." The observations of A.K. Chanda in this connection are noteworthy:

"The best training in any service is provided by the actual doing of the jobs for which the services exist. Much time and wastage can however, be saved by providing a certain amount of basic training to shorten and facilitate the process of learning by doing. Such basic training has to be both 'general' (*i.e.*, applicable to all higher public servants), and 'special' (*i.e.*, relevant to the needs of particular services). The 'general' part comprises the basic knowledge, which all higher public servants should possess. *e.g.*, the main principals of the Constitution, the role of public servants in a Parliamentary Democracy, the organization of the machinery of Government at the Centre and the States, the principals of Public Administration and personnel management and the techniques of public relations. It should also include a knowledge of Economics in general and Indian Economics in particular, and an appreciation of India's social and economic problems.

"The 'special' part of the basic training would cover studying the Acts and Rules relating to the particular service, departmental procedures, etc. The course of training in the I.A.S.

Training School covers both the general and the special parts of the basic training needed by the I.A.S. officers. Arrangements for training of the Audit-service officers. Income-tax, Railways, etc., have been made by the Ministries concerned, but these are confined largely to the 'special' part of the training. It would be of great advantage if, each year, the recruits of the higher services are brought together in some Central Government institution for about six months to receive the 'general' part of the training. This will also enable officers coming from different parts of India to benefit by close contact with each other and lead to elimination of service consciousness. It may also help in reallotting the few officers who, by temperamental or other reasons, prove unsuitable for the service to which they were originally assigned."

The Home Ministry agreed with Canada's suggestions regarding the 'general training' that should be given to the members of specialised services, and, early in 1956, the Home Ministry addressed all the State Governments suggesting a scheme for providing Refresher Courses to officers of All-India Services and Central Services (Class I), and invited them to participate in the proposed scheme, so as to help break down service exclusiveness and to increase the utility of study and discussion of the subject proposed for inclusion in the syllabus for the Refrehser Course. A beginning in this direction was made in 1957, by starting a Refresher Course at the I.A.S. Staff College, Simla, for the I.A.S. officers with a standing of 6 to 10 years. Later, in a statement in the Lok Sabha on April 15, 1958, the Home Minister announced his decision to set up a "National Academy of Training so that the services, wherever they may function, whether as Administrative Officers, or as Accountants, or as Revenue Officers, might imbibe true spirit and discharge their duties in a manner which will raise their efficiency and establish concord between them and the public completely." The various Ministries were then invited to participate in the scheme for setting up an academy for the training of officers of the various services. Almost all the Ministries agreed to the setting up of such a teaching institution in principle, and from July 1959, commenced a combined course at I.A.S. Training School, Delhi, with following categories of officers:

(i) Indian Administrative Service,

(ii) Indian Foreign Service,

(iii) Indian Audit and Accounts Service,

(iv) Indian Defence Accounts Service,

(v) Indian Postal Service,

(vi) Indian Income-tax Service, and

(vii) Indian Customs and Excise Service

Immediately after the commencement of foundational course, the Ministry of Home Affairs decided to amalgamate the two sister institutions, I.A.S. Training School, Delhi, and I.A.S. Staff College, Simla, and to start a National Academy of Administration—now (since 1972) called the Lal Bahadur Shastri National Academy of Administration—At Mussoorie. The Academy started functioning at Mussoorie from September 1, 1959.

The first functional course ended in November 1959. On the basis of experience gained during this course its was suggested to the Ministry of Home Affairs that future courses should (i) begin at the same time for all Service; (ii) last for five months; and (iii) include recruits to the Indian Police Service also who could not join the first course. All these suggestions were accepted by the Ministry of Home Affairs. Each organised Service has today its own training institution to impart training to the new recruits. Recruits to the All-India and Central services are given a five months foundational course at the Lal Bahadur Shastri National Academy of Administration, Mussoorie, and then they go to the training institutions for their respective services. "The idea underlying the (foundational) course is that officers of the higher services should acquire an understanding of the constitutional, economic and social framework within which they have to function, as these largely determine the policies and programmes towards the framing and execution of which they will have to make their contribution. They should, further, acquaint themselves with the machinery of Government and the broad principles of public administration. . . . . The foundational course is also intended to cover such matters as aims and obligations of the Civil Service, an the ethics of the profession—objectivity, integrity, thoroughness, impartiality; etc."[18] Foundational course also develops among recruits to different services a feeling of belongingness to common public service and a broadly common outlook. After competing this five months' foundational course the probationers of the services òther than the I.A.S., leave for their respective training institutions for institutional training, but the I.A.S. probationers stay at the Academy to undergo a further course of institutional training. From 1969, the Government has introduced a new pattern of training called the 'sandwich' course, for the Indian Administrative Service. The new entrants to I.A.S. undergo two spells of training at the Academy with an interval of about a year which is utilised for fundamental course. After completion of the foundational course and spell of institutional training at the Academy, the probationer, as he is called, is sent to the State (to which he has been allotted) for practical training. At the end of this training, he again comes to the Academy for a second spell of training where emphasis is placed on the discussion of administrative problems, the probationer has either encountered or observed in the course of practical training in the state. This part of the training is, thus, more problem-oriented.

The Academy may also organize short courses, seminars, conferences, etc., for the benefit of more senior officers—ordinarily those having about fifteen years of service. The course may deal with the higher problems of government or with special subjects, for instance, social security, fiscal policy, planning interdepartmental coordination, etc. To these courses might be invited both technical as well as administrative officers.

The Academy offers three types of courses mentioned below:

1. A one-year course for the I.A.S. officers to cover the syllabus prescribed under the All-India Services Probations Final Examinations.

2. A six-week refresher course for officers of the seniority of 10 to 15 years. To start with, it is proposed to run this course for I.A.S. officers and, in due course, to throw it open for senior officers of the other services also.

3. A combined course of five months for all the All-India Services and the Central Services, Class I, for training in fundamental subjects.

The purport of these courses is to widen the outlook of the trainees. The course is general in nature, and provides for the imparting of general education in liberal arts to the personnel recruited for posts of specialised nature. This fulfils a big gap which previously existed and is a step in right direction.

The Lal Bahadur Shastri Academy of Administration continues to be located at Mussoorie although sometime back the Central Government had decided to shift it to Delhi. When the Academy was about to be taken to Delhi, the Government cancelled its earlier decision and resolved to keep it at Mussoorie—much to the chagrin of the civil servants. As there has always been considerable bureaucratic pressure in favour of brining the Academy to Delhi, a few comments about its location seem necessary. Delhi is already a crowded metropolis and the governmental policy, in this context, should be to disperse governmental establishments situated in Delhi to other places, certainly not to bring them from outside. There are higher reasons which point to the need for locating the Academy away from Delhi. In the first place, the stay of the new entrants to public services in Delhi is apt to involve them into the not to whole some part of the life and activities in the central secretariat exposing them to the existing groups and lobbies in the administration, and tempting them to evince interest in the matters of posting, transfers, etc. All this is bound to have adverse impact on their impressible minds. Secondly, the stay in Delhi of the new entrants, most of them being conceivably bachelors, exposes them to the tempting gaze of the senior bureaucrats with marriageable daughters. While there is nothing inherently unfair in such dialogues, a direct provocation to take training seriously gets distracted, or he deliberately distracts himself by matrimonial thoughts. Most importantly, imparting training to the members of the All-India Services at the seat of the Central Government is psychologically unfair and unwise. The all-India services are basically meant for states. An initial stay of the new entrants at Delhi is apt to indue in them a feeling of being the employees of the central government, thus, causing grave perceptual distortions. The training of the new recruits in Delhi, and not in the states is, thus, undesirable as well as improper.

Training for Indian Administrative Service (I.A.S.)

Recruits to the All-India Services (including the Indian Forest Service) and central services numbering nearly 350 are required to attend a common course of training, called foundational programme, at the Academy, the underlying idea of which being that officers of all the higher services should acquire an understanding of the constitutional, economic and social framework in which they have to function, as these largely determine the politics and programmes towards the framing and execution of which they make their contribution. In addition, it also develops among the new recruits of various services a feeling of belongingness to common public service and a broadly common outlook. The subjects taught in the foundational course, which is of three and half months duration, are (1) Basic Economics for Administrators, (2) History and Indian Culture, (3) Law, (4) Political Concepts and Constitutional Law, and (5) Public Administration, Management and Behaviourual Sciences. At the end of this course there is an examination and the marks secured in it are added to the recruitment examination.

After completing this foundational course, the probationers of the services other than IAS leave for their respective training institutes for subject-matter training, but the IAS probationers numbering nearly 150 stay at the Academy to undergo further training—called the professional training—of eight months duration introduced since 1969. After completing the first phase of professional training, the probationers go to the state of their allotment for district training the duration of which is one year. During 'district training' the probationers spend some time at the state training institute, and thus acquire knowledge of various aspects of life in the state of their destiny. They learn the language of the state. They are attached to districts where they obtain knowledge of various areas and levels of administration. They undertake socio-economic surveys of villages and this exposure is particularly emphasised as they would be speeding the initial period of their career in rural areas. During the period of district training, probationers remain in touch with the Academy as they have to report regularly to a faculty member.

Training for Indian Foreign Service (IFS)

The recruit to the IFS undergoes a training programme which covers a period of three years. He is attached to a district for some time to enable him to pick up contact with practical work as well as he undergoes a period of secretariat training programme for of IFS, however, puts emphasis upon the study of languages (Hindi and a foreign language) and of subjects the knowledge of which is considered essential to a member of the I.F.S.

Training for India Police Service (I.P.S.)

Entrants to the I.P.S. are trained at the Central Police Training College which was earlier located at Mount Abu (Rajasthan), but was shifted to Hyderabad during the internal emergency (25th June, 1975—21st March, 1977). The subjects of study and the training in drill, handling of weapons, etc., have a direct bearing on the normal work of a police officer. The syllabus of training includes studies of crime psychology, scientific aids in detection of crime, methods of combating corruption and fire and emergency relief. After completing the year's training, the probationer passes an examination conducted by the U.P.S.C. He is, then, appointed as an Assistant Superintendent of Police. But, before this appointment he has to undergo a year's programme of training; he is given practical training by requiring him to do the work of various subordinate officers, under guidance. It is only after this that he is appointed an Assistant Superintendent of Police.

Training for Indian Audit and Accounts Service (I.A. & A.S.)

The recruits to the I.A. & A.S. receive training at the department's training school at Simla. The syllabus of training differs from that of I.A.S. inasmuch as the courses of study have a direct bearing on the work which a member of the I.A. & A.S. has to perform. At the end of this training the probationer passes a departmental examination in subjects directly related to his work. It may also be mentioned that the probationer is also given practical training during the initial training period itself, by making him watch the work of the .A.G., Punjab, and by attaching him to a district treasury and the P.W.E. divisional accounts office. It is, thus, training on the job. After passing the departmental examination, the probationer is immediately posted as an Assistant Accounts Officer.

Training for Income-tax Service

The probationers of the Income-tax Service receive training at the Income-tax Training School, Nagpur. The pattern of training is the same as that of the I.A. & A.S.

Railway Staff College, Baroda

In addition to imparting training to the recruits to the Traffic, Transportation and Commercial Departments and to the Indian Railway Accounts Service, the Railway Staff College at Baroda organizes special and refresher courses for serving officers. The recruits to the T.T. & C.D., undergo three-and-a-half months training at the Staff College—two months at the beginning and one-and-a-half months in the middle of the two-year programme of training. The recruits to the I.R.A.S. undergo the two months' training at the beginning. The course of training is practical and has a direct bearing on the work of these officers.

The Institute of Secretariat Training and Management (Old Central Secretariat Training School), New Delhi

The recruits to the grades of section officers, assistants, and lower division clerks are imparted training at this school, established in May 1948. The courses of training include organisation and methods, office procedure, financial rules and regulations, etc. The training is, thus, closely related to the work of the office. After completion of the training they are posted to different Ministries for practical training. The School also holds refresher courses for those already employed in the above grades. In 1971, the name of the School was changed and it is now called as the Institute of Secretariat Training and Management.

Administrative Staff College, Hyderabad

The Administrative Staff College, Hyderabad, has been established in 1957, on the recommendation of the All-India Council for Technical Education. It is patterned on the

Administrative Staff College at Henley in England. The prospectus says that "the College provides a course of studies which investigates the principles and techniques of organisation and administration in civil life..." that "the College seeks to bring together experienced executives of proved administrative capacity and gives them an opportunity of examining different administrative practices in order to prepare them for still higher responsibilities in future..." and that "the College believes that by bringing together men and women from different walks of life, such as, private industry, commerce, and public service, it would facilitate the maximum interchange of ideas and experience, and thereby enrich the personality of the participants leading to greater administrative efficiency in individual enterprises and higher productivity at the national level." The idea is that after eight to fifteen years of practical experience a man might profitably think of his job from a detached position in company with men from different walks of life, and that this may be the most fruitful educational phase fitting him for higher responsibility. The members drawn from the private sector, the administration, and business in the public sector, are divided into syndicates, generally of ten each. An attempt is made to bring together diversity of experience in each syndicate. The main divisions of the course of studies are structure organisations, internal relations, external relations, i.e., with labour and administration, and maintaining vitality. There is supposed to be no formal teaching, but there are lectures by authorities on certain subjects which might be grouped as (1) economics, economic institutions, planning and development; (2) relations of business, labour and government; (3) working of the Constitution; (4) management sciences; (5) accounts in government and business; and (6) information about particular industries.

The method of training is of study by group discussion. There is a different chairman and secretary for each subject, thus giving an opportunity to everyone for filling these offices. Before the first 'organize' period for each subject, the members of the directing staff brief the chairman and secretary. There is a written brief with a compulsory and additional reading list. In the 'organize' period the study is planned and assignments, distributed amongst the members of the syndicate. The field of study is supposed to be much wider than final report, which must be compressed within the prescribed limits. Most of the subjects are common for all syndicates. Their reports are presented at the Conference when each chairman makes a brief speech.

The character, and content of their training programme of the Staff College, Hyderabad, are based on five major postulates. "These are—first, there are common problems which all administrators have to face in whatever field they work; second, the duties of administrators in both the public and private sectors are becoming increasingly complex and diverse; third, the exact role which each type of administrator has to play in relation to others engaged in his own field and in other fields and in relation to the public interest requires a continuous review and appraisal; fourth, the growing complexity of objectives and organisations in the highly diversified democratic society of today requires for its study a method which is flexible and thought-provoking rather than dogmatic; and fifth, the method of study must seek to evoke qualities and skills which are required in men or women who, as a consequence of their experience and abilities, are likely to be called upon to exercise an influential role in the future development of their concerns."[19]

National Institute of Rural Development, Hyderabad

The National Institute of Community Development under the old name of the Central Institute of Study and Research in Community Development was set up in June 1958, to meet the need felt by the fast-expanding programme for a large number of key-personnel with adequate understanding of the administrative and sociological aspects of the programme. Study Research in Community Development forms an integral part of the work of the Institute. On the Study side, one of the basic objectives is to ensure, through Orientation Courses of 25 days each, that the participants by living and working together are enabled to interchange ideas and experiences; imbibe the past history and latest developments of the movement; get a better understanding of the inter-relationship between the C.D. programme and the overall national plan; appreciate how the respective official and non-official roles complement each other in the achievement of the common national objectives; thereby balance and synthesise the approach to Community Development. Orientation Courses are not in the nature of organised training of the normal administrative pattern, but primarily aim at stimulation of thinking in the key personnel engaged in the programme and exchange of thoughts and experiences. In the words of the United Nations Mission, so far as officials are concerned, "the intention of the course is to get the trainees to take a new look at what may seem to them an ordinary job of administration," to clarify the new dimensions imparted by the C.D. programme in their assignment, and to promote their sense of social responsibility in terms of these dimensions.

The following categories are normally deputed for attending the Orientation Courses:

(i) Development Commissioners, Additional, Joint, Deputy and Assistant Development Commissioners.

(ii) Secretaries and Deputy Secretaries to Government.

(iii) Heads, Deputy Heads and Regional Officers of Technical (Development) Departments.

(iv) Commissioners of Divisions, Collectors and Additional Collectors.

(v) Senior District Planning or Development Officers and Senior Sub-Divisional Officers.

(vi) Selected Block Development Officers.

(vii) Central Government Nominees, e.g., Secretariat Officers.

(viii) M.P.s, M.L.As, and M.L.Cs.

(ix) Chairman of Zila Parishads and other non-officials interested in C.D. programme.

(x) Selected Pradhans.

(xi) Participants from other countries.

The programme of each course consists of:

(i) Presentation of 'My Field Problems' by individual members.

(ii) Syndicate study of selected problems.

(iii) Talks by guest speakers.

(iv) Presentation of papers by individual members.

(v) Consideration of the results of Research studies.

(vi) Book reviews.

The outstanding work in the Orientation Course is the Syndicate study. These studies promote deeper examination of field problems in the light of varied field experiences and policies underlying them. Their object is, therefore, twofold, viz., to provide sound orientation to the trainees as well as to throw up raw material for Central and State Governments, which could be usefully considered by them while formulating policy.

The NICD has been renamed as the National Institute of Rural Development in mid-seventies.

Indian School of Public Administration (1958-1968)

The Indian School of Public Administration was a part of the Indian Institute of Public Administration and its main objects were to provide a liberal education and promote research in public administration. The courses at the School were designed to give students a knowledge of the process of making public policy and of the agencies, tools and techniques for its effective implication. Apart from providing session courses of one or two years, leading to the Master's Diploma in Public Administration, the Indian School of Public Administration ran short-term courses on different aspects of Public Administration. A special feature of the Diploma Course was that any person whether from Public Service or Universities could get himself enrolled for a particular course in which he felt interested.

Indian Institute of Public Administration

The Indian School of Public Administration ceased to exist as a separate entity in 1968. The Indian Institute of Public

Administration has been organizing short-term courses meant for those who are already in the public services or university teaching. These are in addition to the nine-month duration Advanced Professional Programme in Public Administration leading to the award of M. Phil Degree. Generally, persons of the rank of Deputy Secretaries of Central/State Governments attend these courses. These courses have been found to be useful for middle rank officials. The importance of such special courses is that, besides providing opportunity to such officers to exchange ideas about their problems with their counterparts in other states, they bring them in contact with the most up to date thinking on the problems which face them. The lectures are generally delivered either by experienced senior officials of the Government of India or by specialists on the subject. Arrangements for visits to Central Government offices are also made for those officers so that they may see, things as they are run, and return to their respective jobs richer in knowledge and experience. Mention must here be made of nine month educational programme for middle and senior level civil servants which the Institute has been organising since 1975. This is the only training programme of its kind in the whole country.

The foregoing discussion relates to the institutionalised training imparted by various services. The services which do not have such institutionalised training programme provide training on the job. The entrant watches and even actually does the work of the various subordinates whom he will eventually supervise and control when he becomes the junior officer in the service. In addition, he is given some general lectures on specific subjects.

It is, thus, clear that India is steadily becoming training conscious. Institutionalised training programmes are expanding in number, scope and nature. Greater emphasis is being laid on refresher and orientation courses. Seminars, workshops, conferences, etc., are becoming increasingly popular. Recently, the Central Government has decided that study leave should be liberally granted, particularly to scientific, technical and administrative staff, and that in suitable cases the staff should even be encouraged or advised to take such leave. The purposes for which study leave may be granted may also include the studies which may not be closely and directly linked with a Government servant's work, but which are capable of widening his mind in a manner likely to improve his abilities as a civil servant and to equip him better to collaborate with those employed in other branches of the public service. Study leave may as well be granted for a course of training or study tour in which a Government servant may not attend a regular academic or semi-academic course, if the course of training or study tour is certified to be of definite advantage to Government from the point of view of public interest, and is related to the sphere of duties of the Government servant. Study leave may also be granted for purposes of studies connected with the framework or background of public administration. All this is calculated to make the administrator diversify his experience and broaden his vision. Every civil servant is likely to run into a groove, rust and lose the capacity to expand his vision unless he makes deliberate effort to keep alert. Even on the job one must find time to study, bring to it the best current thinking on the subject. But on the job, howsoever much he might try, he is likely to be overwhelmed by the pressure of urgent routine business. An opportunity to look at oneself while away from the daily routine and one's usual surroundings is therefore, valuable. Indeed, it is suggested here that administrators should be attached in mid-career to universities/ institute for higher study while on study leave. They will be away from work and yet not divorced from thinking about it.

Yet the training programmes that are being organised for civil servants are not without many weaknesses. Although the number and variety of training courses have been on the increase, the Government does not appear as yet to take training with sufficient seriousness. The persons sent to the training courses are not always selected very carefully; often only 'sparables' are spared by the Government, Secondly, the contents of training courses are not always relevant and meaningful to the tasks performed by public administration and the challenges encountered by it. Thirdly, training has not yet become integrated with other processes of personnel administration with the result that there is not inconsiderable amount of wasted effort in this area. Indeed, if one were to see the amount of unrealism obtaining in the Government, one has only to examine the relationship (or, the absence of it) between training and placement!

References

1. Nigro, Felix A. *Public Personnel Administration,* New York, Henry Holt & Co., 1959, p. 226.

2. Tickner, E.J. *Modern Staff Training,* London University, 1952, p. 9.

3. Torpey, William G., *Public Personnel Management,* New York, D. Van. Nostrand Company, Inc., 1953, p. 154.

4. *Report of the Committee on the Training of Civil Servants,* London, H.M.S.O. 1944, pp. 10-11.

5. *Report of the Committee on the Training of Civil servants, op. cit.,* p. 11.

6. Nigro, Felix A., *Public Administration—Readings and Documents,* pp. 253-54.

7. *Report of the Committee on the Training of Civil Servants,* op. cit., p. 15.

8. Mandell, Milton M., "Personnel Standards" in Marx (education.), *Elements of Public Administration,* p. 568.

9. Gorwala, A.D., *The Role of Administrator; Past, Present and Future,* Poona, Gokhale Institute of Politics and Economics, 1952, p. 27.

10. *Guide for Internship Training in the Federal service,* Washington, U.S. Civil Service Commission, 1952, Pamphlet No. 46, p. 1.

11. Torpey, William G. *op. cit.,* p. 166.

12. Marx, Fritz Morstein, *The Administrative State,* Chicago, University of Chicago Press, 1957, pp. 186-87.

13. Mandell, Milton, *op. cit.,* p. 573.

14. Pamp, Frederic E., "Liberal Arts as Training for Business", 1 *Harvard Business Review,* Vol. XXXIII, No. 3, May-June 1955, p. 47.

15. Baruch, Bernard, *My Own Story,* New York, Henry Holt & Co., 1957, p. 56.

16. Planning Commission, *Administration and Public Cooperation*, Delhi, Manager of Publications, 1954, p. 121.

17. Bapat, S.B. "Training of the Indian Administrative Service," *Indian Journal of Public Administration*, Vol. 1, No. 2, April-June, 1955, p. 123.

18. *Report on Indian and State Administrative Services and Problems of District Administration* (Chairman: V.T. Krishnamachari), New Delhi, Planning Commission, 1962, p. 14.

19. Adams, J.W.L., "Henley and Hyderabad" *Indian Journal of Public Administration*, Jan., March, 1958, p. 78.

Public Services

Public Services and the Constitution

The Constitution gives pride of place to the Public Services by conferring upon them a constitutional status. Articles 308 to 323 are devoted to 'Services Under Union and the States', providing for the following:

1. Setting up of the Public Service Commission at the Centre and a similar commission for each State.
2. Setting up of all-India services
3. Security of tenure by requiring that no public servant "shall be dismissed or removed by an authority subordinate to that by which he was appointed" and further that "no such person shall be dismissed or removed or reduced in rank until he has been given a reasonable opportunity of showing cause against the action proposed to be taken in regard to him."[1]

Employment Under the Central Government

The number of employees on the payroll of the Central Governments is very large, and, what is more, has been steadily increasing. In 1971 this number was 29.82 lakhs.[2] How this number has been increasing over the years becomes clear from the following table:

Year	*No. of Employees (lakhs)*
1956	18
1963	24
1965	26
1969	28
1971	29.82

Of this number (29.82 lakhs), 14 lakh personnel are employed in the Railways, 4 lakh in Posts and Telegraphs, and 6 lakh in Defence; the remaining 5.82 lakh persons work in the remaining departments of the Central Government.

The class-wise distribution of this strength is as follows:

Class I	0.34 lakh
Class II	0.46 lakh
Class III	15.45 lakh
Class IV	13.37 lakh
Unclassified	.20 lakh
	29.82 lakh

One out of every four Central Government personnel is employed in the administrative, technical, professional, executive and clerical categories and the remaining three are either production process workers or unskilled office workers such as peons, or transport and communications workers. The break-up among the different groups is as follows:

Groups	*Per cent of Total*
1. Administrative	0.05
2. Technical and Professional (engineers, doctors, scientists)	6.4
3. Clerical	17.9
4. Production Process Workers	20.5
5. Other like unskilled workers, transport and communications workers	54.7
	100.00

In 1971-72 this huge number cost the tax-prayer the staggering sum of Rs. 1,000 crores. Since 1971-72, the total salary bill of the central government employees has if anything gone up appreciably. Also, this figure does not take into account what is paid by way of graft, etc., to the governmental functionaries to get work done! Does society get from the civil service full value for the total money spent on it?

Structure of the Central Civil Service

The civil service is organised into four Classes (or groups)—Class I, Class II, Class III and Class IV, corresponding to differences in the responsibility of the work performed and the qualifications required. According to the Third Central Pay Commission,[3] the monetary basis of such a four-fold classification is as follows:

Class I — Post carrying a pay or a scale of pay with a maximum of not less than Rs. 950 per month.

Class II — Post carrying a pay or a scale of pay with a miximum of not less than Rs. 575 but less than Rs. 950 per month.

Class III — Post carrying a pay or a scale of pay with maximum of over Rs. 110 but less than Rs. 575 per month.

Class IV — Post carrying a pay or a scale of pay the maximum of which is Rs. 110 or less per month.

The bulk of the employees fall in Class IV (or group D) which includes messengers, peons, daftaries, jamadars, cyclostyling machine operators and others doing menial jobs. Class III includes clerical jobs. Class II includes both generalists and specialists, and is, basically, the class of first-line supervisors. The 'officer' class begins with Class II and includes, in addition, Class I. In 1971 out of every one hundred central government employees, 45 were in Class IV, 52 in Class III and the remaining three were in either Class I or in Class II.

"Between 1957 (when the Second Pay Commission reported) and 1971, the number of Class I, Class II and Class III posts had more than doubled. The increase in Class IV posts was of the order or about 37 per cent but the proportion of Class IV posts to the total had decreased from 56.3 per cent in 1957 to 45.1 per cent in 1971 while the proportion of class III posts had increased from

42.0 per cent in 1957 to 52.1 per cent in 1971. The Class III and Class IV posts taken together accounted for 97.2 per cent of the total staff. The Class I and Class II posts form about 1.2 and 1.6 per cent respectively of the total in 1971 as against 0.6 and 1.1 per cent respectively in 1957."[4]

Union Public Service Commission

In India a limited role has been assigned to the Union Public Service Commission in personnel administration. It it a recruiting agency, *par excellence:* "It shall be the duty of the Union and the State Public Service Commissions to conduct examinations for appointments to the service of the Union and the service of the States respectively."[5] The fact of the matter is that the Union Public Service Commission partially shoulders and, what is more, in a passive fashion, the staffing responsibility in the Central Government. It is the recruiting agency to the all-India services, and the Central civil services—Class I and Class II—the responsibility for staffing lower services and posts rests with the departments concerned. And, even in the higher services there are two notable exceptions. Under the Union Public Service Commission (Exemption from Consultation) Regulations, 1958, the Atomic Energy Department and the Council for Scientific and Industrial Research have been authorised to recruit directly personnel for Class I and Class II. Contrary to popular belief, therefore, the Union Public Service Commission has only a limited role to play in recruiting governmental personnel. Then, the Constitution endows it with purely advisory functions although there has developed a convention according to which its advice is normally accepted by the Government. There is a high degree of sanctity attached to its advice, for it is required to submit an annual report of its functioning in which it draws particular attention to the non-acceptance, if any, of its advice by the Government and which is discussed in Parliament. It is consulted by the Central Government:

"*(a)* on all matters relating to methods of recruitment to civil services and for civil posts;

(b) on the principles to be followed in making appointments to civil services and posts. and in making promotions and

transfers from one service to another and on the suitability of candidates for such appointments, promotions or transfers;

(c) on all disciplinary matters affecting a person serving under the Government of India or the Government of a State in a civil capacity, including memorials or petitions relating to such matters;

(d) on any claim by or in respect of a person who is serving or has served under the Government of India or the Government of a State or under the Crown in India or under the Government of an Indian State, in a civil capacity, that any costs incurred by him in defending legal proceedings instituted against him in respect of acts done or purporting to be done in the execution of his duty should be paid out of the Consolidated Fund of India, or, as the case may be, out of the Consolidated Fund of the State;

(e) on any claim for the award of a pension in respect of injuries sustained by a person while serving under the Government of India or the Government of a State or under the Crown in India or under the Government of an Indian State, in a civil capacity, and any question as the amount of any such award."[6]

The Constitution does not prescribe the number of members of the Commission. It only says that at least half of the members must be governmental employees with at least ten years governmental experience, that the members would hold office until the age of sixty-five years or for a term of six years whichever comers first, and finally that the chairman is debarred from accepting any employment under the Government of India or under the Government of a State while other members are eligible for appointment to only one position—chairmanship of either Union Public Service Commission or a State Public Service Commission. The last mentioned provision has been made to reinforce the independence, integrity and impartiality of the commissioners. The Commission's office is staffed by personel already in service with the Government with the inevitable result that professionalisation of staff is conspicuous by its absence. The examining techniques employed by the Commission are not up-to-date; the interview method is of a primitive type, and the entire approach to matters of recruitment appears to be pedestrian, lacking push and dynamism. Then, it takes a long time in the processing of applications and in the announcement of the result. In fact, the Union Public Service Commission should maintain ready lists of successful candidates for various types of jobs available in the Government. This would mean that it would be in a position to make candidates available at short notice. Finally, a prospective applicant is required to fill in a large number of forms and, what is more, a large amount of detail about his family and other antecedents. As if all this is not enough, he is even obliged to get these certified by an officer of not less than a gazetted rank! No one has really cared to know how many good candidates have refrained from applying for governmental jobs simply because of such applying procedures.

Historically, the Public Service Commission were originally designed to perform a negative role—namely, to keep the rascals out. It is only after the 'rascals' were kept out that a more constructive role has come to be gradually evolved for them in various countries. Talent-hunting marks the second stage in the history of public service commissions in the world. In India the Public Service Commission of both the Union and the State—has been so structured as to eternally function in the first stage. The Constitution does not envisage any wider or vital role for the Commission in personnel administration.—It is *par excellence* recruiting servant with a purely advisory role, consulted also in certain disciplinary and other matters. Personnel development, in the broad sense of the term, is not its concern.

As said, the Constitution enjoins upon the Government to consult the Public Service Commission in disciplinary matters. The emergence of the Central Vigilance Commission cannot exactly be reconciled with the constitutionally prescribed role of the Public Service Commission. The Central Vigilance Commission may, for instance, recommend disciplinary action of one type against a certain civil servant; the Public Service Commission, in such matters. An embarrassing situation would be created for the

Government if these two bodies fail to agree on the precise advice. Which advice should prevail with the Government? Sanctity and sanction behind the views of the constitutionally created body and the one which is just the creation of an executive resolution are not identical. This potential anachronism could conceivably be resolved by a formal amendment of the Constitution.

Age

Both lower and upper age limits have been prescribed for appointment to various services. For all-India services and Central services—Class I and Class II—the age limit is 21 to 28 years. The upper age was 24 until 1972 (when the government took the decision to raise it to 26 in accordance with the recommendation of the Administrative Reforms Commission) and to 28 from 1979. A lower age group—18-21 years—is allowed to compete for clerical classes. For certain specified Class II and Class III services the age group eligible to enter is 19-23 or 20-25 years. In short, one can hope to enter into governmental service only if one is in the age group 18-28 years. This practice of restricting governmental employment to such an age-group makes the Government rather a closed house permitting to lateral entry and constitutes a serious bottleneck in recruiting for varied skills which a complex administration of today necessarily needs. Deviation from this practice has been made in the case of professional and technical services, and in times of crash recruitment programmes like the Emergency Recruitment of 1947 and 1956. Also a relaxation of age-limit upto a maximum of 5 years is made for members of the scheduled castes and scheduled tribes.

Examination

It may be said that educational qualifications are not very realistically related to the level for which recruitment is made. As each job that the Government has to offer has a bewilderingly large number of people chasing it and also as the phenomenal expansion of education has made degree-holders cheap, and, what is more, caused marked deterioration in overall quality, the Government has fixed educational qualifications at a level higher than is strictly necessary in terms of job responsibilities. As a result, a university degree is the minimum educational requirement for entry into the all-India services, and the Central Civil Services—Class I and Class II (both gazetted and non-gazetted). This is also the minimum requirement for certain specified services in Class III (e.g. Subordinate Accounts Service and divisional accountants in the Indian Audit & Accounts Service). For Class III, however, the minimum qualification generally insisted upon is intermediate or higher secondary. The lower division clerks must at least be matriculates, and for the miscellany of record sorters, cyclostyle machine operators, staff car drivers, etc., a still lower educational level of middle school has been prescribed.

It follows that the Central Government itself is responsible for causing a not inconsiderable amount of academic waste in the country. At any rate, it is encouraging this kind of waste by employing educationally over-qualified personnel in middle-group services. Whether the university degree should be considered a pre-requisite qualification for the public services was examined by the Public Services (Qualifications for Recruitment) Committee, set up in 1955 by the Ministry of Education under the chairmanship of A. Ramaswami Mudaliar. The Committee was not unanimous in its recommendations. The minority report recommended: "We are definitely of the view that there is not sufficient justification for insisting that a university degree must be a pre-requisite qualification for entrance to any non-technical post under the Government."[7] The majority report classified the public services in the following three categories: (i) senior officers—executive and administrative; (ii) junior officers—executive and administrative; and (iii) clerical services, and recommended that (i) a university degree should definitely not be insisted upon for the clerical services; (ii) the university degree should not be made the minimum qualification for entrance into the middle category but graduates should be given an opportunity to compete, if they so desire, (iii) the entry into the top most grades should be restricted to graduates only.

The letter of appointment is issued by the employing agencies but two formalities must be first completed. The first is the police verification of persons to be offered governmental employment. This is done to satisfy the appointing agency about the suitability of a candidate by verifying his character and antecedents before making the appointment. It has been stated by the Government that this verification is not in regard to political opinions held by the candidate. This practice, dating from the British days, admirably suited and alien government but in the altered political situation of today its importance must be played down. The second one is the medical examination of the candidate.

Kothari Committee Report on Recruitment and Selection Methods

There has been growing dissatisfaction against the present method of recruitment to the higher civil service in India. To suggest changes in the methods of recruitment, the Union Public Service Commission appointed in 1974 the Committee on Recruitment and Selection Methods under the chairmanship of D.S. Kothari,. The Committee submitted its report to the U.P.S.C. in March 1976. The scheme of recruitment proposed by the Committee consists of three sequential stages:

1. Civil services preliminary examination (objective type) for the selection of candidates for the main examination.
2. Civil service main examination (written and interview) to select candidates for entry to the Lal Bahadur National Academy of Administration (Mussoorie) for a foundation course of about 9 months. At this stage the candidates will not be allocated to the various services and the marks obtained by them in the main examination will not be disclosed.
3. Civil services post-training test to be conducted by the U.P.S.C. on completion of the foundation course to assess personal qualities and attributes relevant to civil services. In this test, the trainees will be interviewed by an board constituted by the U.P.S.C. and marks assigned to each candidate.

The allocation to various services will depend on the total of the marks obtained by the candidates at the main examination and the post-training test.

The Kothari Committee has recommended that for recruitment to the IAS and other Class I central services there should be a preliminary screening examination and a post-training test besides the main civil services examination (plus an interview worth 300 marks). The suggestion for a preliminary, objective type test to weed out candidates who are not competent enough to write the main examination is sound, for it is only through a device like this that the main examination can be made manageable and meaningful. Today; nearly 40,000 candidates take the main test, and obviously it is senseless to administer it to so many when only about 400 are to be selected. Consequently, the Union Public Service Commission is at present more a rejecting body than a recruiting one, and it has to be rescued from such an image. The screening test should necessarily be of an objective type so that it is a quick and easy way to identify those who have the requisite range and depth of knowledge. The Committee has also proposed a 400 marks post-selection test at the end of the foundational course of institutional training which is compulsory for each selected candidate. The assignment to a particular service is to be done on the basis of the total of marks obtained at the main examination and the post-training test, taking into account the candidates' preferences for the services.

The recommendations of the Kothari Committee have some features worth noting. The Committee recommends a single scheme of recruitment common to the I.A.S., I.P.S. and non-technical, Class I central services. What it means is that no service is called upon to take additional examinations thus adding to its ego and no service is administered a lower test to make it look like a second class service. This is an egalitarian move and is to be welcomed. At the same time, the Report is discriminatory also. The Committee has compiled a list of subjects from which candidates are to choose their optional papers. While most subjects currently taught in the universities are included in the list one finds a popular subject like Public Administration kept excluded. More universities today teach Public Administration than some of the subjects mentioned in the list and equally true it is that more students today graduate in Public Administration than many other subjects figuring in it. Even otherwise, one ought not to ignore or underestimate the importance of the discipline of Public Administration in an examination designed to recruit personnel for public administration. Of what avail is it to deny the nation the services of a pool of competent candidates who might be willing to volunteer for the service?

It is also to be noted that the post-selection test is an interview by a selection board, constituted by the Union Public Service Commission. The Committee thus accords more importance to the interview (carrying 700 marks) than it has now (carrying 400, 300 and 200 marks for Indian Foreign Service). Indian Administrative Service, and other Services respectively, Since human beings evaluate other human beings, an element of subjectivity cannot be completely ruled out.

The Committee is in favour of allocating the candidates to the various services such as I.A.S., I.P.S. etc, after they have completed their training at the LBS National Academy and, secondly, appeared at the post-training test to be held by the UPSC. This recommendation stands in sharp contrast to the present practice under which the successful candidates get allocated to the various all-India and central services before the beginning of the institutional training. The Kothari Committee's view is based on the argument that the exact allotment to various services ought to be made only after watching the candidates' performance during training and in the post-training test and taking into account their aptitudes and preferences. This looks to be a sensible suggestion, but in practice is fraught with dangerous consequences inview of the integrity generally obtaining in the country. The interval between the main examination and the post-training test is too brief to make the 'servicification' really rational and sound. At the same tune, it is long enough to build up powerful lobbies, and thus politicise recruitment.

The Committee has also recommended that the candidates for the main examination should be allowed to answer all the papers, except the language one, in any language listed in the eight schedule of the Constitutions, or English. This, indeed, is a continuation of the official policy first adopted in 1968. The number of those choosing to exercise the option to write in the regional languages has either remained stationery or even declined, the percentage never exceeded 18. This is as much ascribable to the inadequate development of the regional languages as to the snobbish value of English. Also, with uneven development of the regional languages a broadly uniform level of competence is unlikely if not impossible to attain. Besides, this may set into motion rather subjective and political criteria of evaluation, which has to be strictly guarded against.

In December 1978, the Government accepted the scheme of examination as recommended by the Kothari Committee and, thus, the competitive examination to be held by the Union Public Service Commission in 1979 and subsequent years marks a significant departure from the pattern hitherto followed. In other words, the competitive examination for the higher civil service to be held in 1979 and onwards is based on the new scheme.

The salient features of the new scheme are as follows:

1. There is a single examination for recruitment to the Indian Administrative Service, Indian Foreign Service, Indian Police Service and Group 'A' (erstwhile Class I) Central Services.

2. The civil services examination consists of two parts: a qualifying Preliminary Examination (objective type) and the Main Examination (written test and interview).

   (i) The Preliminary Examination consists of two papers, one in General Studies and the second in an optional subject out of the list mentioned below.

   Agriculture; Botany; Chemistry; Commerce; Economics; Engineering (Civil, Electrical or Mechanical); Geography; Geology; Indian History; Law; Mathematics; Philosophy; Physics; Political Science; Psychology; Sociology and Zoology.

Both the papers are of objective type. The paper in General Studies carries 150 marks and the paper in optional subject 300 marks.

   (ii) The Main Examination consists of two parts: the written examination and the interview. The written

examination consists of 8 papers each carrying 300 marks (all conventional essay type) as under:

(i) .... One Indian Language mentioned in the eighth schedule of the Constitution.

(ii) .... English.

(iii) & (iv) ...... General Studies.

(v) & (vi) ...... First optional subject

(vii) & (viii) ..... Second optional subject

The list of optional subjects for the Main Examination is:

1. Agriculture
2. Botany
3. Chemistry
4. Civil Engineering
5. Commerce and Accountancy
6. Economics
7. Electrical Engineering
8. Geography
9. Geology
10. History
11. Law
12. Literature in any one of the following Languages: Assamese, Bengali, Gujarati, Hindi, Kannada, Kashmiri, Marathi, Malayalam, Oriya, Punjabi, Sanskrit, Sindhi, Tamil, Telugu, Urdu, Arabic, Persian, German, French, Russian and English.
13. Management and Public Administration
14. Mathematics

15. Mechanical Engineering
16. Philosophy
17. Physics
18. Sociology
19. Psychology
20. Political Science and International Relations.
21. Zoology.

3. The candidates are given the choice to write their papers, other than English and the Language papers, in any language mentioned in the eight schedule to the Constitution or in English. However, the question papers, for the Preliminary as well as the Main Examination, would be in English and Hindi only.

4. Those who qualify in the written part of the Main Examination alone are called for interview. The marks for interview are 250.

5. The upper age limit for civil service examination has been raised by 2 years i.e., from 26 to 28, with the usual relaxation for candidates belonging to scheduled castes and scheduled tribes.

6. The candidates are allowed 3 chances for the civil service examination. The scheduled caste and scheduled tribe candidates are, however, allowed to take the examination without any restriction on the number of chances, subject, of course, to the prescribed age limits.

7. The minimum educational qualification for appearing at the Main Examination is a University Degree. Candidates are, however, permitted to take the Preliminary Examination while studying in the final year of their degree course, subject, however, to the condition that they have to furnish proof of having passed the degree examination well before the commencement of the Main examination.

The first Preliminary Examination under the new scheme is to be held in June 1979. Only those who qualify in the Preliminary Examination would alone be allowed to appear at the Main Examination.

The Kothari Committee made a recommendation that the selection procedure may include another stage also whereby the allocation to various services is to be made after assessing the performance of the candidates at the Lal Bahadur Shastri Academy of Administration, Mussoorie, on the recommendation of the Union Public Service Commission. This recommendation has not been accepted by the Government on the ground that 'this will involve reorganisation of the Academy'. This means that as at present the allocation of the candidates to different services is made on the basis of the Main Examination and interview taking into consideration their rank in the final examination and preferences.

Management of Public Services

Management of public services in India was until 1970 shared between the Ministry of Home Affairs and the Ministry of Finance. The responsibility of the former pertained to general conditions of service other than those having a financial bearing while the latter was ultimately responsible for laying down conditions of service involving financial implications. "The function of the Ministry of Finance is to consider the financial implications of these matters and that of the Home Ministry to take into account their effects on the efficient functioning of the services in general."[8]

The Ministry of Home Affairs was the Central personnel agency in the Government of India. Its responsibility ran both vertically and horizontally. It administered and controlled the all-India services. Of the Central Services it was directly responsible for the administration and control of the Indian Economic Service. Indian Statistical Service and Central Secretariat Service. It administered the Industrial Management Pool and the Central Administrative Pool. Also it had the responsibility for administration of public services in the union territories. Its responsibility ran horizontally as well: it regulated all matters of general applicability to all services in order to maintain a common standard of recruitment, discipline, and conditions of service. Besides, it looked after the following matters:

(i) implementation of reservations for scheduled castes and scheduled tribes in various services;

(ii) re-employment of displaced or retrenched employees and also persons who join the army during the national emergency;

(iii) setting-up of whitely machinery for joint consultation and compulsory arbitration of unresolved differences between Government and its employees.

Mention has already been made of the dual control of public services in India—control, that is, by Home Ministry and Finance Ministry. The dual control was hardly conducive to their efficient management. Also, this was contrary to the personnel practices in other countries. Personnel administration is a nodal function which according to one school of thought should be located in the office of the chief executive to permit it to take a supra-departmental view and enable it to operate from a prestigious point. The management of public services should according vest in the Cabinet Secretariat, and the Cabinet Secretary should be made head of the public services. Such an arrangement had also found favour with the Estimates Committee: "The Committee recommends that a single agency should be entrusted with control over the services and made responsible for regulating the terms and conditions in respect of the services as a whole. The Committee is averse to the dual control of the Ministries of Home Affairs and Finance over matters relating to services and suggest that although Ministry of Finance may be broadly consulted so far as the functional implications of proposals are concerned, all proposals concerning the services should emanate from, and be finalised by, the agency controlling the services. The Committee feels that it would be in the fitness of things if this centralised agency for personnel management of all-India and other Central services Class I. is placed under any other separate agency independent of any administrative Ministry—preferably under the charge of the Cabinet Secretary. As head of the services, the Cabinet Secretary should be made responsible for advising the Prime Minister in the matter of appointments of senior officers of the rank of Joint Secretary and above. This arrangement is expected to generate greater cohesion in the services. This would also ensure that the Prime Minister would be fully in the picture in the matter of appointment of officers to key positions and that inter-Ministry preferences and prejudices would not be allowed to operate."[9] The Administrative Reforms Commission (1966-70) also recommended the setting up of a separate Department of Personnel which should function under the general guidance of the Cabinet Secretary and be placed directly under the Prime Minister. Accordingly, in August 1970 a separate Department of Personnel was established under the Cabinet Secretariat to function as the central personnel agency in the Government. In February 1972 its name was changed to Department of Personnel and Administrative Reforms. The functions relating to personnel hitherto performed by the Home Ministry were generally taken over by the Department of Personnel and Administrative Reforms. In short, matters relating to the service conditions of public personnel and personnel questions of horizontal concern fall within the purview of the Department of Personnel and Administrative Reforms.

Since 1977 this Department has been transferred to the Ministry of Home Affairs, a move dictated by a national determination to disperse authority which had become unduly centralised into the hands of the Prime Minister.

The Department of Personnel and Administrative Reforms (DEPAR) is the managing authority in the case of the two all-India services, namely (i) the Indian Administrative Service, and (ii) the Indian Forest Service. The Indian Police Service, which is also an all-India service, is managed by the Ministry of Home Affairs. This Department also manages the following Central civil services:

(i) Indian Economic Service (set up in 1961)

(ii) Indian Statistical Service (set up in 1961)

The Department of Personnel and Administrative Reforms advised by the Indian Economic Service and the Indian Statistical Service Boards, is the controlling authority for these two services. There is no one specific Ministry which can be said to be the

Ministry concerned with either the Indian Economic Service or the Indian Statistical Service. As many as 25 Ministries and one union territory are participating in these two services. As it is not possible for any single participating Ministry to administer any of these two services, the Department of Personnel and Administrative Reforms in consultation with the two Service Boards in the controlling authority.

In addition to these services—the two all-India services and the Indian Economic Service and the Indian Statistical Service— The Department of Personnel and Administrative Reforms is the controlling authority of the Central Secretariat Service (selection grade and Grade I); the Section Officers' Grade and the Assistant's Grade of the Central Secretariat Service are decentralised ones since 1962.

Other Central Civil service are managed by the respective Ministries of the Central Government. Thus the Indian Foreign Service is managed by the Ministry of External Affairs, the Indian Revenue Service by the Ministry of Finance, and so on. It must, however be stressed here that the general pollicies relating to personnel in all services and determined by the Department of Personnel and Administrative Reforms.

The Class II i.e., group A civil services are managed by respective Ministries of the Government. As regards the remaining Class III and Class IV services, these are departmentally managed.

Staffing Arrangement

The staffing arrangements for posts of and above the rank of Deputy Secretary in Central Government have been centralised, at the administrative level, in the Central Establishment Board, and, at the political level, in the appointments committee of the Cabinet. The Central Establishment Board; The Central Establishment Board was set up in 1957, and is located in the Department of Personnel and Administrative Reforms "to provide for systematic arrangements for manning senior administrative posts at the Centre, of and above the rank of Deputy Secretary."

Senior and Central Establishment Boards

The practice regarding the placement for posts of Under Secretary and above is centralised in the Department of Personnel and Administrative Reforms. For this purpose, the Central Government has since 1970 constituted two Boards to recommend names for posts of the level of Under Secretaries and above. The Central Establishment Board, presided over by the Secretary of the Department of Personnel and Administrative Reforms, recommends suitable names for posts of and above the rank of Under Secretary but below that of Joint Secretary and most categories of non-secretariat posts. The Senior Selection Board makes recommendations for posts of the rank of Joint Secretary and equivalent non-secretariat posts, and is presided over by the Cabinet Secretary, its other members being the Secretaries of some Ministries. Both these Boards are advisory in character, and their recommendations are required to be placed before the appointments committee of the Cabinet for its final approval. For posts above the level of Joint Secretary, the Cabinet Secretary himself initiates the proposals and the final decision is taken by the appointments committee. The Establishment Officer is the Secretary of the Senior Selection Board and Member-Secretary of the Central Establishment Board.

The Board, as said above, is an advisory one, its recommendations going to the appointments committee of the Cabinet for acceptance. The majority of the recommendations, are however, accepted, for, during 1963-65 there were only 20 cases of non-acceptance.

Establishment Officer

The Establishment Officer to the Government conducts personnel administration in the Government. He is part of the Department of Personnel and Administrative Reforms but reports directly to the Cabinet Secretary. His duties are:

(i) to be the Secretary of the appointments committee of the Cabinet and of the Senior Establishment Board, and Member-Secretary of the Central Establishment Board;

(ii) to receive all communications intended for the appointments committee or the Board and to obtain and communicate their orders to the Ministries concerned;

(iii) to keep himself fully informed of possible or impending vacancies in posts falling within the purview of the appointments committee or the Board and the availability of officers of the requisite seniority and experience for filling such appointments;

(iv) to keep himself in close touch with State Governments, the Comptroller and Auditor-General and the Ministries of Home and Finance for the systematic planning and maintenance of supply of suitable officers for manning the 'deputation' posts at the Centre;

(v) to ensure up-to-date maintenance and proper custody of confidential records of the all officers belonging to or likely to be recruited to Grade I of the Central Secretariat Service, the Central Administrative Pool and other IAS officers of various States;

(vi) to conduct all correspondence with State Governments, the Comptroller and Auditor-General or the Ministries concerned in regard to the selection or reversions of officers connected with appointments within the purview of the board or the appointments committee.

Area of Eligibility for Senior Posts

Only the following categories of personnel are eligible to hold the senior posts.

(a) Officers borrowed from the state cadres of the IAS and from other Class I Services of the States (other than the State Civil Service) on tenure deputation;

(b) Officers borrowed on the tenure deputation from central services Class I including officers serving in public industrial understandings;

(c) Officers of the selection grade of the Central Secretariat Service;

(d) Officers of the Central Administrative Pool;

(e) State Civil Service officers whose names are included in the select list. referred to in regulation 7(3) of the IAS (Appointments by Promotion) Regulations; and

(f) State Civil Service officers other than those mentioned in (e) may also be appointed to senior posts in consultation with the Union Public Service Commission in each case.

Staff Services Commission

The Union Public Service Commission is the recruiting agency for the higher civil service (i.e., Class I and Class II) in the Central Government. Till 1975 there was no centralised agency in the Government to make recruitment to Class III. In absence of a body to undertake recruitment to this class becomes a serious weakness in the personnel system of the country. On 4 November 1975, therefore, the Central Government set up, under an executive resolution, a Subordinate Services Commission (SSC), later renamed as Staff Services Commission.

The SSC has been made responsible for recruiting personnel to non-technical class III posts in the Secretariat, the Attached Offices and the Subordinate Offices in the Central Government. The Railways, the offices of the Comptroller and Auditor-General and the Accountants General as well as the industrial establishments have been kept out of this centralised recruitment scheme. It should be remembered that there is a Railway Services Commission to recruit personnel for lower levels in the Railways. The Staff Services Commission holds competitive examination to fill posts in class III. In particular, it:

(a) conducts competitive examination for recruitment of lower division clerks in the Central Government (except, as already mentioned, in the Railways, the offices of the Comptroller and Auditor-General and of the Accountants General);

(b) holds competitive examination for recruitment to Grade III of the Central Secretariat Stenographers Service;

(c) holds departmental examination for promotion from class IV to Class III of the Central Secretariat Clerks Grade;

(d) conducts typewriting tests in English and Hindi.

The Commission consists of a Chairman, a member and a Secretary-cum-Comptroller of Examinations, all appointed by the Government. The Resolution setting up the Commission is silent about the tenure of its members, thus making their term of office dependent on the sweet will of the executive. The present Chairman is a serving civil servant holding the rank of an Additional Secretary in the Government. The Commission has been given the status of an attached office of the Department of Personnel and Administrative Reforms.

References

1. Article 311 of the Constitution: According to many, this article provides for too much of security to the public servant, which is detrimental to efficiency and discipline. The fifteenth amendment of the Constitution (October, 1963) softens some of the rigidities by expediting the conduct of disciplinary proceedings against public servants. The effect of the amendment is that, instead of having to full-fledged opportunities of defence—one at the time the charges are made and the other at the time when the penalty is proposed to be imposed, the accused government servant can only make a representation against the penalty proposed to be imposed upon him on the basis of the evidence already adduced during the inquiry into the charges against him, without bringing in any fresh evidence or other extraneous matters.

2. *Report of the Third Pay Commission,* Vol. I, New Delhi, Ministry of Finance, 1973, p. 10.

3. *Report of the Third Central Pay Commission* Vol. I, New Delhi, Ministry of Finance, 1973, p. 10.

4. *Ibid.*, p. 12.

5. Art. 320(I) of the Constitution.

6. Article 320 (3) of the Constitution.

7. *Report of the Public Services (Qualifications for Recruitment) Committee,* New Delhi, Ministry of Education, 1936, p. 21. Humayun Kabir, Sushila Nayar and N.K. Sidhana had jointly written this minute of dissent.

8. *Ninety-third Report of the Estimates Committee,* Third Lok Sabha, Lok Sabha Secretariat, 1966, p. 18.

9. *Ibid.*, p. 19.

Government of India's Measures for Administrative Reforms

Administrative efficiency and effectiveness are matters which receive the attention of the Government on a continuous basis. An Action Plan, relating to making administration accountable and citizen-friendly, ensuring transparency and Right to Information and measures to cleanse and motivate Civil Services, was discussed in the conference of Chief Ministers of States and Union Territories held on 24 May, 1997. The Conference resolved that the Central and State Governments would work together to concretize the Action plan dealing with the following themes:

(i) Accountable and citizen-friendly Government;

(ii) Transparency and Right to Information; and

(iii) Improving the performance and integrity of the public services.

1. Measures have been accordingly taken to make the administration accountable, transparent and responsive to the needs and expectations of the people. Several Ministries/ Departments/Organisations with considerable public interface have already introduced Citizens' Charters indicating broadly the quality of service the public would be entitled to, within, a specified time frame. Information and Facilitation Counters have been set up by 45 Ministries/Departments/Central Government Organisations to provide information on procedures and the schemes of the concerned organisation as well as to access information pertaining to the status of individual cases.

2. Steps have also been taken to strengthen the existing machinery for redress of public grievances. Most of the Ministries/Departments have fixed time limits for handling grievances received form the Members of Parliament, and the names of the officers handling grievances have been publicised. A system of categorizing all the grievances and their computerised monitoring has been installed in various Ministries/Departments and this is linked to the main terminal in the Department of Administrative Reforms and Public Grievances.

3. The Government has also taken steps for simplification of laws, rules and procedures. Towards this end over 40 Departments have undertaken, through expert Task Forces or by internal exercises, a detailed review of all the laws, regulations and procedures administered by them.

4. A Commission on Review of Administrative Laws was set up on 8 May, 1998 under the Chairmanship of Shri P.C. Jain with a view to identify proposal for amendment/repeal of existing laws, regulations and procedures having inter-sectoral impact so as to make them objective, transparent and predictable. The Commission submitted its report on 30 September, 1998.

5. The important recommendations of the aforementioned commission include repeal of almost 50% of Central Laws (1382 out of 2500 Laws), expeditious amendments to a list of 109 identified Acts, documentation of administrative laws (rules, regulations, executive instructions) by all the Ministries/Departments, harmonisation of statutes and laws with reference to the perspective of domestic and foreign investors, trade and industry, consumers, exporters and importers, and development of a viable alternative disputes resolution machinery.

6. The Government has constituted a Standing Committee under the Chairmanship of Secretary (Personnel) for monitoring the follow-up action on implementation of the recommendations contained in the report. The Committee has held fifteen

meetings with different Ministries/Departments in groups. Most of the Ministries/Departments have initiated action to make suitable amendments/modifications to or repeal the Acts and Laws being administered by them with a view to improve service delivery and bring about transparency in the functioning of Government.

7. In addition to the specific measures mentioned above, the Government has also taken certain other steps to improve its efficiency and effectiveness. These steps include modernisation of Government offices, a software package to track the movement of files, a scheme to grant awards to members of the public and the employees for suggestions made to improve the overall efficiency, productivity and work culture of the staff, documentation of best practices in Central and State Government organisations etc.

ADMINISTRATIVE REFORMS

Administrative efficiency and effectiveness have been receiving attention of the Government on a continuous basis, measures have been taken to make the administration accountable, transparent and responsive to the needs and expectations of the people. These include the following.

Formulation and Implementation of Citizens' Charters

1. The Citizens' Charter reflects a commitment of the concerned Ministry/Department etc. to provide specific services within a specified time frame as far as possible. The charter assures clearly states standards of services and notifies proper channels for redress of grievances.

2. A Core Group has been set up under the Chairmanship of Secretary (Personnel) for monitoring the progress of initiatives taken by Ministries/Departments with a substantial public interface. So far, 61 Charters have been formulated which include 27 Charters for public sector banks and 4 Charters for hospitals. NCT of Delhi, Goa, Haryana, Rajasthan, Tamil Nadu and Himachal Pradesh are among the States who have formulated Citizens' Charters for selected services.

Information and Facilitation Counters (IFCs)

1. The Information and Facilitation Counters provide a visible face to the Citizens' Charters. They are needed to provide information on procedures and schemes of the concerned organisation as well as to access information pertaining to the status of the individual cases. So far 45 IFCs have been set up by Ministries/Departments. The IFCs are set up outside the security zone of each office with a view to facilitate the dissemination of information to the citizen/user. The information is disseminated through print-outs, brochures, booklets, display boards and sometimes telephonically too.

Redress of Public Grievances

1. The existing machinery for public grievances redress has been considerably strengthened by the Department of Administrative Reforms and Public Grievances and the Cabinet Secretariat. This is, over and above, the efforts of the Prime Minister's Office to monitor the redress of grievances received by it. Most of the Departments have fixed time limits for handling grievances received from Members of parliament and have publicised the names of the officers handling grievances. A system of categorizing the grievances and their computerised monitoring has been installed in various Ministries/ Departments and this is linked to the main terminal in the Department of Administrative Reforms and Public Grievances.

2. This Department in its capacity as the nodal agency for matters relating to public grievances monitors periodically the performance of Ministries/Departments through meetings of Directors of Grievances. This Department also carries out periodic evaluation of grievance redress set up in selected Ministries/Departments having large interface with the public. In this process, the Department also identifies the systemic deficiencies and takes up studies of grievance prone areas with a view to suggesting reforms.

3. A Standing Committee of Secretaries for Public Grievance Redress has been constituted with the Cabinet Secretary as Chairman and Secretary of Ministry of Personnel, Public

Grievances and Pensions; Secretary (Coordination), Cabinet Secretariat; Secretary, Department of Consumer Affairs, Chairman, Railway Board, Secretary, Department of Posts; Director General, NIC and Principal Information Officer as Members. This committee considers proposals for systemic reforms and grievance redress brought out by Department of AR and PG pertaining to Central Government Departments with public interface. It also review the working of the public grievance redress machinery in Ministries/Departments and organisations under their administrative control.

Simplification of Rules

The Government has also taken up simplification of laws, rules and procedures under its policy of preventive vigilance as well as for improving efficiency in the organisation. Towards this end, over 40 Departments have undertaken a detailed review of laws, regulations and procedures administered by them.

Commission on Review of Administrative Laws

1. The Government have initiated action to bring about suitable amendments/modifications in the Acts and laws being administered by them with a view to improve service delivery and transparency in the functioning of the Government. A landmark step in this direction was the constitution of a Commission on Review of Administrative Laws on 8 May, 1988 with a view to identify, in consolation with Ministries/ Departments and client groups, proposals for amendments to existing laws, regulations and procedures so as to make them objective, transparent and predictable as also to identify such laws for repeal, which had outlived their utility.

2. The commission submitted its report on 30 September, 1988. The important recommendations made by the commission include recommendation for:

   (i) repeal of almost 50% of the Central Laws (1,382 out of about 2,500 laws).

   (ii) expeditious amendments to a lits of 109 identified.

(iii) documentation of administrative laws (rules, regulations, executive instructions etc.) by all the Ministries/Departments.

(iv) harmonisation of statutes and laws with reference to the perspective of domestic and foreign investors, trades and industry, consumers, exporters and importers.

(v) development of a viable alternative disputes resolution machinery.

3. copies of the Report of the Commission were sent to all Ministries/Departments of the Government of India and Chief Secretaries of the State Governments/UTs for examination of the various recommendations contained therein and for devising suitable plan for implementation of the recommendations. The Government have set up a Standing Committee under the Chairmanship of Secretary (Personnel) for monitoring the follow-up action on the implementation of the recommendations. Most of the Ministries/Departments have initiated action to amend or repeal the Acts/laws being administered by them.

4. About 46 Ministries/Departments had identified 241 Acts including 109 Acts identified by the Commission for carrying out requisite amendments in a expeditious manner as they were considered to be particularly relevant to the terms of reference of the Commission.

5. Of 241 Acts, action for amendment or otherwise has been initiated in respect of 241 Acts (88%), which are at various stages. Action has also been initiated in respect of 97 Acts (88%) out of 109 Acts.

6. The Commission had recommended repeal of 1,382 Central Acts. A Repealing and Amending Bill has been finalised by the Legislative Department for repeal of 315 Amendment Acts. The issue pertaining to repeal of 700 Appropriation Acts was referred to the Attorney General for advice which has since been received and is being examined by Ministry of Finance.

114 Central Acts relating to State List have been referred, by the Legislative Department, to the concerned State Governments to take necessary action on the recommendation of the Commission to repeal them. Action has been initiated in respect of 216 Acts out of a total of remaining 253 Acts [1,382-(315 + 700 +114 = 1,129) -1,129 = 253] (85%) and is at various stages. These 216 Acts include 6 Acts which have already been repealed and 109 Acts which are not to be repealed, as per the decision by the respective Ministries/ Departments.

7. *Documentation:* All the un-repealed Central Acts of all India application have been placed on the NICNET and INTERNET. An Action Plan has been prepared and communicated to concerned Ministries/Departments for making all the subordinate legislations available on the NICNET within two years.

8. *Simplification/Consolidation of Laws:* Simplification and consolidation of rules and procedures is an on-going process. Several initiatives in this direction were taken before the setting up of the Commission. The Legislative Department has recently taken steps to bring out sector-wise compendia/CD of legislations beginning with a compendium/CD on Election Laws. These initiatives have been taken with a view to make the laws/rules citizen-friendly. The amendments to and repeals of laws taken up in the course of implementation of the recommendations of the Commission would be followed by some more measures to simplify and consolidate the rules and procedures. The recommendations of the Commission would also be kept in view while drafting the Bills in future.

9. With regard to the recommendation of the Commission for improvement in the system of administration of justice, a new Act, namely, the Arbitration and Conciliation Act, 1996, has been enacted while repealing the Indian Arbitration Act, 1940. This new Act has, for the first time, introduced the concept of conciliation in India in consonance with the UNCITRAL (United Nations Commission on International Trade Laws) model. Further, in order to provide necessary

infrastructural support, the Department of Legal affairs has taken the initiative to set up the International Centre for Alternative Dispute Resolution (ICADR), as a private registered society, Under the Legal Services Authorities Act, 1987, Lok Adalats have been constituted at various levels under the guidance of the Legal Services Authorities set up at the national, state and district levels.

Freedom of Information Bill

1. An Inter-ministerial Working Group was set up under the Chairmanship of Shri H.D Shourie, Director, Common Cause to examine the feasibility and need of introducing a full-fledged Right to Information Act so as to meet the needs of an open and responsive Government. The report of the Group has been processed and a Bill for freedom of information has been drafted. It is under examination for introduction in Parliament.

Anti-corruption Measures

The Government is fully alive to the need to remove corruption at all levels of administration. The endeavour of the Government to check malpractices in administration and Government Departments is a continuing process. Policies, in this regard, have been formulated and are being continuously monitored and modified in order to make them more effective and responsive to the needs of a changing environment. The efforts of the Central Government in combating corruption in public administration have been considerably stepped up during the last few years. The Annual Action Plan prepared by the Ministry of Personnel, Public Grievances and Pensions envisages a three-pronged strategy comprising preventive vigilance, surveillance and detection and deterrent punitive action. It was initially launched in 1985-86 and is being continued on an annual basis.

Lok Pal Bill

In order to maintain purity and integrity in high public offices, the Lok Pal Bill, 1998 was introduced in the Lok Sabha on 3.8.1998 by the Prime Minister. The Bill, *inter alia,* covered the Office of Prime Minister. Before the Government could take a final view on the various recommendations made by the Parliamentary Standing Committee on the Bill, the Lok Sabha was dissolved in April, 1999 and consequently, the Bill also lapsed. The Government have initiated action to reintroduce the Bill in Parliament.

Strengthening of Central Vigilance Commission

In pursuance of the directions of Supreme Court in Vineet Narain and Others Vs. Union of India and Others (popularly known as Jain Hawala Case) to confer statutory status upon the Central Vigilance Commission, the Ministry of Personnel, Public Grievances and Pensions promulgated the Central Vigilance Ordinance on 25.8.1998 (as amended on 27.10.1998) and thereafter the Central Vigilance Ordinance, 1999 on 8.1.1999. The Central Vigilance Bill, 1999 replacing the above mentioned two Ordinances was passed in the Lok Sabha on 15.3.1999. However, the Bill lapsed consequent to the dissolution of the Lok Sabha in April, 1999. The Government have initiated action to reintroudce the Central Vigilance Bill in the Lok Sabha.

The Total Quality Management in the Government

1. The ceoncept of quality has been widely applied in private sector to improve the performance of organisations and to endow them with a competitive edge. The watchword is continuous improvement. The relevance of TQM in Government originations has been highlighted by increasing focus on citizen friendly, transparent and accountable Government.

2. The Ministry of Personnel, Public Grievances and Pensions is implementing a project on introducing TQM in Government initially in training institutions. The current project is funded by the Department of International Development, UK through the British Council Division. This is being coordinated by the Lal Bahadur Shastri National Academy of Administration, (LBSNAA) Mussoorie.

3. The Department of Administrative Reforms and Public Grievances has recently made an arrangement in collaboration

with the Quality Division of the Confederation of Indian Industries (CII) to introduce TQM practices in the Department. A TQM seminar was organised on 6 August, 1999 to generate awareness about the concept of TM among senior civil servants. The Department of Administrative Reforms and Public Grievances, in collaboration with the LBSNAA and the Quality Division of CII also organised a one-day concurrent session on 'Quality in Government' during the Seventh Quality Summit conducted by the CII from 17-19 November, 1999.

Apart from the above, the Government has taken several other steps to improve the efficiency and effectiveness of the functioning of the Central Government

(i) Modernisation of Government Offices

A plan scheme has been introduced with effect from 1987-88 to help the Ministries/Departments to improve their work environment through adoption of functional lay out creation of open offices to facilitate better supervision, better services to the people, more efficient management of data through reduction in paper work by using modern aids as well as cost and space effective records management. The budgetary allocation under this scheme for the current year is 1.83 crores.

(ii) Award Scheme

An Award Scheme for Central Government employees as well as members of the public to come up with innovative and workable suggestions for iproving the quality of public service and making it more customer friendly has been formulated. The scheme is being implemented in the Department of Administrative Reforms and Public Grievances from 1998-99. Under the Scheme, the suggestions received from employees as well as members of the public are required to be scrutinised by the respective Departmental Evaluation Committees of Ministries/Departments, and the recommendations of the Departmental Evaluation Committees are considered by an apex committee constituted under the Chairmanship of Secretary (Personnel). The suggestions which are finally found to have potential to lead to financial saving through reduction of manpower material or which enhance efficiency/ productivity through procedural improvements and reduced paper work/time taken etc. in Government officer are awarded. The Scheme also provides for awards to the Central Government operation staff for their meritorious services.

(iii) Office Procedure Automation

A software package on 'Office Procedure Automation' was developed by the NIC to help computerised recording and tracking of papers and files in each Department and to monitor easily the pendency of cases. All Ministries/Departments have been advised to adopt the package and its implementation is being monitored by the Department of Administrative Reforms and Public Grievances.

(iv) Progressive Computerisation of Government Operations

All the Ministries/Departments have been requested to convert into electronic form all the non-classified rules, regulations, procedures, circulars and information relating to work of different Ministries/Departments. They have also advised to make a 5 years plan for increasing Information Technology usage. The Planning Commission has advised the Ministries/Department to allocate 2-3% of their plan budgets for promotion of Information Technology. A High Powered Committee has been set up under the Chairmanship of Cabinet Secretary for improving administrative efficiency of the Government by using IT.

(v) Organising Seminars and Symposia etc.

As a sequel to a conscious decision to hold seminars etc. in different parts of the country in pursuance of the Action Plan adopted by the Chief Ministers' Conference held in May, 1997 and also in conformity with the National Agenda for Governance to make the administration accountable, transparent and responsive to the needs and expectations of the people, 10 seminars etc./have so far been organised by the Department of Administrative Reform and Public Grievances in different parts of the country in collaboration with the respective State Governments. Its basic objective is to create an awareness about the various initiatives taken by the Central Government as also to benefit from the best practices available with them.

—Vivek K. Agnihotri

Suggestions for Administrative Reforms

Details regarding changing the laws, procedures, office orders etc. are very important. But this is one area in which 'reform' with its usual connotation of 'slow changes' would be disastrous. There has to be a 'Total Change'—immediately, ail within a span of one or two months to be effective.

The laws identified to be obsolete and irrelevant by Mr. H.D. Shourie Committee to be 'nullified' by a single ordinance or Bill. No point in trying to research on them or deliberate on them. Even assuming that there are a few mistakes, the gain is fae more than procrastinating on useless order derived two and half centuries ago from a Colonial Master.

Another crucial issue is to nullify plethora of orders or communications or O.M.' s or Dear Secretary letters sent by the Cabinet Secretariat, the Finance Ministry etc. on from 1960 onwards on various methods of functioning. Let new orders be issued, be it on recruitment, or economy etc. with a clear statement "In suppression of all earlier orders and instructions in this regard". (This can be done within two months). Nothing will be lost if a good order it nullified in this process. One can later insert it after deliberations. Correspondingly instruction can also be issued that ready reckoners like Swami's compilations are all invalid with new orders. Let new Swami versions come out. Today' 'Yath Pinde that brahmande' is ruling the Government in its vulgar form: it is a micro-micro rule that determines how a Joint Secretary, Secretary or Minister works. Let the new rules remove the diarchy were the Finance Ministry, Personnel are ever present, no responsibility-sharing Monarchies. Let the Finance Ministry concentrate on macro economic and issues fixing budgets firmly. Let Personnel concentrate on reducing Government in a systemic form i.e. spin off institutions to autonomy, private sector etc. or close down with VRS.

There are a number of items good in Fifth Pay Commission Report. They should be accepted. Still it has not questioned the very basis of the organised services. That has to be questioned and changed. At least 50% of the top echelons of the Government have to be changed with 'new mutants', if the changes has to be effective. Therefore running the Government with the top of the existing structures of only with IAS, IAAS, IFS etc. have to be changed except for the Armed Services and the Police. Also the unwritten rule that the Cabinet Secretary should be only from the IAS has to be changed; I am not suggesting that it is free for all or have a raw Professor or an economist or scientist there. There are several other options. Today this "IAS fixation" has introduced systemic problems. Life, and even organisations in life, are open-ended systems. If we close its 'algorithms' to a few, it will collapse.

BASIC PRINCIPLES

System Time Constants

While the details are important it is not enough to be after them. We will be lost, if we are after a few small changes. That is where the earlier attempts failed. It is not merely the case of "will". One should understand the overall system context. First and Foremost in this case is the system time constants. I have done several case studies which will clearly illustrate that in the Indian-time-rate-of-interaction the unit time is about one-year. It takes about 7 to 10 years for any idea (on which everybody agrees) to fructify into action. (This is another Raj Krishna type number, we should be worried about!).

Whether it is Cogenitrix or Tata SIA or take anything else like our beginning to understand WTO implications (First round started 1986 and it came to force in 1995 and we debate not merely Government but the elite, media etc. in 1999 when bulk of its first phase "has come into effect" in January 1, 2000 and most will be by January 1, 2005).

There is deliberate and urgent need to change the time constant. What is a good number? Let us see what Prof. Andrew Lippman of MIT has told in an interview to the Times of India of January 3, 2000 "The rate of change of society is the function of age at which you gain access to the dominant technology of the time. The dominant technology of today is computing. The rate of change of computing is four years. A society driven by car changes more slowly than one based on computers".

We cannot say that we don't have so many computers and be laid back. The external world has it! The Foreign company or government or even a hijacker! So we cannot ignore the time constants set by dominant technology.

Let us also not that our administrative system was designed at the time when the dominant technology was shipping and later was adjusted to Railways and telegraph. We did not adjust it for aircraft, satellite communication or fax!

The question now is: how to change the time constant?

It cannot be gradual. There has to be a non-linear step change. The suggestion to have an Apex Cabinet Level Committee on Administrative Reforms is a good suggestion, provided they decide to work differently: not to look at individual rule. Existing organism will try to make them do so, as the Committee of Secretaries (COS) meetings have tended to be. The GOAL of that Apex Committee should be to reduce the time-constant to say a time-rate-of interaction of about 2 to 3 months from one year and overall total project completion time about 3 to 4 years from the present 7 to 10 years.

This means not merely clearance of files in a week or less but decision making in 3 to 4 months irrespective of the size of the project of issue. For every unresolved issue (or involving multi departments) one Ministry need to decide as NODAL by the APEX Committee. It should be their responsibility to decide within 3 to 4 months (Note the simplified new rules would exist and they need not be engulfed in the self-made marsh of referrals to thousands of O.M.'s etc.). If they have any problem they can refer to the Apex Committee which shall decide. [Note: There has to be an understanding that those who refer too often to the Apex Committee shall have a negative marks, as they will be empowered to decide; it is not the diarchy of Ministry Finance etc. sitting on judgement on everybody!]. Decision does not mean always accepting a proposal or saying always yes.

If this method is followed, the productivity and efficiency will become the inherent nature of the system. Functioning of the Groups C& D are but creatures of the existing system. They are not to blame for the inertia!

Metsystem

The laws of nature cannot be violated, even if we wish to. The life systems and social systems are complex adaptive systems. We may, at a given point of time, not know all the details of the rules or even all the laws. The role of the sciences—natural and social—and to discover these laws and apply them. More complex is, the cause and effect interact considerably. Notwithstanding these complexities it is well known cybernetic principle that the problems or inadequacies of the subsystem have to be solved in a system and it cannot be solved at subsystem itself. So when the whole system is dysfunctional; the solutions come about by going for a meta system. The crucial point is that the existing system has introduced crucial institutional infirmities, which in turn have induced individual infirmities in those who populate those institutions; they in turn stymie the institutions; the vicious circle has continued for decades. The task is to cut the vicious circle. One cannot expect those who are in the system to do it because most of them are well adjusted in if and are happy about. This is not to deny some mutants within the existing systems. (That is the reason why some top Government functionaries attended ICSSR meeting and spoke freely and frankly and on specifics and there may be dormant ones who may be activated when opportunities arise!) In our administrative system we have been tottering at the end of its evolution. A few mutants inside have died or are lying low. But no change is taking place. If we allow it as it is, it will crash and be extinct as an evolutionary end. Result can be total anarchy or chaos, (Already appears in many parts of India!). The better method is to help it redesign itself with new mutants pushed into the systems in large numbers. The change has to be total. When people call for global tender for better governance (it is partly done jocularly or in anguish; but it also contains a desire for external mutants). I would suggest as suggested by Mr. K.P.S. Gill that we should empower about 1500-2000 people (selected differently, not by the usual processes of the existing system) with sufficient back up from the Apex Committee and State Apexes. Also introduce more changes in the economic sectors, foreign affairs etc. (all aspect of governance). Have a long tenure 6 to 7 years (long enough to make change even with the existing time constants but their goal should be to do changes in 4 years and sustain it for sometime more so that things stabilize).

But administrative change has to be Total (not reform); all round; judiciary included; CAG etc. included. This addition of sizeable mutants from outside coupled with mutants inside with the meta system, required for change. In addition, expand their horizon of thinking so that their existing system becomes small and get interconnected with something else, thus creating new spaces of meta systems. (Let them all be innovative).

Administrative reforms are not merely to be isolated to Government Ministries and their agencies. Government had taken over in the past the functions of education, running universities, colleges, scientific laboratories, industries etc. They need to be covered by administrative reforms. If we just say the are left to themselves and freed from Government, it is not enough. They all have terrible "bureaucracies" of their own: for example, academic bureaucracies are 'terrible'; the hierarchies and bureaucracies in the institutions run by scientists are also suffocating. These are understandable as the 'system is one and subsystems develop their own toxic products based on the overall algorithms of the system!

Resistance to Change—Provision for Protection of change Agents

Till the change stabilizes say for a decade or so, the change agents would require a fair degree of protection from misinformation and disinformation. Public information and the media are subject to various forms of manipulation. There will be a demand for openness, which is good. There has to be openness to avoid elitism or an 'emergency' like operations.

But we should bear in mind what the Nobel laureate Prof. Murray Gell-Mannn says, in his seminal work Quarks and the Jaguar, 'Unfortunately, that information explosion is in great part a misinformation explosion. All of us are exposed to huge amounts of material, consisting of data, ideas, and conclusions—much of it wrong or misunderstood or just plain confused. There is a crying need for more intelligent commentary and review".

It is easy to damn a good change agent by quoting 'convenient' portions of the advice. A super specialist may think he or she has been slighted and go on attack. Some others may attach 'equal' weightage to all the opinions (informed or otherwise) and arrive at a different solution and damn a person in the system who-decided on the issue earlier. Also there could be mischievous attempts of misinformation and attributing malafide intentions. The actual decision making process is more complex. No 'objective model exists for decision-making given the multiple inputs. Also one should not be trapped in paralysis by analysis syndrome. Therefore in the final analysis, the decision making has a certain crucial component of subjectivity. In fact part of the reason why a bureaucrat shuttles files is to insulate himself or herself from accusations or audit remarks. etc. She or he spreads the risks of decision making. Especially when one is trying to do a major change, the 'affected' parties or 'vested' interests are many and they would like to strike.

Therefore, there has to be an insulation or a saving provision not to penalise a person for a decision taken or for the advice given. There has to be no 'witch hunt'. This is very important when the files are opened to public. However, there has to be simple checks for Integrity: i.e. no "pecuniary benefit" for the person for taking a decision or advising; and no personal hatreds are involved. This mechanism for such integrity checks has to be simple and innovative. Not necessarily uniform all over. As the new system evolves it will become self-correcting over a period.

Ability for Making Continuing Changes: Providing for the Future

So far all of us have been addressing the problems of the past because we have a huge stock of unsolved and ever-growing problems. It is important to address them and effect a Total Change. Then the "hare" should not sleep. Technologies, and businesses and therefore societies and people would change fast during this phase of human history. Therefore, there has to be a constant look into the future and projection of changes. People have to be kept informed of the changes. Then their informed feedback will be there to take into account the changes required to be done. We need not cry against after 10 years or later that our system is obsolete and is not meeting the aspirations of people, society, business, etc. and international needs. In such a future looking studies and for interacting with people, organisations like ICSSR have an important role to play.

On the whole, I hope an integrated set of actions will be taken urgently taking into account the above factors, noting that the reforms are too serious a matter to be left to any one section alone. Metaphorically speaking, gone are the days when there was one major central computer processor catering to several workstations attached to it (subordinate to it). We are now in an era where there are multiple parallel processing nodes (which can process autonomously and also in synchronism) tackling much bigger tasks than were ever done before. Similarly there is no longer a major database being accessed by everybody; millions of small data bases or information bases accessible through Intranet/ Internet etc. is the power tool available for millions. The administrative systems we need, should be in a manner to respect, to utilize the talents, of, and to meet the aspirations and needs of—individuals, local groups, larger groupings and the nation while also keeping a world view.

—Y.S. Rajan

12

The Second Generation Reforms: A New Approach

Now that the dust of elections has settled down, and government is in office, there is a lot of debate in the media about the second-generation reforms. Issues focused in the second-generation reforms are:

- Opening up of the insurance sector
- Reforms in the banking sector
- Reforms in infrastructure
- Regulatory agencies in different sectors like telecommunication, power and so on.

Is the current agenda for second-generation reform adequate? I am afraid, that the second-generation reforms which are now being discussed, suffer from the following defects, which also form the basis of the criticism of the first generation reforms.

- The prime focus is on attracting foreign investment. The Indian entrepreneur may feel that he is given a second class treatment.
- The basic approach seems to be guided by the Washington Consensus to open up the economy for global trade.
- The opponents of reforms always point out that the reform agenda is of interest only to the elite. The common man and the poor are completely left out of the process.

In this context, is it possible seriously to think of a second generation of reforms, which will achieve all the goals of the current promoters of reform and at the same time satisfy the pro poor critics of current reforms? A new approach based on following three points may succeed.

- Zero tolerance of corruption
- Increasing tenfold the velocity of government operations.
- A focus on productivity to make the investments already made in different sectors yield the promised benefits.

The first item in the second-generation reform should be a frontal attack on corruption. The Prime Minister has already given a lead to the country by calling for zero tolerance of corruption. The Mahbub Ul Huq Centre at Islamabad in its Human Development in South Asia Report 1999 has pointed out that if corruption levels in India were reduced to those in the Scandinavian countries, investment rates could increase annually by some 12% and GDP growth rate by almost 1.5% each year. After all, the promoters of second-generation reforms are talking about attracting foreign direct investment and promoting growth. Why not focus on corruption and practice zero tolerance so that the common man also who is an everyday victim of the menace of corruption in our country can breathe more easily? In this way the second-generation reform can become more popular.

A three-point strategy can be a broad framework for such an onslaught against corruption. The first is to simplify the rules and regulations so that the scope for corruption is eliminated. The second is to empower the public so that they know their rights and can have access to information. In this context, the need for a Freedom of Information Act becomes very vital. The third is effective and prompt punishment of the corrupt.

Here I would draw attention to a weakness in the power structure of Lok Sabha and Rajya Sabha as of today in carrying out the second-generation reforms wherever any new law has to be enacted. While the ruling coalition has the majority to pass a bill in the Lok Sabha, in the Rajya Sabha it does not have the necessary majority to carry out its will. This will mean that every legislative measure will have to be the result of a political compromise. The danger of the baby being thrown out with the bath water in such compromises cannot be ruled out.

Is there a way out? I think there is. All that is needed is for the government to decide that the main thrust of the second generation will not depend on passing laws but effective implementation by executive action. For example even without a Freedom of Information Act, every department can declare what information it will make available openly to the public. Once the departments take this initiative, people will become automatically empowered and there will be greater transparency.

That brings us to the second point of the second generation of reforms namely a total attack on red tape and delay in our system. We must aim at a tenfold increase in the velocity of government transactions. If every department of government of India and all state governments were to take a simple decision that whatever is the transaction time taken today to handle cases will be brought down to 10% of the time taken, there will be a dramatic increase in the velocity of business transactions. A focus on using IT extensively in governmental systems will automatically increase the velocity of business in government tremendously. Automatically this will also eliminate the scope for corruption. In today's global context, investment is attracted where there is greater velocity in decision making. Time is money in today's business. The objective of the current champions for second generation reform for attracting foreign direct investment will thus be served more effectively. Incidentally, the domestic entrepreneurs and citizens also will stand to benefit.

A major issue that is always discussed in the second-generation reform is that we need a very large amount of capital upfront especially to improve our infrastructure. We do not have this capital and therefore we have to go in for foreign investment or assistance from multilateral agencies. But have we ever thought whether we use whatever infrastructure we have, effectively? For instance in successive five-year plans, the irrigation engineers used to get large amounts allocated for irrigation projects. There was always a difference between the area claimed to have potential for irrigation and the actual area irrigated. Why not in the second stage of reforms, focus on issues like this and examine whether from whatever infrastructure we have created, are we getting optimum promised results? This can be in the area of irrigation, telecommunication, power generation etc. Everybody knows about the transmission losses of the order of 22% in power sector. A focus on productivity must be the third point of the second generation reforms.

I wonder whether the champions of reform who believe in the *mantra* of the Washington Consensus and the pro-poor critics of reform will come together to implement the second stage of reforms on the lines I have indicated.

—N. Vittal

13

Mobility Between Government and Other Sectors

Mobility of employees refers to their capacity, in terms of flexibility in service conditions, to move in the course of their career to other services or posts in the Central Government itself, or in State Government, public enterprises, autonomous organisations, international agencies, foreign Governments and even the private sector. Conditions of service of Government employees, particularly those relating to forwarding of applications, retention of lien in the parent department while working in other departments/ organisations, transfer of pensionary benefits in cases of permanent absorption or transfer, etc., have been liberalised and improved periodically so as to remove impediments in their movement to other sectors. But the extent of mobility is as yet quite insubstantial.

A Liberal Exit Policy

A number of demands have been received by us urging that a liberal exit policy should be formulated to enable Central Government employees to accept employment in the private sector or abroad while retaining their lien in their parent departments. It has been contended that, apart from earning foreign exchange for the country, this would also help in restricting the size of government organisations. It has been suggested in this context that employees should be sanctioned extraordinary leave for the purpose, as it being done by certain State Governments like Kerala and WestBengal, as well as some public enterprises. Lateral entry of person from other sectors into government service has also been advocated.

Position in State Governments

In Kerala, State Government employees are permitted to avail of leave without pay and allowances, whether continuously or in broken spells, for a total period of 15 years to accept alternative employment either within the country or abroad

Position in PSUs

The National Hydroelectric Power Corporation Limited permits, on a selective basis, its employees who have been declared surplus to retain their lien for a period of two years to enable them to secure alternative employment in private organisations. Employees of Himachal Pradesh State Electricity Board are permitted to accept assignments in companies in the private sector which have entered into memoranda of understanding with the State Government. Such assignments are normally tenable for two years, but can be extended up to five years. The period is treated as *dies non* for all purpose.

Present Position in the Central Government

In terms of the Central Civil Services (leave) Rules, 1972, not more than five years' leave may be sanctioned at a time to Central Government employees. These further prohibit the employees from accepting any employment either within the country or abroad or undertaking any commercial activities while on leave.

Retention of Lien for Employment in Private Sector—Our Recommendations

After careful considering, we are of the view that it may not be desirable, as a general principle, to permit all Government employees to accept employment in the private sector or abroad while retaining their connections with the Government. Quite obviously, acceptance of the demand would be detrimental to the interests of efficiency in government. The existing provisions in the rules requiring them to resign from government before accepting such employment are considered to be salutary and deserve to be retained. It may, however, have to be recognised in this context that many employees are apprehensive about exploring alternative careers in other sectors because of the uncertainties involved and doubts about their being able to adjust in an alien work environment. One of the major thrust areas of the Commission is also to devise measures for rightsizing the government machinery. For this purpose, it may be essential to ensure that exit from the government sector is easy and painless. Therefo e, as an experimental measure, certain specified categories of employees could be permitted to retain lien in their posts in government for a very limited period, say two years, while being employed in the private sector or abroad. During this period, it should be possible for them to make the transition from the government sector and to adjust themselves in the new work environment and to decide whether they would prefer to continue in their new assignment after resigning from government service or return to the post earlier held by them. This measure could conceivably act as an incentive for persons to consider quitting government service after being exposed for a limited period to a new work culture and environment. To begin with, this facility could be extended only to those categorised as Executives.

Forwarding of Applications

The present rules governing the forwarding of applications for alternative employment from serving employees are considered to be adequate. These provide enough mobility while safeguarding, at the same time the right of government to retain such of those employees as have been trained in specialised fields at government expenses and are, therefore, obliged, in terms of bonds executed by them, to serve government for specified periods. They are not retrained, however, from accepting employment in State Governments, public enterprises and quasi-government organisation. In such cases, the bonds are transferred to the concerned organisation.

Exemption from Appointment on Permanent Absorption in Autonomous Organisation

At present, Central Government employees can accept appointment in a public enterprise or autonomous organisation only on severing all connections with government. It view,. however, of the fact that this restricted the capacity of those autonomous bodies which had only small cadres to obtain the services of personnel in specialised fields, detailed guidelines have been issued by government listing the cases in which exemption can be sought from the applicability of the provisions relating to permanent absorption insofar as appointments in autonomous organisations are concerned. Besides, appointment of Chief Executives and the zonal and regional chiefs on deputation for a period of five years are also permitted in those Central public enterprises which are required to maintain continuous liaison and ensure coordination with State Government is considered essential for organisational efficiency. In the specified cases, the autonomous organisations concerned are required to obtain the necessary exemption from the Department of Pension and Pensioners' Welfare. We are however, of the view that once the guidelines themselves specify the cases where the requirement of permanent absorption may be dispensed with, a formal exemption from the Department as envisaged should not be necessary. Instead, the autonomous organisations may be given the discretion to appoint Central Government employees on deputation to the specified posts.

Transfer of Pensionary Benefits

Reciprocal arrangements presently exist to ensure that the services rendered by a Central Government employee in a State Government and *vice versa* are counted for pensionary benefits. The earlier provision in the rules which required the transfer of the pro rata pensionary liability to the borrowing government has now been deleted. On the same analogy, it has been demanded that this provision which still exists, should be dispensed with in the case of appointments in autonomous organisations as well.

This is on the ground that the autonomous organisations are fully funded by government grants. However, appointments in autonomous organisations, irrespective of the source of their funds, are not comparable, with those in the Central or State Government. The present arrangements in this regard may, therefore, continue.

Lateral Entry in Government Service

Lateral entry of persons from other sectors into General Government service could also be considered as the experience and expertise gained by them could be utilised with advantage in government. They must be encouraged to join on a time bound contract basis.

14

Need for Contractual Employment

EMPLOYMENT

Introduction

One of the main points of criticism against government employees is that once they are appointed, they are there for life and no one can get rid of them. It is, therefore, necessary to see how in the new atmosphere of liberalisation, we can devise novel methods of recruitment which would not necessarily involve life-time employment. Contractual employment is the obvious alternative.

Present Position in Government

Appointments on contract are generally not resorted to in the arena of public employment in the Government of India, except in a few areas requiring specialisation. A contract appointment is one under which an employee signs a legal contract with his employer to perform assigned tasks for a specific period on the terms and conditions (including remuneration and perquisites) specified therein. The need for contract employment particularly arises when a project work of a purely temporary nature is required to be undertaken for completion within a specified period or certain specialised skills and inputs are considered necessary for short durations. Generally, recruitment to all posts in government, which are likely to continue beyond a period of one year, is made on a regular basis, the general understanding being that persons so recruited shall continue in service on a long-term basis. Thus persons recruited for temporary jobs are shifted to another project or jobs of temporary nature and they are ultimately assimilated in the permanent work force.

Why We Need Contract Employment

There is, therefore, a crying need to recognize time bound temporary contract employment as a legitimate and accepted form of employment. The need for such employment also arises in the context of labour laws and general attitudes of courts, which had to protect the interests of labour and convert causal workers into permanent regular employees even if they are recruited for specified jobs on a purely temporary basis. Providing security in employment thus assumes greater importance than ensuring that the work of the Government is done at the minimum possible cost. The need for contract employment is also felt for the purpose of lateral entry for various positions at sensor level where services of an expert in a particular area of specialisation are needed. Such outside talent brings a whiff of fresh air into the musty corridors of Government and deserves to be encouraged.

SCHEME FOR CONSULTANTS

Details of the Scheme for Engagement of Consultants

A form of appointment for temporary work that is prevalent in the Government of India is the scheme of engagement of Consultants to undertake specific jobs of a specialised nature. Consolidated instructions on the subject were issued by the Department of Personnel and Training in their O.M.No. 16011/6/93 Estt. (Allow) dated 31st December 1993. These stipulate that Consultants can be appointed to the extent of 10 per cent of the total number of posts at the level of Joint Secretaries and above within a Ministry, including attached and subordinate offices. In the case of the Planning Commission, this restriction can be relaxed upto 25 Consultants in all. In the case of appointment of retired/ retiring employees as Consultants, their total number in a Ministry/ Department is not to exceed to at any given time. Employment of such Consultant is not to be made for work of a regular nature. In case this is resorted to under exceptional circumstances, the post earmarked for such work is required to be left vacant. The maximum period for which such appointment can be made is not to exceed two years in case of employment of outside experts and 6 months in the case of retried/retiring employees of the Ministry/ Department. However, this scheme does not respond to the need for contract employments at all levels in Government, whenever work of a temporary nature arises.

COMPARATIVE POSITION ELSEWHERE

Positions in Other Countries

Temporary work is a common form of employment both in industrial and developing countries. According to a report of the International Labour Organisation (ILO), in some developing countries, the percentage of temporary work ranges between 30 and 50 per cent of the total employment, while in the industrialised countries, an average of 10-20 per cent is most common. Government of most developing countries readily acknowledge the deployment of temporary personnel, though only very limited statistical data are available on such deployment. In certain developing countries like Bahrain, Kuwait, Zimbabwe, etc., Which have a significant number of expatriate non-technical advisors, the only legal manner in which they can be recruited is on temporary contract. Contract employment for temporary work is regarded as very useful in structural adjustment programmes in the context of reforms in public service, reduction in size and reduction in job security. Contract employees, who are more vulnerable to termination than workers with a permanent status, go first when staff cuts are unavoidable. Any reduction in the workforce is the light of an economic crisis is easier to implement if the proportion of temporary workers is higher. It is easy to ensure smooth structural adjustments in a situation necessitating reduction in the size of the public service. Some countries however, discourage temporary employment on the ground that most of the personnel recruited for temporary work lack professional skills and are not recruited by competition. The legal framework for such employees is also being constantly improved upon in a manner that they do not retain only a temporary status for a long time and, even while on contract, service conditions are more or less at par with those on permanent employees.

Position in Private Sector

Appointments on contract are comparatively more popular in the private sector in India. The contract form generally used in the corporate sector for employment at higher levels provides in detail the duties and responsibilities, remuneration including perquisites like accommodation, office equipment at home, soft furnishing of home, servants, etc. It also provides for conditions of termination of service. Whereas a notice of two months is generally prescribed for termination of services from either side, services can be terminated by the employer without any notice when the employee is found to be guilty of misconduct, unpunctuality, neglect of duties, unauthorised absence, breach of confidentiality, etc. Such contracts also have a clause about applicability of current Indian legislation on employment contracts.

OUR RECOMMENDATIONS

Recognition of Contractual Employment

Taking into consideration all the factors discussed in the preceding paragraphs, we recommend that employment on contract basis in Government needs to be recognised as one of the legitimate forms of employment and should be resorted more frequently in certain situations like (i) replacement for temporarily absent personnel for a considerable duration ranging from one to five years (ii) time-bound special projects, which are not likely to continue (iii) specialised jobs not normally required and (iv) for the purpose of maintaining a certain flexibility is staffing both for the purpose of lateral entry of experts, moderating the numbers deployed depending on the exigencies of work and ensuring availability of most competent and committed personnel for certain sensitive specialised jobs.

Amendment in Regulations

At present, appointment against any post likely to continue beyond period of one year is to be made on regular basis through UPSC. In Employment Exchange etc. In case contract appointments are to be make concerned Ministries/Departments, it shall be necessary to amend the UPS (Exemption from Consultation)

Regulations, 1958 to provide for exemption of all job-specific contract employment, which is to be continued upto a maximum period of 5 years. Regular appointment through UPS should be required to be made only where it is likely to continue beyond period of five years.

Amendment in Labour Laws

It may also be necessary to amend the labour laws in the country send a clear signal to the courts that short-term employment should be recognised as a legitimate mode of engagement of labour, and job secure should not be accorded the preponderant attention that it has received in the past.

Model Agreement Forms

The Model Agreement Forms circulated by Ministry of Finance in 1955 for contract appointment shall need a re-look and updating in the context of changes in employment/labour laws during the last four decades. The model should also provide for the description of duties/specific details of the job for which such contract employment is to be made.

Modification in the Scheme for Consultants

The scheme of the Government for engagement of consultants' shock be modified to provide for such appointments on contract basis. There should be a provision that the appointment of a consultant on contract base should be made only after proper notification/due publicity of the vacancy and should not be made in an arbitrary manner. Similarly, appointment of retired officers of the Ministry as consultants on project posts funded by UPSC bilateral agencies should also be brought within the framework of present guidelines on engagement of consultants about tenure, proper notification publicity for appointment etc.

Training and Development

Importance

All the recommendations on administrative reforms will work only if a proper training programme to effect necessary changes in the work ethos of government officials is designed and implemented. The proposal re-structuring of the government offices and work procedures would cause a large scale re-deployment of existing staff—especially those in groups 'D' and 'C' categories—who will have to be re-trained for taking up new jobs. In the new environment with emphasis on "customer orientation", attitudinal changes in the supervisory and executive cadres would also be necessary. Besides, training facilities will also be required for responding to rapid technological changes taking place at present.

EXPERIENCE OF OTHER COUNTRIES

Training Mechanisms in Other Countries

Canada

In Canada, despite a series of cut-backs in opening budgets, expenditure on training and development has been maintained at previous levels or even increased. Employees are given total freedom to opt for a training of their choice. A substantial part of the training effort is delegated to individual departments. Public servants undergoing training in colleges etc. in their own time are reimbursed part of the cost incurred thereon and employees are encouraged to organize briefings and information sessions in their free time.

United Kingdom

In the United Kingdom, greater responsibility for training and development of employees is delegated to individual departments. The focus of training has been shifted to bring about necessary changes in the skills for better customer service. Training courses are devised on the basis of practical experience of different business houses which have improved their performance through proper training of their staff. Simultaneously, employees are encouraged to identify their own job-related development needs and managers are given the responsibility for regularly catering to such needs.

Malaysia

In Malaysia, training has been identified as a vital component in the implementation of the total quality management concept and the clients' charter. Provisions are made for training at all levels in the civil service. Attachment programmes to send Government employees to certain specified business houses in the private sector for exposure to practical aspects, practices of management and intricacies of business operations have been initiated.

The Present System in India

The Indian Government has taken numerous steps to provide training facilities to its employees. Direct entrants to Group 'A' services undergo several institutional and in-service training programmes. Such programmes for Group 'C' and Group 'D' personnel are, however, else common. A Central Training Division exists in the Department of Personnel and Training which is responsible for promoting and coordinating training programmes of the different Central Ministries and Departments, providing guidance and help, sponsoring or arranging training courses on aspects common to different services and maintaining liaison with the State. This Division is also responsible for the training of Trainers and Coordinators of different Departments and Ministries.

In the government, there are various institutes conducting different training programmes. The Lal Bahadur Shastri National Academy of Administration at Mussoorie imparts training to IAS officers. Apart from conducting training progrmmes for these IAS probationers, it runs refresher courses for senior IAS officers. A week-long vertically integrated training is also being imparted annually to all IAS officers. There are other specialised institutions like the National Academy of Direct Taxes, Sardar Vallabhbhai Patel National Police Academy, etc. Which provide training to officers of the IPS/Central services. These academies run foundational courses for direct recruits to the All India and non-technical central group 'A' services.

There are autonomous institutes like the Indian Institute of Public Administration, Administrative Staff College of India etc. which conduct several courses on administrative leadership, policy planning and so on. Some State Governments have set up training institutes for specialised course. A large number of officers are also nominated for training abroad.

Lacunae in the Existing System

Training in India suffers from the twin ills of low priority and ad hocism. There is no well thought out perspective plan for training. Frequently there is no integration between training and performance or career development Modules imparting the spirit of "Customer orientation." Amongst government employees are sadly lacking. The priority assigned to training is low and more often than not, an official is sent for training only because he happens to be free. Training needs of the staff are seldom identified. Due to lack of proper incentive, a posting as a faculty member of a training institution is not valued. Feedback obtained from the trainees is not properly analysed, and this leads to perpetuation of ineffective training programmes. While individual training divisions for imparting specific training have been created in some large ministries/departments, these do not exist in smaller departments.

Recommendations Made in Consultancy Reports

In the sponsored study on 'Restructuring the Government Office' Indian Institute of Technology (IIT), Delhi as well as Tata Consultancy Services (TCS) have made certain observations on this subject. IIT has observed that the present level of skills among the staff of government offices is very moderate, thereby indicating a need for better training. The training needs of staff are seldom identified and there is a growing need for adequate training mechanisms for multi-skilling and redeployment of staff. TCS has propose setting up of a training division in each department, which should compile an inventory of knowledge, skills and attitudes required for performing different jobs so as to rectify any gaps by proper training for performing different jobs so as to rectify any gaps by proper training in a planned manner. The need for establishing a system for proper feed-back and periodical assessment of the impact of training being given to the employees, as well as linking training with other HRD functions like performance appraisal, promotions, recruitment, etc. has been emphasised.

DEVELOPING A NEW SYSTEM FOR TRAINING AND DEVELOPMENT

General Strategy

In the liberalised scenario where the government has to reduce its size while simultaneously increasing the productivity, the thrust of training for groups 'C' and 'D' employees, which form a bulk of the work-force, will have to be towards multi skilling. All group 'D' staff should be trained in different skills so that they can simultaneously perform various functions presently being carried out by a plethora of auxiliary staff. In the case of groups 'C' office staff in the Secretariat, proper training, enabling them to perform all the functions of executive assistants, should be devised. This should include training in use of computers and other modern office gadgets, shorthand, typing drafting, noting and attending to phone calls. For groups 'A' and 'B' employees, the emphasis has to be on brining about an attitudinal change which is crucial to the success of the administrative reforms. Some specific recommendations on different aspects of training and equipment follows.

Creation of Training Groups under HRD

An adequately equipped training group for analyzing regular training needs as well as for arranging department-specific, post-specific and individual—specific training should be created in every department as part of the Human Resource Development team. This group should work out a detailed training plan specifying the kind of training required for each level and identify suitable training institutes and trainers therefore.

Common Courses for all Services

DOP & T has already identified a number of institutes for running general training programmes funded by it. These institutes should run common courses for different services/departments so as to bring about a better interaction and commonality of approach between them.

Foundation Courses

Presently LBSNAA, SVPNPA and NADT conduct foundational courses for all direct recruits to the All India and non-technical Central Group 'A' services. Lately, IAS recruits are only sent to LBSNAA for the foundational course and only the recruits of the other All India and Central Groups 'A' services are sent to the other two academies. This defeats the very purpose of the foundational course. We recommend that all probationers, irrespective of their service, may be distributed equally amongst these three academies. Further, direct recruits to Central Group 'A' Technical services may also be sent for these foundational courses.

Linkage with Private Sector

There is a crying need for exposing government employees to the work processes, mode of functioning and pressures existing in private sector jobs. Accordingly we favour initiation of a new scheme of attachment of Probationary executives of the Government to certain selected and efficiently run private sector organisations for short durations. During this attachment, the probationers should be asked to perform some specific tasks which should be assessed for incorporation in their appraisal sheets. Short duration workshops and seminars with top ranking managers of private sector should also be organised for senior executives of the government in order to facilitate exchange of ideas and experience.

New Methods

New methods for imparting training should be evolved and, as far as possible, employees should be allowed to choose their own training schedule.

Linkage with Career Plan

There has to be a direct relationship between the career plan of an employee and the training imparted to him. Although the present performance appraisal form has a column for training undergone and future training needs, not much importance is attached to it. We recommend that various training courses undergone by an employee should be counted for assigning proper gradings at the time of promotion and deputation to posts should be linked to the officer having successfully completed training in a related field. Besides, refresher training courses tailor-made for honing the skills required for handling specific levels may be conducted at regular intervals. All officials, after putting in specified years of service, should undergo these courses mandatorily, followed by a test. Employees who fail to clear the test even after two attempts should be classified as unfit for promotion. Furthermore, certain prestigious courses should be evolved on the Staff College pattern in the defence services, to which only officers whose performance has consistently been outstanding and who have been identified as potential leaders for the future are sent. Such officers, on successful completion of the training, should be picked up for manning the most sensitive and important assignments in the departments.

Foreign Training

There is clamour amongst government officials to rush for any kind of foreign training, irrespective of the fact whether it is related to their work or not. This tendency needs to be curbed. We recommend that government officials should be sent only to such foreign courses and training as have a direct relationship to their work and can be used for developing their skills further.

Training of Executives as facilitators

In view of changes envisaged in the functioning of the government, there will be need for carrying not refresher courses for executives at all levels, for effecting attitudinal changes to prepare them for taking up the role of "Facilitators" instead of being mere regulators.

Special kinds of Training

In the case of professional services like medical and engineering, there is a need to introduce a proper training schedule at the middle level for broadening their horizons, updating their technical skills and fitting them for higher policy assignments. Similarly, in generalist services, there may be a need to re-orient them towards broad sectoral specialisations at a certain stage in their careers.

Feedback

Adequate review mechanisms for gauging the effectiveness and relevance of training programmes have to be developed. All training divisions should establish a system for receiving a proper feed back on the effectiveness of a course from participants. Based on such feedback the training divisions should develop mechanism for pinpointing any lacunae in their training programme and institute immediate remedial action.

16

Performance Appraisal

Objective

Performance Appraisal covers a broad ground and could be defined as the overall methodology by which an organisation is entitled to assess the performance and capability of an individual employee. Such appraisal is made every day, every hours, every minute by the superiors, colleagues, subordinates, clients, the courts, the media, members of the public. Organisations have periodic review meetings or are monitoring performance through which the performance of individual officers can be adjudged. But the chief, most commonly used, weapon is the Annual Confidential Report.

Annual Confidential Reports on the performance of government servants provide the basic inputs for assessing their suitability for being confirmed in service, crossing efficiency has for drawal of further increments, promotion, deputation and other special assignments. Aimed primarily at improving the performance of employees, the main focus of the report is envisaged as being developmental rather than merely judgmental. It is intended to be true indicator of the strength and weaknesses as well as achievements and shortcoming of an individual government servant and is thus an essential tool for proper personnel management. The system of writing annual confidential reports, therefore, has two principal objectives, which a Reporting Officer should be clearly aware of. The first is to improve the performance of the subordinate reported upon in his present job and the second is to assess his potential and prepare him, through appropriate feedback a guidance for further advancement.

Present Position

Major changes were introduced in the system of writing the confidential reports on three occasions in the past in 1975, 1978 and 1986. The formal of the Report currently in force was introduced in 1986 after detailed deliberations in a workshop organised in the context of certain demands from the staff side in the National Council of the Joint Consultative Machinery that there should be greater openness in the system, assessment of the fitness of lower level functionaries for promotion should be dispensed with, etc. This format is based on the concept of management by objectives' in government and is the outcome of an attempt to made the system more objective and achievement-oriented. It envisages the evolution of new work culture based on performance and results and the assessment is, therefore, both quantitative and qualitative. Instructions currently in force also provide that the reports on Group 'D' employees need not be maintained if they are not employed on sensitive jobs.

ABOLITION OF CONFIDENTIAL REPORTS

Discontinuance in Specified Cases

We have received a number of suggestions that the Annual Confidential Reports should be discontinued. This has been justified on the ground that the system is defective and causes a great deal of dissatisfaction to the employees and that, instead of achieving the primary objective of improving employees in a positive manner, it has become an instrument of harassment and victimisation. Other suggestions in this regard are that (a) the reports should be written only during the initial ten years of service of an employee and discontinued thereafter (b) the system may be retained only in respect of employees in Groups 'A' and 'B' and such of those Group 'C' employees as are eligible for promotion to Groups 'B' posts; and (c) The reports should be discontinued in respect of posts to which promotions are made entirely on the basis of seniority-cum-fitness, i.e. by the non-selection method.

Our Views

Quite obviously, in the absence of other effective methods of performance appraisal, it would not be desirable to restrict the writing of the Annual Confidential Reports only during the initial years of an employee's service. We understand that reports in respect of Groups 'C' personnel employed in some of the State Governments are required to be maintained only if the are eligible for promotion to Group 'B' posts. We also recognize that the Annual Confidential Reports are only of limited utility in determining the suitability of personnel for appointment to posts to which promotions are made on the basis of seniority-cum-fitness alone. Though these factors might justify a review of the necessity for the continuance of the system in certain specified circumstances, the benefits under the Assured Career Progression Scheme separately recommended by us would be available only to those whose performance conform to the prescribed standards and who fulfil all other prescribed criteria for regular function promotion to posts in the relevant higher scales of pay. Besides, we have also recommend elsewhere in the report introduction of Performance Related Increments for all employees, including the Group 'D' personnel, purely on the basis of their performance during the year. An appropriate mechanism for the purpose will be necessary and the Confidential Reports would form the basis of assessment of performance for regulation of increments. In this circumstances, we are of the firm view that it will not be desirable to discontinue the system of Annual Confidential Reports. In fact, in the context of our recommendations aimed at improving employees productivity and relating increase in compensation to performance, this should be reintroduced even in respect of Group 'D' personnel.

REFORMS PROPOSED

Summary of Suggestions

There is a widespread demand for greater openness and transparency in performance appraisal so as to eliminate, as far as possible, any subjectivity in reporting. Some of the suggestions received by us in this connection are: (a) the contents of the reports should be disclosed to the employee concerned so that he is aware of his capabilities and shortcomings and can strive to improve his performance; (b) the performance of an entire team should be assessed whenever necessary; (c) employees should be assessed not only by their superiors but also by their colleagues and subordinates; and (d) additional monetary benefits should be provided for employees whose performance is consistently of a high order and who are graded as such. It has also been urged that more than one report with an average grading should be treated as adverse and communicated to the employee concerned. A few have also suggested, on the other hand, that the grading of employees in the reports should be dispensed with and the reports confined only to a general appraisal of an employee's performance during the years.

Nodal Ministry's Views

The Department of Personnel and Training appears to be averse to the communication of an average report to an employee on the ground that "average" performance is not considered to be adverse though it is not complimentary. It also appears that the demand for reports on performance of employees being open documents was considered in the early eighties, when the concept of an open system was not favoured. Instead, the present system which provides for a self appraisal by the employees themselves and assessment at two levels by the Reporting and Reviewing Officers was considered to be suitable for our conditions. According to the Department, this has been working reasonably well.

We find that there is already partial openness in the Armed Forces in the system of appraisal of the performance of Officers, who are shown the assessment of their performance, excluding the observations on their fitness for promotion. Openness of varying degree has been introduced by the State Governments of Kerala. Tamil Nadu and West Bengal. Some of the public enterprises have also introduced a participative system of performance appraisal for their Executives. The trend internationally is also to place a greater emphasis on detailed job assessment of every employee and understanding between a manager and his subordinate about their duties and responsibilities, the appraisal of an employee's performance and contribution now takes place on parameters known and agreed upon by the employee. This enables the manager to be more responsive in a more satisfied and productive work force. The traditional approach to performance appraisal, which is primarily concerned with the past and usually, leads to salary review or promotion in being replaced by a new approach, a forward looking process known as Self Development Review, having its primary emphasis on the future of the employees and the organisation.

Our Recommendations

In order to keep pace with the significant changes taking place globally, and in the context of our emphasis on increasing employees' productivity and relating increments to performance, we are of the view that certain changes in the present system of employees' appraisal are called for. Our recommendations on the reforms necessary are contained in the succeeding paragraphs.

Grading of Overall Performance

Under the present system of grading employees as "Outstanding", "Very Good", "Good", "Average", or "Proof", the finer and more subtle distinctions between different employees are not readily discernible. For instance, an employee may not qualify to be graded outstanding, but his performance may well have been shades better than merely very good, which would rightly justify his being considered superior to another employee who may have earned only a very good grading. Finer distinction in grading would be of considerable utility in ensuring that the most deserving among different employees are elevated to posts promotions to which are based on selection and merit. These would be of particular relevance in the case of appointments to executive and senior duty posts. A more exhaustive and comprehensive assessment of personnel based on a point rating system is already in vogue in the Central Police Organisations and the Armed Forces, and even individual traits and attributes are measured against a ten point scale. The grading system followed in respect of civilians employees is, however, somewhat restricted in its scope and ambit.

Grading on 10 Point Scale

In order to remedy this deficiency in the present system, grading of officers on a ten-point scale could be introduced for the Executive cadres. This need, not, however, be as comprehensive as in the Armed Forces or the Central Police Organisations but could be confined only to the final, overall grading. The present system may, however, be retained without any change in respect of all other employees below the level of Executives.

Rating of 6 and Below

A rating of six and below on the ten-point scale, which would have adverse implications for promotions based on selection for bench marks are prescribed, should be treated as being not good enough and communicated to the executives concerned. This would enable him to represent against the grading, should be feel aggrieved for any reason.

Detailed Orders to be Issued

In the context of our proposals to relate increments to performance and to facilitate the extension of financial benefits under the Assured Career Progression Scheme as well as promotion based on selection. Reporting and Reviewing Officers may be specifically required to assess and indicate the suitability of all categories of employees to (i) draw one or more increments, (ii) derive the benefits of the Assured Career Progression Scheme, and (iii)for promotion to higher posts, appropriate columns being included in the report form for the purpose.

Openness and Transparency

In order to ensure transparency in reporting and to serve the intended objective of providing a feedback to employees to improve their performance, partial openness may be desirable. For this purpose, the final grading of employees, as recorded in the confidential reports, should be conveyed to them. Besides, grading of an employee as " Average" is as harmful as adverse entries in the reports. This is sometimes resorted to by Reporting Officers in order to overcome the associated problem of communicating an adverse grading to the employee concerned and having to justify such grading. In the process, the employee reported upon is denied the opportunity to be aware of the quality of his performance and contribution, so as to enable him to improve or even to represent against the grading. In the circumstances, we are of the view that grading of an employee as an average performer should be treated as adverse and should be communicated. In fact, it may even be desirable to treat any grading below the benchmark prescribed for promotion to the next higher post as adverse and to communicate such grading to the employee concerned so as to afford him an Opportunity to represent against an assessment that may already affect his career advancement. While receiving the communication regarding an adverse entry or grading, the employee should also have access to the confidential report in its entirely.

Employee Appraisal to be a Continuous Process

With a view to securing greater objectivity in reporting and ensuring that the Annual Confidential Reports and more focused and contain specific, and not vague or terse comments, assessment and appraisal of employees' performance should be a continuous process. For this purpose, officers responsible for reporting on their subordinates should maintain a weekly or monthly record of their impressions about the performance and contribution of subordinates, indicating *inter alia* important achievements, shortcomings, adherence to schedules for completion of specified tasks, etc.

Assessment to Include Teams and Department's Performance

To be realistic and objective, performance appraisal should not also confine itself merely to an assessment of the traits and attributes of an individual employee. It has to be recognised that an employee does not function in isolation and that his performance and contribution are often influenced by the team and work environment in which he is required to function. Reporting and Reviewing Officers should, therefore, also endeavour to assess the performance of an individual employee in the overall context of the performance of his team including his individual performance and contribution as compared to that of other team members, as well as the entire office or department, identifying clearly the constraints in achieving the stated goals and objectives. The employee should thereafter be graded, assigning appropriate weightage for the contribution of the team and the office/department with reference to his own functional responsibilities.

Inconsistencies in Reporting

If the entries in the confidential report of an employee for any particular year or period are inconsistent or entirely at variance with those recorded in the reports of earlier years, which could be attributable to bias or subjectivity on the part of the Reporting or Reviewing Officer, the employee concerned should have the right to get himself transferred to work under another Reviewing or Reporting Officer. In such a situation, the report in question should not be taken into account for determining the employee's suitability for promotion, increments, etc. However, if the reports for the subsequent year or periods are also similarly adverse, the earlier report should not be ignored.

Assessment of Suitability for Advancement and Other Benefits

Normally, Confidential Reports of the immediately preceding five years along should be considered by Departmental Promotion Committees to assess the suitability of employees for career advancement and other benefits, unless reference to reports of earlier years is considered to be absolutely essential.

Quinquennial Review

At present, an exclusive reliance is placed on the Annual Confidential Reports for assessing the personality traits and performance of individual employees. For obvious reasons, the reports may not always reflect fully all the achievements and contribution of an employee or aspects of his functioning that may not be entirely complimentary or praiseworthy. We are, therefore, of the view that it would also be desirable to introduce a system of quinquennial review of the performance of personnel in the Executive (Group 'A') cadres by a group of officers. Apart from affording an opportunity to the executives concerned to present their achievements before the group and to dwell upon the constraints under which they have had to function, such occasions should also be utilised to apprise them of any adverse reports on their functioning as may have been reflected in media reports, anonymous complaints, etc. and to ascertain their versions on such reports. In our opinion, the quinquennial review would reveal various facts of an executive's personality that are generally not discernible from the confidential report, however objectively these may have been written. This would also be useful in determining whether the executives concerned are fit for further retention in service or whether they should be compulsorily retried by invoking the provisions of Fundamental Rules 56(j). The group of officers to be associated with the review should be senior to the executives concerned and should have been closely associated with the departments or divisions in which the executives had worked during the period to which it relates.

Counselling

Counselling of employee, which would be of particular significance in the case of employees adversely reported upon, should also form an integral part of performance appraisal. This could be done by a group of officers intimately acquainted with the work of the concerned employee, including the Reporting and Reviewing Officers. The counselling would serve the twin objectives of providing the necessary feedback to the employees and improving their future performance.

DELAYS IN SUBMISSION OF REPORTS

Measures to Eliminate Delays

A major problem brought to our notice is that meetings of Department Promotion Committees are not held in many cases because of the non-submission by the Reporting or Reviewing Officers, which result in promotions being deferred, causing avoidable hardship to the employees concerned. We are of the firm view that employees should not suffer because of the failure of the Reporting or Reviewing officers to ensure timely finalisation of the appraisals. Apart from obtaining special reports in such cases, it should be ensured that the schedule prescribed for the submission of self-appraisals and confidential reports is scrupulously adhered to by all concerned. The concerned employees should also be informed of the non-receipt of reports for any particular periods so that they could also make efforts to have them written. The present instructions which envies that the reports should be written even if self-appraisals are not submitted by the employees to be reported upon should be strictly enforced. Delay on the part of

Reporting Officers should also be adversely commented upon in their Confidential Reports. Computerisation of data relating to Annual Confidential Reports of employees by all departments would greatly facilitate proper monitoring and follow-up action. For this purpose every officer should establish a Confidential Cell as has already been done by certain organisations like the Border Security Force, which has sep up a compurised Personnel Management Information System.

17

Establishing an Efficiency Programme

HISTORICAL PERSPECTIVE

Administrative Reforms in India

It cannot be said that the realisation of the critical importance of the public service to the overall development of the country is recent. There have been several attempts at administrative reforms, starting from the Secretariat Reorganisation Committee, which submitted its report in August, 1947. The Committee suggested various steps for administrative reorganisation in the context of British withdrawal from India.

Ayyangar Committee

In 1949, Gopalaswami Ayyangar sumitted a Report on Reorganisation of the Machinery of Government. Besides suggesting the regrouping of Ministries, he advocated the establishment of an Organisation and Methods Division to keep a continuous watch over the performance of the administrative system and to improve the standards of efficiency therein.

Constitution of India

In 1950, the Constitution of India came into force. It was by itself a fundamental instrument of administrative reforms. It laid the ground rules guiding the relationship between the citizens and the State, and the State and the civil servants.

Gorwala Committee

In 1951, A.D. Gorwala submitted his Report on Public Administration in which he made a number of recommendations particularly with regard to introduction of Organisation and Methods procedures in Government departments.

Appleby Reports

Two reports which had a significant impact were Paul H. Appleby's 'Public Administration in India: Report of a Survey, 1953' and "Re-examination of India's administrative system, 1956". As one of the outcomes of his 1953 Report, and O & M division was set up in 1954 in the Cabinet Secretariat. The attempt here was to effect improvement in paper management through manualisation and a system of inspections.

Second Pay Commission

The Second Pay Commission (1959) recommended the pooling of the Secretariat and the attached offices into a single headquarters organisation, as also the establishment of a Whitley council type of machinery for negotiation and settlement of disputes.

Santhanam Committee

In 1964, the Santhanam Committee looked into the problem of corruption. Its recommendations led to the establishment of the Central of the Central Vigilance Commission and amendment of the conduct rules.

Department of Administrative Reforms

In the same year, a Department of Administrative Reforms was set up in the Ministry of Home Affairs and the O&M Division transferred to it. In 1965, a Bureau of Public Enterprises was set up to provide an in-house management consultancy agency for public enterprises.

Administrative Reforms Commission

In 1966, Government set up the Administrative Reforms Commission under the chairmanship of Shri Morarji Desai. From 1966 to 1970, the Commission submitted 20 reports which led to many major changes. The Department of Personnel was set up, the role of the Department of Administrative Reforms was redefined, new systems of Secretariat working including the desk officer system were introduced, performance budgeting was adopted by all developmental ministries, financial and administrative power were delegated to the maximum extent and the Bureau of Public Enterprises was strengthened.

National Police Commission

The National Police Commission (1977-87) examined the role and functions of the police and modernisation of law enforcement, and suggested arrangements for preventing misuse of powers by the police.

Ministry of Personnel

In 1985, a full-fledged Ministry of Personnel/Public Grievances and Pensions was set up directly under the Prime Minister, and a new Ministry of Programme Implementation was established to improve the overall economic management of the country.

Jha Commission

The Economic Administrative Reforms Commission under L.K. Jha (1983) advocated the need to move towards accountability in the positive sense, so that greater importance was given to performance than mere adherence to rules and procedures. The concept of Management by Objectives was introduced in the form of Annual Action Plans for Ministries and Departments and Memoranda of understanding with Public Sector Undertakings. Similarly, an on line monitoring of managerial performance in infrastructure sectors was initiated.

Lessons from the Past

Although the many reforms introduced in the last 50 years have borne some fruit, there has been a tendency for dynamic initiatives to peter out once the prime movers behind them were removed. Thus the Systems of performance budgeting, annual action plan, management by objectives, organisation and methods, memorandum of understanding etc., which started off as highly innovative responses to systematic states, got converted into routine, ritual exercises bereft of any meaning. Organisational reforms have tended to be more in form than in real substance, leaving little impact on the efficiency of the system. What has been lacking is a congruence between strategy, structure and substance. Indian experiments with reforms do not get institutionalised, they often fade away with the personalities who introduced them.

INITIATIVES TAKEN ELSEWHERE

International Experience

The Commission had the opportunity to peruse the excellent publications titled "Current Good Practices and New Developments in Public Service Management" brought out by the Commonwealth Secretariat in respect of different Commonwealth countries. It also had the opportunity of visiting the United Kingdom, Canada, Malayasia and New Zealand in order to have a first-hand interaction with those connected with the public service reforms. Some of the initiatives taken in other countries have been discussed in the succeeding paragraphs.

THE UNITED KINGDOM

Reforms in the United Kingdom

The U.K. Civil Service consists of over half a million People. The most notable attempt to reform the Service was the Report of the Fulton Committee, but the administrative culture still remained bureaucratic. In 1979, the Conservative Government led by Margeret Thatcher sought to reduce public expenditure in order to reduce direct taxation. The view was taken that the U.K. was over-governed and it would be in everyone's interest for Government to play a small role. This started the drive for Civil Service reforms.

Efficiency Unit

In 1979, the Prime Minister's Efficiency Unit was created and it has typically comprised two civil servants and three seconded industrialists with a support staff of three. The Unit developed a methodology based on Scrutiny Exercises on narrowly focused and short-term studies in order to reduce Expenditure and improve efficiency of a department. It is not responsible for conducting screening exercises; it is responsible for ensuring that such exercises are conducted by the departments themselves. There are twenty exercises done, every year and these are stated to have produced savings of rounds 200 to Pounds 300 million annually.

Financial Management Initiative

As the exercises recorded fundamental flaws in the civil Service approach to management, the Financial Management Initiative was introduced in 1982. Managers in Government Departments were given responsibility for managing their own budgets. Output was measured and the cost-effectiveness of their work evaluated. Each department was required to operate within a limit for its manpower and total running costs.

Next Steps

In 1988; the Next Steps study recommended that Executive Agencies should be established to carry out the executive functions of government within a policy resources framework approved by the Minister. Each agency would be under the direction of the Chief Executive who would have freedom from day-do-day involvement of minister. By April, 1994, 60% of the civil servants were working in Agencies and other organisations operating on Next Steps lines.

Citizens' Charter

In 1991, the Prime Minister launched the Citizens' Charter Initiative. This is a ten-year programme designed to raise the standards of public service. It has six key principles—setting standards, information and openness, choice and consultation, courtesy and helpfulness, putting thing right and value for money.

Lessons from the U.K. Experience

The conditions that have been shown to be critical for the success of the programme are:

- sustained political commitment to change on the part of the Government and a degree of cross-party agreement on policy principles
- pressure to secure the most efficient use of resources

- pressure to reduce the number of people in the Civil Service
- opportunities for civil servants to participate in analyzing the problems that are faced
- responsibility for implementation being firmly placed with those responsible for sustaining the changes and
- programmes of staff development directly linked to the reform programme.

NEW ZEALAND

Reforms in New Zealand

In New Zealand, reforms were initiated by the Government elected in mid-1984. Their key overall concepts were transparency and consistency and these translated into the following organizing principles for the reforms process:

- The State should not be involved in any activities that would be more efficiently and affectively performed by the community or by private business.
- Trading enterprises would operate most efficiently and effectively if structured on the lines of private sector business.
- Departments would operate most efficiently and effectively with clearly specified and non-conflicting functions particularly with policy and operational functions separated, and with commercial and non-commercial functions separated.
- Departmental managers would perform most effectively if made fully accountable for the efficient running of their organisations, with the minimum practicable central control of inputs.
- The quality, quantity and cost of products offered by the State departments should be determined by the purchaser's requirements rather than the producer's preferences.

Legislation Passed

These principles were reflected in three important pieces of legislation:

- The State owned Enterprises Act, 1986 which provided the basis for converting the old trading departments and corporations into business along private sector lines.
- The State Sector Act, 1988 which made departmental chief executives fully accountable for managing their organisations effectively.
- The Public Finance Act. 1989 which changed the basis of state sector financial management from a focus on inputs to a focus on out puts (the relevance and effectiveness of actual products) and outcomes (the overall results of the outputs from the Government's point of view).

Structural Reforms

The reforms process had four main stages as under:

- As part of the structural reform large departments were abolished and most of their functions assumed by State-owned enterprises. Many of these were subsequently sold and most of the remaining enterprises are viewed as potentially marketable. The State has almost entirely withdrawn from direct involvement in trading enterprises.
- Department restructuring began in 1985, to rationalize the functions and shape of the core public service, and moving much of the service delivery functions to a new tier of non-departmental entities called 'crown entities'.
- In 1988, government began a major restructuring of the education sector. Local education boards were abolished and their functions transferred to elected boards of trustees. Similarly, health authorities have been replaced by appointed regional health authorities with founding responsibilities and Crown health enterprises operating commercially as service providers.
- In 1988, chief executives became individually accountable to the ministers, through limited term contracts which were performance related. The role of the State Services Commission changed from employer of all public servants to employers of the chief excutives.

Review of the Programme

A review of the reforms programme in New Zealand show that three aspects have been extremely successful. Transparency in the activities and processes of the State, the liberation of managers from central input controls, and a new financial management and accounting systems are revolutionizing the way in which departments and officials works. New Zealand's economy has recovered, its audit rating has been regraded upwards, inflation has been reduced to less than two per cent and employment has been growing steadily. The 1993 World Competitiveness report ranked New Zealand first in quality of government and second on business community optimism.

Lessons from the New Zealand Experience

The New Zealand experience suggests that there are seven key elements to a successful reforms process. These are:

- unflinching political determination;
- very clear objectives, agreed at the highest levels, and based on an intelligent appreciation on the community's tolerances;
- a set of comprehensive and well-integrated basic principles, agreed at the highest levels;
- sound legal architecture that re-defines the rules outright;
- a demanding but realistic time-table;
- a core of unified, highly motivated, experienced and imaginative senior public servants, provided with sufficient resources and discretion to manage implementation; and
- very effective information and public relations systems.

MALAYSIA

Administrative Reforms in Malaysia

In Malaysia, the Government established the Development Administration Unit (DAU) as a centre for administrative reforms in 1966 and six years later the National Institute of Public Administration (INTAN) was set up to develop skills and expertise among public sector employees. The Malaysian Administrative Modernisation and Management Planning Unit (MAMPU) was set up in 1977 under the Prime Minister's Department, to initiate administrative changes and innovations to the Public Service. Some of the important measures introduced during the eighties included the downsizing of the Public Service through privatisation, the introduction of the Malaysian Incorporated Concept and the inculcation of positive values and work ethics. Efforts were also made to improve the quality of counter services as also to streamline systems and procedures.

Vision 2020

In February 1991, the Prime Minister of Malaysia unveiled his Vision 2020, which states the national aspiration to attain a fully industrialised and developed nation status within the next three decades. This vision can be achieved only if there is an excellent Public Service to meet the challenges of rapid development in a constantly changing environment. The Public Service has identified seven fundamental values which are deemed necessary for this purpose. These are quality, productivity, innovativeness, discipline, integrity, accountability and professionalism.

Quality

In Novermber,1989 the Government launched a nation-wide Excellent Work Culture Movement which stresses quality as the foundation for success. The Public Service adopted Total Quality Management in order to create customer-focused organisations capable of delivering quality outputs and services to customers. Agencies were advised to form Quality Control Circles as an effective mechanism to mobilize expertise, experience and employee creativity in problem-solving. The Malaysian Incorporated Policy is based on the underlying philosophy that collaboration between Government and business is essential for accelerated national competitiveness in the global marketplace. The Government has also adopted the Clients' Charter which ensures that each Government agency provides a written commitment to its customer that goods and services will comply with declared quality standards.

Productivity

The Public Service places equal emphasis on productivity. The Government has identified eight critical factors which influence productivity. These are manpower, systems and procedures, organisation structure, management style, work environment, technology, materials and capital equipment. Productivity measurement and evaluation is also part of the improvement effort. Various steps have been taken to introduce better file management, work simplification, form design, office automation, information technology, etc.

The professionalism of the civil servant has been further enhanced with the introduction of the New Remuneration System. This involves major changes to the organisational structure, remuneration and reward system, and terms of service. This has resulted in creating a cadre of innovative, creative and talented employees who have readily embraced a work culture that emphasizes performance, quality and productivity.

Strategies for Success

Five main strategies have been adopted to ensure the successful implementation of administrative reforms. There include consensus building, documentation and information dissemination, training, follow-up and follow-through, and recognitions and awards. The reforms are coordinated at the highest level by the Panel on Administrative Reforms to the Civil Service which is chaired by the Chief Secretary and acts as a think-tank and prime mover. Consensus is also built through discussions in four major permanent committees of Public Service top management comprising Secretaries General of Ministries, Heads of Services, Heads of Federal Departments, representatives of State Governments and Chief Executives of Statutory Bodies.

Political Support

A major reason for success is the personal interest shown by the top political leadership, especially the Prime Ministers of Malaysia who have been the leading propellants of reforms.

CANADA

Public Service 2000

The starting point for the Government of Canada's Journey on the road to administrative reform is the process entitled "Public Service 2000". This was mainly the effort of the federal public service itself. Although it had political interest and support, it was not closely directed and actively managed by the politicians. Thus it does not bear the imprint of a particular political agenda as in some other countries.

Key Themes

Public Service 2000 staked out some key themes. The Public Service must strive to provide a high quality service and increase client satisfaction. The Public Service must become more engaged, more open, more visible and more consultative. Public Service managers must create organisations in which people are valued for their skill, dedication, energy and loyalty. Public Service must invest move heavily in the development of its people. It must reduce the burden of internal controls so that intelligent, well-motivated managers have greater latitude to improve service quality and client satisfaction.

Initiatives Taken

Among the initiatives to improve service quality is the establishment of an inter-departmental quality network and an attempt led by the Treasury to establish service standards for all departments. The reduction of central agency constraints is being addressed by increased delegation of authority for human resource management to departments, and for financial management through the mechanism of Operating Budgets and increased flexibility at the end of the fiscal years. Special Operating Agencies have been created to give service units within departments direct responsibility for results and increased managerial flexibility. Even in an era of fiscal constraint, the Government has been increasing its investment in the people who constitute the public service. A new special operating agency called Training & Development Canada has been created and the Canadian Centre for Management Development established to focus on the needs of the executive level. Employing new information technology is emerging as a key way of achieving objectives such as improving service and reducing cost.

Future of Reforms in Canada

There are several reasons to believe that the process of public service reform will continue for many years. First, there is a major economic problem that gives it urgency. As result of very substantial budgetary deficits in the last two decades Canada finds itself in the uncomfortable position of being a major international debtor. Thus there is a demand for major reductions in the operating cost of the public sector. Secondly, Canada has always been in the forefront of advances in communications technology. The Canadian public sector will draw upon this expertise to apply leading-edge information and communication technology to the provisions of public services. The final factor is the commitment of public servants to reform. The values that public Service 2000 has espoused are taking root within the culture of the public service in Canada, at all levels of government.

Establishing the Need

Looking at the experience elsewhere, it is apparent that there is a world-wide movement for public service reform. We have seen that their success depended initially on the firm commitment to reforms at the highest level. Such reform can come about in India only when there is an appreciation that launching an efficiency programme is critical for the socio-economic development of the country. This realisation has to come at the highest political level and nothing short of a personal commitment of the Prime Minister himself will do. It has also to be realised that this is not a political issue. Thus a national consensus needs to be developed, cutting across party lines, so that the process of reform once initiated is not allowed to peter out merely because of a change of Government.

Developing the Apparatus

Once the overall commitment is forthcoming, what is then required is an apparatus which will spearhead the reforms and constantly monitor it. For this purpose, the following steps need to be taken:

- The Department of Administrative Reforms should become the most important Department of the Central Government. It should be headed and manned by the most brilliant and outstanding officers available in the Government.
- It should be a separate Department headed by a senior Secretary.
- There Department should cease to be an adjunct of the Department of Personnel and may be placed directly under the Cabinet Secretary and the Prime Minister.
- The should be a Cabinet Committee on Public Service Reforms, which should meet once a month. It should consist of the Prime Minister, Finance Minister, Home Minister, Defence Minister and the Cabinet Minister in charge of Public Service Reforms. This Committee should take final decisions on proposals put forth by the Committee of Secretaries and Chief Secretaries.
- There should be a Committee of Secretaries on Public Service Reforms under the chairmanship of Cabinet Secretary. It should meet once or twice a month, as may be warranted, to consider specific proposals of administrative reforms.
- Another Committee of Chief Secretaries should meet once a quarter under the chairmanship of Cabinet Secretary to review and monitor the public service reforms in the States.

Approach to Reforms

With this apparatus in position a step-by-step approach to public service reforms should be adopted as follows:

- The Core functions of Government should first be defined;
- The distribution of work between the three tiers of governance will have to be restated;
- The number of Central Ministries and Departments should be reduced drastically;
- The size and constitution of Central Ministries and Departments should be redefined in order to fit them for their newly stated roles;

- All functions that should be performed by the State Governments and Panchayati Raj institutions may be transferred to them;
- All functions that do not involve formulation of policy should be delegated to agencies, which may be public sector enterprises autonomous bodies or cooperative institutions;
- Recruitment to the different services may be reduced;
- There should be a sound legal architecture that redefines the rules outright;
- The Government office itself will need a heavy dose of restructuring;
- The financial management and budgetary system will have to be totally re-written;
- There will have to be a simplification of procedures and formulation of accountability norms in Government.

A time-table for action

Above all, there is need for a demanding but realistic time-table for achieving the major objectives of the reform process. There will have to be some short-circuiting of procedures, some ruthlessness in implementation and some strategy for management of change. This will try to the utmost Government's skills in dealing with the opposition parties, the unions an associations of Government employees, the press and the general public. But if there is a basic sincerity of purpose and a strong determination at the very top, tangible results can be shown in two to three years.

18

Re-defining Functional Goals

Introduction

The efficiency programme has to start with a redefinition of the functional goals of Government. Unless the objectives of governance are made clear and specific, there will always be a tendency for expansion of the bureaucracy in accordance with the inexorable Parkinson's Law.

Historical Background

There was a time when governments were instruments of political power and their main function was to maintain law and order inside their territories and to defend their boundaries against external aggression. Over time, there was an enhancement of the rôle under the influence of welfare, Keynesian and Marxist ideologies, till the State threatened to become an overbearing presence, exemplified by the 'Big Brother is watching you' syndrome. The last two decades have send a reversal of the trend, mainly due to the burgeoning budgetary deficits, forcing governments of all persuasions to cut back on staff, subsides and functions.

In India, also, the same trend exhibited itself. In the fifties and sixties we were trying to find a middle way between the Soviet and the Beveridge models and this gave rise to the 'socialistic pattern'. Latter, nationalisation combined with de novo establishment of public sector enterprises became the buzzword and PSUs occupied an increasingly large area of industry and commerce. The fiscal indiscipline of the eighties finally led to the ignominious crash of 1991 and to the reversal of the trend.

Proliferation of Departments

Proliferation of departments is a sure index of the widening net of the Government. Against only 35 ministries and departments in 1962, we had 50 in 1972 and there are 81 ministries and departments at present. Despite the economic reforms, in 1995 we had unedifying spectacle of five new departments being set up at the Centre. Industry, which is already fragmented into several departments, got an off-shoot with industrial policy and promotion being separated out. Urban Development Ministry carved out a separate area of urban employment and poverty alleviation and so did the Ministry of Rural Development branch off into 'rural employment and poverty alleviation'. A Department of Animal Husbandry was set up in the Ministry of Agriculture and a Department of Consumer Affairs in the Ministry of Civil Supplies.

CONCEPTS AND METHODOLOGY

Activity Analysis

All this is a result of confused and woolly thinking. Instead of only looking for political slogans or how new slots can be created for ministers and secretaries, we have to start by asking ourselves the following basic questions about any particular activity:

- Does the job need to be done at all?
- If so, does the Government have to be responsible for it?
- If so, which level of Government?
- If it is the Central Government, does it have to carry out the job itself?
- If so, is the organisation properly structured for the job?

If a Group of three, who combine in themselves objectivity, knowledge and dynamism, look at the Central Government with the above questions in their mind, the answers will stare them in the face.

CONSULTANCY REPORT

Classification of Government Offices

The report of the Tata Consultancy Service have suggested

a three-fold classification of Government offices, on the basis of the role performed by them. They can be Core, participatory or Auxiliary.

Core

The offices under this category perform roles which are given by the constitution, which Government has to perform at all times, which are governed by societal expectations and where the Government has exclusive responsibility to deliver social goods and services. Examples are: Atomic Energy, Science and Technology, Space, Defence, External Affairs, Finance, Forests, Home, Law, Planning and Rural Development.

Participatory

These cover areas where the Government has both a policymaking and enforcement role but private and public sectors are allowed to participate in deliver of goods, where the Government has responsibility of ensuring a desired level of delivery of services through direct or indirect intervention in the sectorial markets and industry, and where Government has a responsibility towards production and trading of goods and services. These may include Coal, Education, Health and Family Welfare, Energy, Petroleum, Steel, Chemicals and Fertilizers, Industry, Information and Broadcasting, Railways, Surface Transport Telecommunications, Posts, Urban Affairs and Civil Aviation.

Auxiliary

Here the Government has only policy making responsibility but not for delivery of goods and services, or Government may enter for regulation of markets, trade practices etc. Examples are Art and Culture, Food Processing, Sports, Tourism, Consumer Affairs, Labour, Water Resources, Wasteland Development and Textiles.

Validity of Concepts

The above classification is highly arbitrary and simplistic, and there is scope for endless refinement both of the definitions as well as the list of Ministries which fall under one or the other category.

The main point to appreciate is the need to undertake such an exercise so as to be clear about what has to be done by the Central Government itself, where it has to regulate and participate and where it need act only as policy maker and arbitrator.

Even within the Core category, the functional goals need to be sharpened further. Let us take defence which is definitely one of the key functions of the Central Government. We are left with the lingering impression that the threat perception as perceived by the Government as a whole after looking at the political, diplomatic, military, strategic and economic aspects has not been clearly articulated, to enable the armed forces to develop a long-term manpower policy perspective. This is a blatant example of fuzziness in our perception of functional goals. Such examples can be multiplied.

Mission Statements

At the level of individual organisation, what is required is a mission orientation which provides clear and understandable goals fully owned by the senior management and accepted by the operational staff. The purpose of establishing a mission orientation is to:

- clarify the goals of the organisation in the mind of the management;
- clarify for staff the purpose of their jobs in meeting organisational goals;
- make clear the policy of the Government to ensure that it is interpreted accurately by staff;
- engender pride in belonging to the organisation;
- provide targets to aim for, against which results can be assessed.

Preconditions

The basic pre-conditions for this are:

- understanding customer needs;
- top management commitment to goals expressed in the mission statement;

- clear grasp of mission concepts by management and staff;
- full explanation and training to staff.

Conclusion

A study of the experience of other countries underlines the importance of redefining functional goals, both the Government as a whole as also of each governmental organisation in particular. The concept of mission statement is an effective tool in this process and is recommended for adoption.

19

Contracting out of Services and Privatisation

Introduction

The rightsizing of Government and the structural reform of the bureaucracy can get off to a flying start if the Government decides to privatize both public sector undertakings as also departmental enterprises within a strict time-frame while at the same time contracting out many of its own activities to the private sector.

Experience of Other Countries

International experience suggest that the areas of privatisation and contracting out of services are very fertile and yield a rich harvest in terms of a diminished government presence in the life of a citizen, a reduction in the draining out of public funds in a vain endeavour to bolster sick public enterprises, improved and more cost-effective services to customers and better value for money.

United Kingdom

In the United Kingdom, the Government departments use market-testing to assess whether the services for which they are responsible can best be delivered in the public sector or the private sector. The objective is to promote fair and open competition and find the supplier of a service whose combination of price, quality and other factors offers the greatest value for money in the long term.

In general, activities which have been found to particularly suitable for market-testing are of the following types:

- resource intensive;

- relatively discrete;
- specialist or support services;
- subject to fluctuating work patterns;
- subject to a quickly changing market;
- subject to a rapidly changing technology.

The White Paper 'Competing for quality' (1991) set out the Government's plans to achieve better value for money, in particular by opening up more public services to competition from the private sector, while making it clear that Government had no dogmatic preference for private or public provision of services.

Candidates for market-testing are identified by each department by asking the following questions:

- Is the function or activity essential? What are the implications of not doing it? Or of doing it in a reduced or combined form elsewhere?
- Can the activity be performed more economically by other means?
- What is the full cost of the level of service presently provided and that which is considered necessary?
- Is that function or activity organisationally discrete?
- What are the working methods, organisation and use of capital assets? What use is proposed of existing staff and assets?

The attempt is to define the user-need for the service and to establish the cost of the existing service. A specification for the service is drawn up and this is part of the invitation to tender. The providers of the current service are encouraged to submit an in-house bid. Eventually, the line management decides on whether the service should be retained in-house or contracted out.

New Zealand

In New Zealand, the mechanism developed to facilitate the divestiture of the state trading agencies was the State Owned

Enterprises Act of 1986. The process of economic liberalisation led to a major restructuring of the public sector, first through corporatisation and in many instances subsequently through privatisation. Government owned enterprises in field such as banking, forestry, insurance, transport, communications and broadcasting were transformed into corporate entities and were later fully privatised.

The move to corporatise organisations was consistent with the Government objective to open up many sectors of the economy to internal and external competition. State-owned enterprises were now statutorily required to operate as successful commercial business and emulate the efficiency and profitability of their private sector counterparts. If Government wanted such an enterprise to provide a no-commercial service, it had to contract to do so. These enterprises were expected to fund their spending from unsubsidised private sector capital sources and to pay taxes and dividends.

For the privatisation process, no standard formula was applied. A range of routes and methods was adopted, depending on conditions in the market place, fiscal considerations and political factors. They tended to follow two routes:

- an equity route, where shares were sold in clearly defined commercial organisations.
- An asset route that entailed selling of assets because of the less commercial nature of the organisation.

The process of privatistion proved more controversial than corporatisation. Particularly in the initial years, mistakes were made in privatisation before the Government and the public service gained experience. In the privatisation of assets, as long as safeguards were installed, there was no restriction on foreign ownership.

Although most of the large scale privatisations involving organisations such as Telecom, New Zealand Rail and Air New Zealand have been completed, privatisation is an ongoing process.

Malaysia

The privatisation policy of Malaysia has been introduced in order to relieve the administrative and financial burden of

Government and to improve efficiency and productivity. IT was first announced in 1983 and the first stage consisted of dissemination of information to the public. Guidelines on privatisation were published in 1985 and the Privatisation Master Plan was launched in 1991.

The privatisation programme can be implemented in a number of ways. There are:

- Sale of Government assets or equity or sale of Government companies' equity, whether in part or whole.
- Lease of assets for a specified time period.
- Management contract which uses management expertise of the private sector to manage Government entities.
- Build-operate-Transfer or Build-own-Operate systems, generally used for new infrastructure projects and public facilities. Under this method; the public facility is built by the private sector using their own finances and is run by them during the period of concession, at the end of which it is surrendered back to the Government.

The planning of privatisation is done in the Economic Planning Unit of the Prime Minister's Department and involves the identification of privatisation candidates. In-depth studies are undertaken and these lead to two-years rolling action-plans. An interdepartmental committee on privatisation discusses the plan and, after the approval of the government, evaluates the various possible modes of privatisation.

These are Government-initiated privatisation projects and therefore subject to competitive bidding. But there are also private sector-initiated proposals which are evaluated and if found to be acceptable, an award is made by the ministry concerned. Further, the private sector is allowed to initiate projects not yet identified by Government, provided that their proposals contain unique features by offering a unique solution to an economic problem or by using the exclusive patent right or technical know-how of a particular party.

The efforts at privatisation have been very successful, as they have not only reduced the administrative and financial burden of the Government but also enhance the efficiency and productivity of the privatised entities. In Malaysia therefore, the implementation of the privatisation programme will continue to be accelerated.

Policy perspective for India

In the light of the international experience as also the peculiar genius of Indian institutions, a comprehensive policy perspective for corporatisation, privatisation and contracting out of services needs to be drawn up. Some sporadic efforts have been made by individual departments but there has been no conscious policy thrust initiated and monitored at the highest levels of Government. The general parameters of such a policy perspective could be the following:

(a) Corporatisation

No activity, which involves manufacturing of good or the provision of commercial services should be undertaken by a Government department. All such activities should be transferred to existing public sector undertakings or new PSUs be set up to look after them. Outstanding examples are ordnance factories in the Ministry of Defence, mints, currency presses and opium factories in the Ministry of Finance, rail coach factories in the Ministry of Railways, telecom factories in the Department of Telecommunications etc.

Corporatisation could also be a necessary half-way house on the road to privatisation. There are certain advantages of privatisation which can be achieved through corporatisation, and corporatisation is always less controversial than privatisation.

(b) Privatisation of activities where Government does not need to play a direct role

There are a number of areas where Government, either directly or through its PSUs, has been compelled to play a role. If an objective and dispassionate review reveals that such a role is unwarranted, Government should take expeditious steps to disentangle itself from the same.

Examples of such areas abound. The National Textile Corporation need not be a PSU. The clothing and vehicle factories in the Ordnance Factories Board can be privatised with advantage. All printing presses, dairy and other farms of the Ministry of Defence, Telecom Factories, Delhi Milk Scheme, Mail Motor Service, sale of postal stationery, stamps and postal orders, Song and Drama Division of the Ministry of Information and Broadcasting etc. are outstanding candidates for privatisation.

(c) Activities which should continue to be the exclusive responsibility of the Government

There are activities like defence, atomic energy, space, development of railway infrastructure provision of security to sensitive installations and so on which have to be the monopoly of the Government. These should continue to be so. All we can do is to explore possibilities of linking the private sector as a source of raw materials, components, sub-assemblies and even some non-sensitive finished products.

(d) Areas which should retain the mixed economy concept, but with greater competition

We should identify clearly those areas of the economy where for reasons of public welfare it is not desirable either to keep them exclusively in the public sector or in the private sector. The private sector should play an increasingly active role in these areas, but there should be a substantial presence of the public sector so as to ensure that quality services are provided at reasonable rates to members of the public.

Such areas would include road, rail and air transport, telecommunication services, banking, insurance, power, medical and educational services, courier services, construction and maintenance of defence aircraft, ships, tanks and other equipment, production of blank coins for mints etc.

(e) Contracting out of services

There is a widening area of services which are currently being performed in-house in the Government, but which can be conveniently outsourced to the private sector.

These may include designing, construction and maintenance of Government buildings, factories, workshops, residential colonies, railway stations, equipment and transport, cleanliness, sanitation and housekeeping, maintenance of monuments, lawns, and gardens, catering (including catering in airlines, trains, canteens), provision of transportation services (to replace the fleet of staff cars), postal deliveries, carriage of mail, security of all non-sensitive buildings and installations, reservations in railways and airlines, printing, reprography, photography, audiovisual publicity, translation, interpretation, computer-related services, maintenance of accounts etc.

Routes for Privatisation

As far as privatisation is concerned this can also take a variety of routes as in other countries:

- There could be straight disownment of Government equity in public sector enterprises.
- Lease of assets could be tried out.
- In certain areas, management contracts could be given to private companies.
- There could be private participation for improvement of a public service.
- We may also try out the Build-Operate-Transfer kind of schemes, so, that the assets revert to the Government after the private company has realised its investment.

INITIATIVES ALREADY TAKEN IN INDIA

Several initiatives have been taken in the wake of the recent economic reforms. Some of these are:

(i) The Build-Own-Lease-Transfer (BOLT) scheme has been launched by the railways in order to attract private finance in railway projects on leasing terms. At the end of the lease period assets are transferred to the Railways on a nominal payment. Efforts are being made to attract private capital for manufacture of rolling stock, gauge conversion, doublings, electrification, Telecommunication etc.

(ii) An Own Your Wagon scheme has also been initiated for investment by rail users in acquisition of wagons by the Railways in return for assured allotment of wagons and lease charges to be paid by the Railways.

(iii) Maintenance of railway station and colonies are being tried out for privatisation.

(iv) All future catering in trains is being sourced out to private contractors.

(v) Printing of postal stationery has been partly privatised.

(vi) A scheme of Licensed Postal Agencies existed upto the late eighties but there were complaints of misuse of authorisation and opposition from Staff Federations.

(vii) Carriage of mail through private and public transporters has been successfully undertaken for several decades in rural and semi-urban areas.

(viii) In the Department of Telecom, value added services and cellular phone sector has already been privatised fully.

(ix) Several departments have contracted out sanitation, maintenance security, computer, reprography, canteen and transport services.

(x) Some military dairy farms have been closed down.

(xi) MES contracts out its building works and has started giving out maintenance work also to private contractors.

(xii) Several ordnance factories are buying components from the private sector.

Disinvestment Commission

Some progress has also been made in respect of disinvestment of Government equity in PSUs. Disinvestment was first conceived primarily as a method for reducing the fiscal deficit, but it go bogged down in controversies. Recently, the Government has set up a Public Sector Disinvestment Commission which is expected to suggest a comprehensive overall long-term disinvestment programme for about forty PSUs referred to it by the Core Group. It will prioritize the PSUs in terms of the overall disinvestment programme, recommend the preferred mode of disinvestment (domestic capital market/ international capital market/auction/private sale to identified investors/ any other mode), suggest the appropriate mix between primary and secondary disinvestment, advised Government on possible capital restructuring of the enterprises etc.

Present trends indicate that Government may concentrate, in the short run, on reforming the PSUs by grant of greater autonomy and flexibility, greater delegation of powers, introduction of greater accountability by means of performance-related pay and a system of hire and fire and other similar measures. The issue of transfer of ownership of these enterprises may get deferred.

Whatever the shape disinvestment may take, observers feel that it would be good for consumers as the Government will relax such controls on private enterprises as had been imposed in order to protect the public sector enterprises from competition.

CONCLUSION

Role of Trade Unions

It will be apparent from the above discussion that although some steps have been taken towards corporatisation privatisation and contracting out of services in India, these have been ad hoc, unsystematic and halting. What is required is a clear and comprehensive policy in this crucial area, so as to progressively reduce the role of the public sector in the industrial and commercial activity of the nation. There are bound to be hurdles on the way. The main opposition will come from the trade unions and associations. They will have to be handled with care and circumspection. There may be a need for a new policy on the formation of trade unions, on the pattern of what has been attempted in other countries. Workers will also have to understand that in the perspective of globalisation, we have to compete or perish.

Need For Transparency

The other problem would be to keep the process of disinvestment and privatisation as transparent as possible, so as to obviate the criticism of partisanship and malfeasance. Even in advanced countries these have attracted virulent controversies and India can be no exception.

Value for Money

Lastly, we have to keep the public interest paramount in our minds. Privatisation should not become a fad, as nationalisation had become at one stage. We should choose the private sector, the public sector or a mix of the two, according to the nature of the commodity or service to be produced and the only touchstone should be that the ultimate customer should get the best value for his money on long-term basis in as competitive a market as is humanly possible.

20

Restructuring the Government

INTRODUCTION

Reinventing the Government

The entire machinery of Government has got to be reinvented. This is a mammoth task. It is not possible for us to go into the details of the restructuring exercise that such a reinvention would entail. In this chapter, we would like to take up the Ministries of the Central Government as an example and demonstrate how the restructuring could help.

Expansion in the Bureaucracy

We had 8 posts of Secretaries, 18 departments and a total workforce of 14.40 lakhs in 1948. Today, we have 92 Secretaries, 79 departments and a workforce of more than 41 lakhs. No doubt, the work has expanded, but the expansion of the Government is disproportionate to the increase of workload.

Earlier Attempts at Restructuring

There have been many attempts at reforming the Central Government. Some of these are:

- setting up of Organisation and methods Divisions in the ministries.
- setting up of a Department of Administrative Reforms.
- setting up of a Department of Personnel, Public Grievances and Pensions.
- setting up of Staff Inspection Unit.

- introduction of Desk Officer system.
- introduction of Financial Adviser system.
- introduction of Annual Action Plans.
- introduction of Performance Budgeting.

Consultancy Studies

We had awarded two studies on restructuring of the Government to IIT, Delhi and Tata Consultancy Services.

IIT, Delhi

The IIT, Delhi, identified the major objective of restructuring to be goal achievement and service orientation, through flexibility and efficiency. The restructuring options involved interventions at the level of situation, action and process. At the level of situation, action and process. At the level of situation, the physical environment, the operating environment and the socio-cultural environment was to be changed. At the actor level, both systemic and attitudinal changes were required. At the process level, the interventions related to operations processes and strategic processes.

Interventions Suggested

For Phase I, the interventions found feasible at situation level were: conductive physical working conductions; openness to environment; federalism; delayering; and decision-oriented system. At the actor level these were: Training for multi-skilling; involvement in clarifying goals and objectives; quality and work consciousness; sense of dignity and individuality; promoting self-help; and receptivity to technology-based solutions. Process level options identified were; simplifying system of checks and balances; horizontal communication processes; minimal and appropriate reporting and documentation; upward feedback process; privatised support services; reorienting strategically to liberatize; shedding functions to affiliated autonomous bodies, installing learning processes; reengineering work flows and continuous change in work processes.

The Office of the Future

The findings of the study point towards a decision oriented, facilitative, flatter, flexible, Information Technology supported, participative and elegant Government officer effectively achieving goals with service and client orientation.

TCS Study

The TCS Categorised various Government offices into three broad types Core, Participatory and Auxiliary. Based on the decision-making matrices in these offices, the study concluded that one of the major changes in the organisational structure was to reduce the levels in the hierarchy from nine to seven. A flatter hierarchy would ensure speedy decision-making and be able to respond quickly to the demands of the environment.

The levels proposed were:

- Chief Executive
- Senor Executive
- Middle Executive
- Junior Executive
- Supervisory
- Assistant
- Support/Attendant

Grades and Levels

Eighteen grades were proposed in these seven levels. The grades within a level would only be for promotional purposes and not form a hierarchy for reporting. The promotional channels were increased to provide career growth for the employees. Thus the hierarchial levels were delinked from promotional grades.

Decision-making More Important

The study laid emphasis on decision-makers rather than on assistants. It proposed that each section within a department should have just one Assistant level position. Decisions should be hastened, and files and papers should be disposed of at the level to which they were addressed.

Utilisation of Redundant Staff

The support staff that would be rendered redundant could be utilised in the following manner:

by training them in computer applications so that Government departments could redeploys them in those functions.

- by transferring them to new activities or projects, after giving them adequate training in the new skills.

Three-fold Restructuring

The TCS study considered restructuring in three streams. The first was organisational structure. The second was a comprehensive human resource development system to achieve greater efficiency, responsiveness and productivity, and to bring in sustainability in the organisation. The third concentrated on the two major office systems-record management and dak system, office equipment, information technology and work environment.

In this chapter, we shall concentrate on the first stream viz. organisational restructuring in the context of the Ministries and Departments of the Central Government.

OUR PROPOSALS

The Three Basic Questions

The first exercise we must have is to survey the entire gamut of governmental functioning and ask the three usual basic questions:

- Does this need to be done.
- Does this need to be done in Government?
- Does this need to be in the Central Government?

Things that Need Not be Done

The answers to these questions, if attempted in an objective and dispassionate manner, will show that some activities need not be undertaken at all. For example, we do not need the large and expensive memorials which have taken up so much of prime land and building space besides involving heavy recurring expenditure. The moment we identify this as an activity that should be stopped forthwith, a number of action points emerge.

Things that Need Not be Done by Government

In the second category, we may conclude that bread, milk or condoms need not be manufactured in Government. In the third category, we may decide that 90% of our effort in education, health, agriculture, law and order etc. should be with the State Governments. Our honest replies to the basic questions will show us the areas in which restructuring can yield rich dividends.

Number of Ministries

One of the basic objectives of restructuring is reduction of staff. It is best to begin with the top most category of Secretary. There is a general feeling that we have too many Secretaries to the Government of India. Health is a State subject. Do we really need three Secretaries in the Ministry of Health, looking after Health, Family Welfare and Indian System of Medicine? We would like to recommend that there should be just one Secretary for the whole Ministry.

Ministry of Industry

Similarly, industry is a State subject. We have separate departments of Industrial Policy and Promotion, Industrial Development, Public Enterprises, Heavy Industry, Small Scale Industries. Agro and Rural Industries and Textiles. With the reduced emphasis on licensing, one Secretary could look after all these subjects in a single ministry.

Suggestions on Merger of Departments

Similarly, it does not seem necessary to deploy Secretary each for Animal Husbandry, Inter State Council, Official Language, Programme Implementation and the like. We have appended a small list at Annexe 9.1, suggesting some realignments of departments

Size of a Ministry

The most major restructuring effort would be in determining the size of a Department of Ministry. The general formula that we would like to suggest in this regard is the following:

- If it is a Core Central subject, we may not take it up in the beginning.
- If it is a Core State subject, it cannot be a Core Central subject too. In that case it should be high on the list of Ministries to be reduced in size.

- As we move from Core subjects to Participatory or Auxiliary subjects, the need for sizeable Ministries becomes more and more questionable. Such Ministries should be axed first of all.

Organisations Attached to Ministries

Ministries have certain organisations or activities which may either be an integral part of the Ministry, or an attached or subordinate office. Very often, such organisations have no business to be in Government. They would be much better managed if they were in the public sector, the cooperative sector or as an autonomous body. Just one example of each type will suffice to clarify the point being made:

- Ordnance Factories would be better managed as PSUs.
- Delhi Milk Scheme would be better off under the NDDB.
- The Central Institute of English at Mysore would be best managed if it were an autonomous body.

Delayering

Coming to the organisation of A typical Department of a Central Ministry, we would like to recommend delayering as an antidote to delay. There should be a general rule that no file would be allowed to travel to more than three hierarchical levels before a decision is taken. The TCS study has hinted at the solution by delinking hierarchical levels from promotions. We have separately approved modified version of the hierarchy suggested by TCS as under:

- Top Executives
- Senior Executives
- Executives
- Supervisory Staff
- Supporting Staff
- Auxiliary Staff

ACP and Delayering

Thus there will be only six levels in the hierarchy. The TCS have suggested that promotions to grades within a level should be for purposes of financial benefit, but need not have any relationship with a higher decision-making level in the hierarchy. We have adapted the TCS recommendation to provide for the Assured Career Progression Scheme, by which all non-executive cadres will receive two financial up gradations on a time-bound basis while executives will benefit form three such financial upgradations. The ACP has been designed to delink hierarchy from financial upgradations, and should therefore help in delayering of the Government set up.

Level Jumping

Another method of quick disposal, which is quite related to delayering, is known as level lumping. Here there is conscious attempt to bypass rungs in the hierarchy. As early as September, 1968 the Administrative Reforms Commission recommended that there should be only two levels of consideration and decision below the Minister viz. (i) Under Secretary/Deputy Secretary and (ii) Joint Secretary/Additional Secretary/Secretary. This observation led to implementation of a scheme of direct submission of cases by senior Assistants to Branch Officers in 1974, 1978, the scheme got a push when it was said that a case should either be seen by an Under Secretary or a Deputy Secretary/Director but not by both. The concept of level lumping, though known in Government, has not been effectively implemented so far. What is required is a firm guideline that at the executive level, the third level should be the last, where a decision is taken.

Desk Officer Concept

A major pieces of organisational restructuring was the enunciation on the Desk Officer concept. The attempt here was to convert the Central Secretariat into an officer-oriented system. The Desk Officer system was introduced in January, 1973 in selected wings of Ministries where at least 40% of the work related to strategic policy making, planning and problem solving. Each desk comprised two officers of the rank of Under Secretary or Section Officer or both. The Section Officer submitted cases directly to the Deputy Secretary, while the Under Secretary submitted his files direct to the Joint Secretary. The idea was to abolish the Section, which has too much of supporting staff in the shape of assistants, UDCs, LDCs, Daftaris, Peons etc. The aim was to reduced the number of levels by at least two, to reduce the accent on nothing and to lay stress on oral discussion, to foster greater participation in and commitment to organisational goals among officers at the base of the Secretariat structure. Each desk was given a well-defined area of functioning. SOs appointed as Desk Officers were allowed to authenticate order and sanctions in the name of the President and to dispose cases on their own responsibility.

Why it Has Not Made Headway

Currently, there are 1816 Sections and 427 Desks in the Government of India. The Desk Officer system has not made much headway due to the following reasons:

(a) Section Officers appointed as Desk Officers got all the responsibility but without much monetary incentive. They were allowed a special pay of Rs. 150/- p.m. which proved insufficient to motivate them.

(b) The staff unions saw the Desk Officer system as an attempt to reduce the dependence of the Secretariat on the supporting staff like Assistants, UDCs, LDCs etc. Whose numbers are very large. They asserted their position in the JCM and forced the Government to slow down the implementation of the new system.

(c) There was just one desk attached or P.A. attached to the desk, with the result that no memory could be built up, as in the case of the section. The working of a desk got disrupted even by the proceeding of one of its members on leave.

The New Desk Officer Concept

It is our considered view that no restructuring of the Secretariat can go very far unless the Desk Officer system is reintroduced in a highly effective manner. We propose to remove the defects in the earlier system by adopting the following strategy:

(a) The Desk Officer should be a separate and distinct post, not a mere honorific for a Section Officer, with a pittance as

special pay. That is why we are suggesting that 25 per cent of the posts of Section Officers be converted into Desk Officers in a higher pre-revised scale of Rs. 2500-4000.

(b) The percentage of 25 per cent should gradually be increased to an optimum level so that the bulk of the work, baring that pertaining to housekeeping and routine administration, is finally done in the desks and not in the sections.

(c) Each Desk should contain two officers and two Executive Assistants. With a numerical strength of four, the absence of one or two members will not lead to a collapse of the Desk.

The Executive Assistant Concept

The next step that is necessary to restructure the supporting staff in the Central Secretarial is to create a multi-skilled position called Executive Assistant. He should replace the present posts of Assistant, UDC, LDC, PA and Stenographer. The qualifications prescribed for this functionary should include:

(a) graduation in any discipline

(b) the qualifications presently prescribed for a stenographer

(c) ability to work on computers.

Training to Executive Assistants

The training imparted to an Executive Assistant should be such as to enable him to discharge all the skills of noting, drafting, filing, stenography, typing, public relations, receiving telephone calls and visitors and so on. The idea is to have a multi-skilled employee capable of performing all the tasks required for a competent secretary in organisations other than The Government.

Multiskilling in Group 'D'

We have to inject the concept of multi-skilling at the Group 'D' level too. Here we may finally arrive at the ideal worker who may be called an Officer Attendant and can really attend to all the auxiliary tasks in an office. But in the short run we are suggesting a rationalisation into four occupational groups—office attendants, security attendants, cosmetic attendants and malis..

Office Systems

There is a whole area of office systems, about which the TCS study has thrown up a number of ideas. Restructuring of office systems has to make the office more efficient and effective. This can be done by:

- reducing unnecessary movement of files.
- reducing the number of files with various officers at any given time
- preventing wastage of time in locating the files
- freeing officers from routine maintenance of records
- eliminating repetitive tasks
- making the dak system more efficient etc.

COORDINATING AGENCIES

Planning Commission

Lastly, we come to the coordinating agencies in the Government. The most gargantuan of these is the Planning commission. There was probably some justification for its size and range of authority when our objective was a centrally controlled economy on the Soviet pattern. Now that such centralised planning models have been abandoned even in the country of their birth and we are moving towards an open, liberalised economy, we have to considerably reduce the size of the Planning Commission. Japan has a small Economic Planning Unit under the Prime Minister's Office. In our case, we can have the Planning Commission as a separate entity with much more reduced functions than at present. It should be an advisory body performing an idea generating role and providing alternatives before the national economy in a fast changing and technology-driven world.

Department of Programme Implementation

The Department of Programme Implementation also had a coordinating and monitoring role at one time. Somewhere along the way, it has lost its mandate. It should be abolished.

PMO

The Prime Minister's Office has emerged as a coordinating office of sorts. It may be of advantage to have a less visible role for it.

Cabinet Secretariat

The Cabinet Secretariat is officially charged with the task of coordination and is geared for it. This position should be recognised and the Cabinet Secretary charged with the responsibility for ensuring coordination at the bureaucratic level. There may be need for some amendment in the Rules of Business to provide for certain matters to be resolved at the level of Secretaries through the intervention of the Cabinet Secretary, and at the level of Ministers through the intervention of the Prime Minister. This will impart the necessary edge to both the offices, in keeping a grip on the governmental machinery, so that all actions of Government are seen to move in the same general direction and in mutual harmony.

Conclusion

We have provided certain broad directions on the restructuring of the Central Secretarial. Similar solutions will also apply to attached and subordinate offices. It is our fervent hope that organisational restructuring of the Governmental machinery would lead to a more effective, more efficient and service-oriented set-up.

ANNEXURE

Merger of Departments in the Central Government

Sl. No.	*Department(s) to be merged*	*Ministry/Department in which to be merged*
1.	Department of Administrative Reforms	Cabinet Secretariat
2.	Department of Animal Husbandry and Fisheries	Department of Agriculture and Cooperation (to be renamed as Department of Agriculture)

3.	Departments of Jammu & Kashmir Affairs, official language and Inter-State Council	Ministry of Home Affairs
4.	Department of Consumer Affairs	Department of Civil Supplies and Public Distribution
5.	Department of Fertilizers	Department of Chemicals and Petrochemicals
6.	Departments of Family Welfare; Indian System of Medicine and Homeopathy	Department of Health
7.	Departments of Industrial policy and promotion; Industrial Development Public Enterprises; Heavy Industry; Small Scale Industries; Agro and Rural Industries and Ministry of Textiles	To be merged into a new single department called Departments of Industrial Development
8.	Departments of Culture; Youth Affairs and Sports; Women and Child Development	Department of Education
9.	Departments of Food Procurement and Distribution; Food Processing Industries	Department of Food
10.	Ministry of Non-Conventional Energy Resources	Ministry of Power
11.	Department of Rural Employment and Poverty Alleviation: Department of Waste Land Development	Department of Rural Department
12.	Department of Urban Employment and Poverty Alleviation	Department of Urban Development
13.	Department of Statistics	Department of Planning
14.	Anticorruption wing of the C.B.I.	Central Vigilance Commission

21

Work Methods and Work Environment

Introduction

Today, the government office is seen as a dusty, moth-eaten, dingy, paper-infested hovel chockfull of babus, which is feudal in its outlook, hierarchical in structure, antediluvian in its procedures, dilatory in examination of issues and secretive in its dealings with customers. Despite being one of the largest providers of services, there is a complete lack of customer orientation in various government departments. Consequently, the common man views the government functionaries as exploiters rather than facilitators or providers. The reality has been changed somewhat on account of various measures taken by the government in the recent past. However, the process of change has been tardy and much more needs to be done to improve the existing work methods and work environment in government offices.

Three Types of Offices

Government offices can broadly be divided into three categories: Those incharge of–planning and policy formulation; monitoring and control; and operations. The work methods and environment in all these categories of government offices needs to be improved, albeit in different ways.

The Present Scenario

While office procedure manuals detailing the procedures to be followed for performing any work and guidelines enumerating specific space and facilities to be given in staff/officers of different levels do exist in the government, these guidelines are observed more in the breach. The elaborate office systems and procedures being observed presently generate unnecessary file work, reports and returns. Filing system in most of the offices is antiquated. Proper accommodation is also not available is most offices and while senior officers do have separate individual rooms, the staff usually sits in cramped conditions. The furniture is very old and in poor condition, and not available in adequate quantity. Sections where the staff sit are usually noisy, under-illuminated and poorly ventilated. Many buildings housing government offices are very poorly maintained and lack in basic amenities like safe drinking water and clean toilets. The conditions in service departments of the government, which provide an interface with the general public, are the worst, with customers having to suffer the lackadaisical attitude of functionaries coupled with physical discomforts like lack of proper sitting space.

Comparative Profile

While current state of work methods and work environment in most of the State Governments is similar to that existing in Central Government, public sector undertakings have effected certain changes in this field. Most public sector offices today have an open layout wherein modular partitions and modular office units are extensively used. In the offices of the Reserve Bank of India, Such an open layout is being used where grade 'A' and 'B' officers sit in the open space along with the staff.

International Experience

In most of the countries where large scale administrative reforms were effected, proper attention was paid towards establishment of streamlined work methods and a conducive work environment for the staff. In Malaysia, the open office concept heralded closer supervision, Congenial working atmosphere and effective communication and interaction. In the United Kingdom, the individual departments were given flexibility to tailor their own systems of work methods within the general framework. In New Zealand, the Chief Executives were given complete control over establishment of appropriate work methods and environment so as to deliver the agreed output at the contracted price to the concerned

Minister. As would be clear form the experience of other countries which have been successful in implementing the administrative reforms, proper work methods and a good work environment are inherent constituents of such reforms and no organisation can hope to be efficient and effective without proper emphasis on these aspects.

Consultancy Studies

In the Commissioner's sponsored consultancy studies on "Restructuring the Government Office", Indian Institute of Technology (IIT) and Tata Consultancy Services (TCS) have in their reports, commented on the general state of work methods and work environment in the government offices.

Both the organisations have found the existing level of amenities and facilities in government offices inadequate and the prevailing procedures for file movement, dak disposal and filing cumbersome and time-consuming. TCS has proposed a new system of filing and file movement wherein creation of "File Libraries" containing all the section-related files has been suggested. Under this system the concerned official can call for the relevant files, as and when required, by sending a requisition to the library. The official would only keep the file with himself in case he is still processing it at the end of the day. In all other cases, the file would be returned to the section library. The Section File Library will keep all the current files, with non-current files being sent to a Central File Library for purposes of record. File retrieval and subsequent return to the Central Library would be through the Section Library. The concerned official would submit a file requisition form to the Sectional Library Incharge who would then procure the file from the Central Library. Apart from the filing system, both these studies have also suggested changes in the work environment wherein an open centrally air conditioned office for seating of all non-executive staff, with junior executives being provided shared cabins and individual cabins being limited to only senior executives have been suggested. Other measures like use of modular furniture, permanent and semi-permanent partitioning and diversion of area above fire cabinets for storage shelves have also been recommended.

OUR RECOMMENDATIONS

Reducing the Paper Work

Paper work in government offices should be reduced by abolishing all necessary reports and returns, reducing the number of circulars, increased use of computers etc.

Streamlined File Movement

The existing system of file movement needs to be streamlined. Files may be replaced by floppies, queries and letters by phone calls, fax messages and electronic mail. Officers may be given the freedom to destroy all useless paper immediately on receipt. These devices not only result in speedier file movement and decision-making, but lead to a more efficient functioning of the office.

There is a need for greater inter-ministerial and inter-departmental co-ordination. Instead of moving files for every case, discussions and decisions should be issue-wise with individual matters being finalised within the concerned department/ministry in the light of general decisions taken inter-ministerially. Unnecessary and irrelevant questions should not be raised. All points needing clarification should be raised only once.

Reorganising SIU and IWSU

Staff Inspection Unit (SIU) and Internal Works Study Units (IWSU) should be re-organised in terms of their style of functioning, as presently these units follow thumb rules without any analysis of actual situations. At times, they also lack expertise on the subject matter under review. Instead of having such units which operate from outside, efforts should be made to develop in-house mechanisms like "quality circles" to constantly review their own working and suggest innovations and improvements. Often SIUs and IWSUs are not welcome in most of the organisations as they are perceived to be instruments for downsizing the staff. The proposed system from within would develop space for creativity and build confidence among the participants that any decision taken would be in the overall interest of the organisation as well as the individuals by improving their effectiveness, productivity and also the rewards. Apart from SIU, the Government should also make increasing use of outside management consultants to streamline the Government machinery.

Reducing the Supervisory Levels

The number of supervisory levels should be curtailed with individual officers being given smaller charges with complete autonomy so that they are fully accountable for any lapse. Simultaneously, multiplicity of checks in the form of internal audit, technical audit, external audit etc. Should be replaced by a single agency for effecting suitable checks.

Service Departments

In order to minimize the differences in the quality of services being provided, there is a need for laying down strict guidelines regarding accountability norms and standards for government servants, to be strictly adhered to while providing the service. The people delivering the services and the physical environment where these services are delivered are crucial. This has been one of the most neglected areas in the service departments of the government. Of late, a few departments have made efforts to improve the physical environment of such place but there is immediate need to make them cleaner, aesthetically pleasant and more congenial.

Training

The public servants who have an interface with the people should be given intensive training in behavioural science, so that they are seen as helping hands with the smiling face rather than as exploiters.

Common Typist Good

All the available typists in an office should be placed in a common typist pool. Any official requiring typing assistance may utilize the services of any typist of this pool. We should depart from the prevailing practise of giving individual typists to officers.

Heralding an Officer Orientation

All government work has to be made officer-oriented. Matters may be considered and disposed of only at officer level and full authority must be delegated to each officer.

Work Environment

Work environment includes office layout and furniture, office decor and amenities. We have considered all the three aspects of work environment separately.

Office Layout

Office layout concerns the arrangement of equipment within the available floor space. Presently most of the government offices have a number of private rooms. Such rooms are given to employees on account of their position or prestige or because the work needs a higher level of concentration or is of a confidential nature. The concept of private rooms is now changing and the image of prestige built on separate rooms has to be abandoned because they hamper close supervision of the subordinate staff, occupy more floor space and are generally more expensive to build and maintain. Accordingly, efforts should be made to design offices with large open areas where all the staff/junior level executives (up to the rank of Under Secretary) should sit. For limited privacy, partial modular partitions can be provided. Adequate lighting, ventilation and acoustical sound proofing should be provided. Modular furniture should be used and the area above file cabinets Should be converted into storage shelves. Mobile racks should be used for storing all files in a sections. The personal assistants should not be given private rooms but be placed in foyers outside executive offices. While middle and top executives may be given private rooms, the same should be constructed by using movable partitions so as to provide flexibility for any future changes. Proper area should be provided for visitors and reception.

Office Decor

Officer decor gives a pleasing appearance to the office, thereby reducing the boredom of sitting in once office for years.

Decor also helps to improve the image of an organisation. Most of the government offices are found to be wanting in this area. As a short-term measure, different ministries/ departments may initiate steps for ensuring better ventilation, lighting, air conditioning sound-proofing through provision of carpets, proper maintenance of office equipment and furniture, proper colour scheme, use of potted plants, wall clocks, curtains, wall paintings, etc. Long-term measures can include provision of piped music/art galleries in the corridors/reception area, utilisation of space on the ground floor for small museums displaying articles relating to the historical background of the particular department etc.

Amenities

Provision of basic amenities is a necessity, as their absence can spread dissatisfaction amongst employees and customers. We have observed that most of the government offices at present lack proper basic amenities. Provisions have to be made in every government office for providing drinking water with water coolers, clean toilets, vending machines for tea and coffee and a small recreation room/library. Government should also consider taking concrete steps for providing facilities like creche, ladies' common room, gymnasium, sports facilities as well as departmental stores well stocked in items of daily consumption in all large offices.

Ensuring Uniformity Across Offices

We view with concern the tendency of vocal and powerful officers to get more space and amenities for their personal and functionally related staff. The government should take adequate measures and form proper guidelines to ensure that uniformity is maintained in provision of these facilities to different offices.